THE PRICE OF THE COMMON GOOD

THE PRICE OF THE COMMON GOOD

MARKETS, CORPORATIONS, and POLITICAL ECONOMY

MARK HOIPKEMIER

University of Notre Dame Press
Notre Dame, Indiana

Notre Dame, Indiana 46556
undpress.nd.edu

Published in the United States of America

Library of Congress Control Number: 2024947138

ISBN: 978-0-268-20897-4 (Hardback)
ISBN: 978-0-268-20900-1 (WebPDF)
ISBN: 978-0-268-20899-8 (Epub3)

GPSR Compliance Inquiries:
Lightning Source France, 1 Av. Johannes Gutenberg, 78310 Maurepas, France
compliance@lightningsource.fr | Phone: +33 1 30 49 23 42

FOR

NAOMI

CONTENTS

TABLES

PREFACE

What's wrong with this picture?

> Strings of plastic beads are a staple of the carnival scene at Mardi Gras in New Orleans. The colorful beads are tossed from parade floats to revelers, who then swap the strands with one another in a sort of drunken mating ritual. The beads are usually thrown away as soon as the party is over, leaving a festive carpet of trash on the most popular streets of the French Quarter. No one at Mardi Gras is curious about where the beads come from. In fact, the beads are made in a factory in Fuzhou, in southeast China. The factory's workers, mainly young women of little education, work six to seven days a week in twelve-hour shifts, endlessly repeating single tasks in the complex process of shaping, stringing, and painting polystyrene. They sleep in dormitories and have to bribe guards to leave the factory compound. The workers at the factory are just as ignorant of the beads' ultimate use and cultural meaning as New Orleans crowds are of the beads' origins. The only members of this long human chain who can see the whole picture are the American wholesaler and the factory's Chinese owner, who brings home $1–2 million per year for having cornered the bead market. His employees are paid by the piece, about one cent for every bead string, usually earning less than $75 per month. When the women of the factory are informed by a documentary filmmaker about the retail cost ($1–20) and meaning of the beads on Bourbon Street, they are shocked and

bewildered. Likewise, New Orleans revelers are conscience-stricken to hear about the conditions and wages at the far-off factory that has made their party possible.[1]

Consider two stereotypical responses to a story like this, from opposite ends of today's political spectrum. Partisans of market efficiency would see a normal stage on the sometimes-bumpy road to prosperity. Bead production moved to China because labor costs and legal hurdles are low, while workers in the bead factory presumably tolerate the poor wages and conditions because it is the best option they have. The anonymity of global trade, far from being a problem, allows complete strangers on opposite sides of the world to benefit one another, with competition leading over time to better, more affordable products. On this view, so long as everyone involved is free to take part or not, the only thing fundamentally wrong with this picture would be that the workers and revelers are bothered to discover how their world really works.

A typical response from the political left, on the other hand, would excoriate the inequalities on display between the laborers, consumers, and businesspeople of the bead trade. The fact that the manufacturer earns a thousand times more than his employees seems itself morally repugnant, and in practice it prevents them from obtaining a fair share of the wealth. The revelers can live with themselves only because layers of middlemen screen them from the poverty of the workers who serve their whims. On this second view, until that day when regulation or redistribution levels the playing field and effectively recognizes the equality of all concerned, everyone is right to be ashamed of the secret life of beads.

Each of these differing perspectives can be found in sophisticated theoretical treatments from economists and philosophers as well as vernacular judgments in the press and on the street. Certainly, both points of view have something to say for themselves. But notice what they share. They agree that the bead trade should be judged ultimately by material output and who lays hold of it. More broadly, though left and right disagree whether it is more pressing to grow the economic pie or to cut it into fairer slices, they agree on the basic ingredients of the pie: it's about making money.

We should call this verity into question. As a matter of respectable public discussion, the primacy of private gain may seem almost self-evident.

Yet it is curiously out of sync with the suffering and sympathy of the actors in the bead trade. Both the workers and the revelers have an obscure sense of being caught up, in the very act of working or trading, in human projects that go beyond their personal actions and interests. Normally they have no meaningful way to assess their place in the larger landscape, which is shrouded by distance and middlemen. But when the veil is lifted for a moment, what bothers them is not the discovery of the size of someone else's pile. They suddenly find themselves shaping the lives of others in ways that they can scarcely understand or affirm.

Political economy as a human affair is more capacious than the elemental concern for wealth. There would be more to a truly healthy commerce in beads than benefiting all the relevant pocketbooks more, or more equally, or both. Indeed, there is already more at stake, which is why the women of Fuzhou cannot rest content with their inability to connect their work to a shared horizon of meaning. It is the reality, indeed the primacy, of a shared dimension in the firm and the market that this book aspires to confirm, clarify, and press against anyone who would reduce the point of enterprise, either personally or politically, to the pursuit of private gain.

ACKNOWLEDGMENTS

This book has traveled a long road in terms of ideas, years, and miles, and I have incurred debts of all sorts and sizes along the way. Publicly avowing my debts is hardly tantamount to paying them off, I admit. But even were it possible, I would not want to make all my intellectual creditors entirely whole, since this would mark an end of common action rather than its fulfillment in friendship. Strangers Selling Stuff may want to settle up and close the account book, but I do not. All those named here, please accept my gratitude as a small down payment, with the balance to be made good in our continued search for wisdom together and in the common product that lies before you. As to responsibility for its shortcomings, the usual caveats apply.

The foundations for this book were laid in my graduate studies at Notre Dame, where I learned and drew support from more people than I can list here. Many thanks are due to my dissertation committee: Patrick Deneen, Mary Keys, and especially Russell Hittinger, whose mentorship and intellectual example have helped me as much as his pathbreaking approach to common goods. I can hardly thank all my fellow students who have encouraged both me and this project, but I offer special thanks to Kevin Vance, Theresa Smart, Zack German, Scott Hefelfinger, Rob Wyllie, Liam de los Reyes, and Brian Boyd. Special thanks to Ross McCulloch for his decisive contributions to the "power-practice-profit" matrix of common good analysis that features in chapter 3. Among my exemplary teachers and mentors I remember Michael and Catherine Zuckert, Dan Philpott, Christian Smith, and Rick Garnett. I am compelled also to thank the crew at my second intellectual home from my doctoral years, the Lumen Christi Institute at the University of Chicago, for their hospitality at Gavin House, Berkeley, Oxford, and elsewhere, and especially to Thomas Levergood, may he rest in peace.

The actual text of the book was written largely at the Institute for Advanced Studies in Culture at the University of Virginia, an incomparably beautiful and convivial setting to work. Thanks to James Davison Hunter and the IASC staff and leadership for their generous support over three years. Thanks to John Owen and Joe Davis for wise mentorship, and to all the participants in a valuable manuscript workshop Joe organized: James Bernard Murphy, Colin Bird, Tal Brewer, Andy Yuengert, and my scribe Jim van Dyke. Thanks to Matt Crawford for your example and advice and to David Ciepley for your support and example before, during, and after our shared time at the IASC. Thanks for innumerable conversations to IASC fellows: among the younger set Andrew Lynn, Kyle Williams, Cassandra Nelson, and Paul Nedelisky, as well as more senior colleagues Paul Scherz, Isaac Reed, and Brad Wilcox. Thanks to my Navarra colleague Alejo Sison for steadfast friendship, to Megan Levine of University of Notre Dame Press for her editorial support, and to Bob Banning of Turning Leaves Editorial for his deft copyediting.

I should also like to thank audiences and commentators that have kindly allowed me to share some of this work with them: at the University of Pennsylvania and the Collegium Institute, University of St. Thomas (Minnesota), Universidad de los Andes (Bogotà, Colombia), Holy Cross College, UPAEP (Puebla, Mexico), the economists of the CREDO seminar, and the University of Navarra as well as annual meetings of the American Political Science Association and the Association for Political Theory. Of the many colleagues from institutions other than my own who have helped me by conversations, feedback, and general encouragement, I should like to remember especially Mary Hirschfeld, Dan Finn, Brad Lewis, Stefan Eich, Kirk Doran, Nic Teh, John Buchmann, Fr. Aquinas Guilbeau, O.P., and Émilie Tardivel.

For incalculable support in the intellectual life and so much more, I offer my filial gratitude to my parents, David and Rory Hoipkemier. You may have actually read the manuscript as it grew readable in the final stages, for which I thank you particularly. The best way to cope with this unpayable debt is, I suppose, to try to love my own children as well as you loved me.

My most comprehensive and least payable debt is to Naomi, my rock of support and encouragement, who has been at the back of this from the beginning, before the Hermitage was a twinkle in the mind's eye. You haven't read this book in its entirety yet, but I hope you will, as I dedicate it to you with all my love.

INTRODUCTION

Merchant versus Citizen

The gap is growing between the human experience of the marketplace and the terms of public debate about it. Open the newspaper on any given day. The front page gives the GDP or unemployment or another economic indicator. A few pages later, the financial section recounts the fortunes of leading corporations, compressed into statistics and ciphers. When politicians put their spin on the economic situation, it is the numbers they are spinning. There is no lack of public interest in these matters, but the kinds of questions that citizens are encouraged to ask are curiously truncated. Whatever cannot be said in the language of the spreadsheet usually goes unsaid. Why do we speak as if merchants had nothing to do with the project of making a social world together beyond supplying it with money?

The language of wealth is dangerously impoverished, when it comes to articulating the role of merchants and markets in public life. Consider a troubling political development: the growth of authoritarian populism in the US and abroad. Certainly, populism has been nourished by decades of widening wealth inequality, as the global market has left behind France's yellow vest protestors (*gilets jaunes*) or the Trump-voting "deplorables" of middle America.[1] Yet their grievances do not concern only their pocketbooks. They object also to their diminished place in the common world and to the public scorn heaped on the things they hold dear. To express populists' concerns in terms of material resources alone, as their opponents have often done, only feeds the mutual miscomprehension that is all too common in partisan politics today. There is something at stake beyond the pursuit of private goods, which we overlook at our peril.

A similar inarticulacy surrounds the working lives of young adults. Their aspirations are far less mercenary than the typical wealth-oriented view would admit. According to a 2016 Gallup report, the millennials (born 1980–96) are looking for more out of their jobs than any previous generation.[2] They want purpose at work, not just a paycheck. The rising generation is much more committed and loyal when they see their contribution to a mission-driven organization and its role in society. Often enough, millennials don't find what they seek. The wide-ranging implications of their disappointed quest, for themselves and others, cannot be reckoned in dollars and cents. Yet like the political populists, millennials frequently lack the vocabulary for expressing their economic aspirations and frustrations in a way that is both resonant and realistic.[3] The dominant discourse of self-interest and free exchange is tongue-tied when it comes to shared dreams and projects.

This book revives the concept of common goods to redescribe the moral architecture of today's dominant economic institutions—the business firm and the market. They pull citizens, often unwittingly, into common projects answering the deepest political questions of how to live together. Treating business and trade in narrow money terms, as we so often do, only obscures their full civic cost as well as the larger goods they serve. We need a richer vocabulary. Though the phrase is often just a slogan, deeper reflection on "the common good" yields a powerful grammar for analyzing economic orders as transformative moral projects that cannot be fully explained, much less justified, in the language of self-interest. Prices and private gain do play a crucial role, of course, but a grammar of common goods allows us to map the fundamental and often-overlooked dimensions of the firm and market that go beyond price.

In the book's two main sections, I argue that the idiom of private gain obscures the different modes of solidarity at play in business or the market respectively, and then suggest how common goods might be better kept in view. The firm is an especially clear case, because it is itself a communal endeavor. The collaborators in a business inevitably suffer injustice when their shared practice, friendship, and authority are instrumentalized for the profits of others. Business flourishes over time, both morally and materially, by integrating private gain into common ventures that are pursued as ends in themselves. Unlike firms, price-centered markets are not typically communities in their own right, because they do not involve merchants in any collaboration around shared ends. Nonetheless, the marketplace has always been a publicly constructed space of private action, instituted in service of a common vision. Market patterns draw on a common life and should be ultimately evaluated, at least in part, in terms of the solidarities on which they depend. We need not subscribe to rosy ideals of virtuous, public-spirited commerce (though in some cases we should not shrink from higher aspirations) in order to live up to the common goals built into the market economy as we know it.

FIRMS AND MARKETS

This book turns to the firm and the market as centrally important institutions in their own right, and also as illuminating examples of how and why to think our way past the balance sheet. In a society where everyone is "in some measure a merchant,"[4] as Adam Smith puts it, the real-world influence of firms and markets is beyond dispute. Getting their moral architecture right or wrong will deeply affect the working lives, indeed the whole lives, of billions of people. (By "moral architecture" I mean the pattern of normative ties among different persons/positions in a given institution.[5] *Who* makes claims on *whom*, and in *what* do these claims consist?) The firm and the market pose an especially tantalizing puzzle for a civic idiom of common goods and goals, because we tend to think of commerce ultimately as a vehicle of self-interest. No one could plausibly deny that firms and markets are centrally concerned with material wealth, and have proven rather good at getting it. Still, I shall argue that this morally unambitious picture does not adequately capture either institution. One might say that a stunted view of how firms and markets actually *do* work (e.g., "they run on private exchange alone") cuts off a full sense of the shared human goods they might ideally realize. Or one could say that a narrow pecuniary ideal (e.g., "their real goal is just to make money") obscures the modes of solidarity that are actually at work. In fact both institutions are built around communal action and irreducibly shared goals. In conversation with leading analytic theories, I will show how the firm and the market in their familiar forms already embody a commitment to common goods, which we ignore only at the price of injustice.

If the book's constructive project has an antagonist, it is the Chicago school of economics (along with Austrian fellow traveler Friedrich Hayek), because of its extremely influential account of the firm and the market in terms of individual goods alone, excluding common goods. The Chicago school's political and intellectual clout peaked in the 1980s, thanks to its confident, quasi-scientific application of individualistic market models to phenomena as disparate as family and crime.[6] Since then, like an aging champ taking on all comers, Chicago's ambitious project has been critiqued from all points of the compass in economics, political science, business ethics, and law. The 2008 financial crisis put a definitive end to "markets in everything" as a practical policy agenda, and also rekindled scholarly discussion on the moral limits of markets.[7] Nonetheless, Chicago's intellectual paradigm still sets the terms of debate, even among its critics. For instance, many normative theorists and institutional economists rightly object that the corporate firm is a mode of cooperation under authority, not a market, but still assent to the basic Chicago tenet that the firm's raison d'être is profit or gain.[8] Likewise, leading neo-republicans have adopted wholesale the Chicago claim that the market is necessarily devoid of arbitrary power, even though their overall program of "nondomination" would be anathema to many disciples of Milton Friedman.[9] Chicago has drawn them into its way of thinking, and its intellectual influence will continue until a rival framework of comparable cogency and explanatory power supplants Chicago's fundamental focus on private exchange. By marking out common action and common ends as essential categories for explaining economic institutions, I hope to contribute to that more capacious vision.

Rather than reemphasizing the limits of the market, as many normative theorists have rightly done, this book takes the fight to Chicago's home turf. It is not only the case that politics and family are not markets, though that is true enough. Even the market itself is not a market in the individualistic sense that the Chicago school alleges. Still less could we say of the business firm that it is oriented to profit alone. Of course, the idea of holding firms and markets to a standard beyond money is nothing new. It is a staple of moral and political argument among both the defenders and critics of capitalism.[10] But, given a social imaginary that divides the world of the merchant from that of the citizen,[11] neither side can easily maintain that shared moral goals are native to the allegedly neutral economic domain. Too often, therefore, Chicago's critics from normative theory adopt a finger-wagging, moralizing tone, as if their concerns required merchants to sacrifice hard "economic" thinking to a foreign normative standard.[12] I hope to enhance their arguments by clarifying the common ends already built right into economic institutions as we know them. One contribution of the present book is to fashion a language of critique that cannot be shrugged off by the "tough-minded realist" who focuses on material productivity rather than airy ethics. Lying just below the surface of the market and the firm are shared moral projects that are essential to their practical function. What we need is not a *moralized* firm or a *politicized* market, nor a greater concern for equity at the expense of efficiency, but firms and markets that are more fully themselves.

MANY SOLIDARITIES

The intellectual backbone of this book is a basic distinction between two kinds of goals that we might legitimately pursue in interacting: divisible private goods and essentially shared common goods. The former can be achieved or enjoyed apart from the collaboration at hand; the latter cannot. If you and I both sign up for a mutual fund, the success of the fund can be legitimately assessed by our separate bank accounts. But where cooperation is intrinsic to our goals (as for the quarterback and the community organizer) or simply is our goal (as in romantic love), we pass beyond the realm of divisible private goods. Suppose a couple files for divorce: she gets the house and he gets the car, but who gets the marriage? No one, of course. Loving intimacy is something that "we" achieve together, as a common good, or not at all. When a heap of private goods is all that is left of a shipwrecked union, the sense of loss testifies to the additional dimensions of the relationship when it was thriving: mutual enjoyment and deliberation (and likely quarreling), moral formation and solidarity (and the potential for exploitation), and all that comes with being caught up in a venture larger than oneself.

As a practical matter, the different logics of acting together around common and private goods are familiar to everyone. No one has trouble distinguishing the players on a sports team from its fans or suppliers, in terms of their rights and duties or the moral scope of their commitments. Athletes themselves apply different norms and expectations at the contract-negotiation table (where private goods are salient) than on the field. But without a vocabulary for articulating the distinctions that we enact every day, it is hard to persuasively connect personal relationships or private associations with the larger questions of politics and economics. This book develops a conceptual "grammar" for thinking about common goods in any setting, centered on the claim that each form of common action is to be reckoned as a form of solidarity built around common ends of its own. I call this normative framework "Aristotelian pluralism": "Aristotelian" in that communities' real ends are not reducible to private gain, and "pluralism" because of the legitimate multiplicity of common goods.

The members of any community share a moral goal, which is that their collaboration flourish as whatever kind of emergent social form it is—firm, school, family, polity, and so on— by achieving its ends with justice. Their allegiance as members is due primarily to this common good; in collaborating, members should pursue private interest only to the extent of a just share in the common benefits and burdens. The emergent ends of common action, which typically "alter not only what you do but what you want to do,"[13] are a matter of embodied practice as well as shared understandings. Modeling the point of common action as an aggregate of private goods, as economists recommend, does not alter the formative power or the moral priority of socially embodied ends. As an orchestra is more than forty-odd soloists,[14] any collaborative achievement is more than a sum of private contributions and cannot be assessed without distortion unless one attends to intrinsically shared dimensions of culture, authority, and formation. We can get at the normative goals of a given social order by asking three key questions: To what ends is it characteristically oriented? Who participates in them? How could their shared ends be justly achieved?

It is important at the outset to distinguish this grammar of common action from traditional political theories about The Common Good.[15] Though my argument owes much to Aristotelian and civic republican insights, I keep my distance from their large political claims, the better to benefit two distinct audiences. First, to help the proponents of The Common Good more trenchantly to apply this often hazy concept. Second, and perhaps primarily, for those who are skeptical of The Common Good in politics, Aristotelian pluralism shows why and how to consider common goods in the firm and the market. The skeptics' own normative views will be enhanced if they do so, for the price of ignoring the full scope of acting together, in any domain, is error and injustice. They can sign on to Aristotelian pluralism because it is a conceptual language for articulating an architecture of shared rights and duties, not a full-fledged theoretical rival to their own views. Compelling political judgments will have to flesh out this skeletal framework with further, always contestable claims about justice and human flourishing. Though my two rival audiences should both adopt the framework of Aristotelian pluralism, they will vehemently disagree on these further moral questions, and I will not try to settle their dispute.

The proponents and the skeptics might both think that inasmuch as I skirt the grand questions of political theory in their full breadth and depth, this book is scarcely even addressing The Common Good in its traditional, directly political sense. They are right. For the Aristotelian pluralist, the shared project of citizens is only one kind of common action around common ends, albeit an especially influential one. To describe the goods pursued in common by players on a team, or workers in a firm, is not to say anything about The Common Good shared by citizens, except insofar as the two forms of common action are actually linked. (The actual links are not negligible, so one cannot help adverting to politics at least as a backstop for the plural common goods of markets and firms.) Admittedly, there is a real danger of confusion between my pluralist usage of "common goods" and the dominant terminology. Out of respect for the traditional parlance, I have adopted the convention of denoting the putative supreme goal of politics as "The Common Good," capitalized and singular. When referring to any other ends or goals shared by anyone other than citizens qua citizens, I will use a variety of other terms: common ends, common goods (in the plural, noncapitalized), common goals, common projects, and so on.[16]

An analogy may help to clarify the ground I mean to occupy. It is too seldom noticed that what drives most substantive theories of The Common Good is the formal distinction between private goods and the ends of common action. This intellectual engine has been traditionally linked with a number of further claims (of Aristotelian or civic republican inspiration) about what is best for humans to seek or to be. Together these components generate a full-bodied political theory, which we might imagine as the complete race car of Team CG (the proponents of The Common Good). Yet we should not mistake the engine for the whole car. What I do in this book is akin to extracting the engine—the distinction between private and common goods—and hitching it to a stripped-down test chassis, the better to canvass dimensions of the firm and the market that would otherwise remain unexplored. Whoever wants to drive on this difficult terrain needs Team CG's engine, even if they reject the rest of the vehicle. I will not try to convert the opposing teams (the skeptics) to support their rival's car, only to convince them that there is technology under Team CG's hood that they should take seriously. The loyal supporters of The Common Good, on the other hand, should take heart that it is indeed their engine that I am using. Drivers can learn from mechanics, and I believe that Aristotelian pluralism can help Team CG more insightfully to apply their own intellectual machinery to the distinctive challenges of today's world. I pause to address these two distinct audiences in turn.

Team CG: It is easy to forget how a reliable engine works, unless you tinker with it in the way of repair or enhancement. The broad discourse of The Common Good is lamentably prone to hazy moralizing, which fails to ask how particular human goals are shared and by whom, on the assumption that true human flourishing is a common concern for all citizens merely as such.[17] Speaking roughly, most traditional accounts focus first on what is good, largely ignoring how it might be held in common. Equally roughly, Aristotelian pluralism does the reverse, asking first about what ends are already common and what demands they make upon us, leaving provisionally unsettled the question of the ultimate good. Whether or not we ever approach anyone's ideal of shared flourishing, we need to be able to discuss the projects we actually share. Firms or markets cannot be directed toward healthy communities and flourishing lives without first asking the questions that this book's grammar of common action is designed to clarify: Is a market oriented to private gain, or something more? And for whom? What is a market, anyway? The same can be asked of the firm. The adherent of The Common Good may wonder why the present book, having posed such questions, self-consciously declines to take the next step and propose a full normative ideal. Ultimately, I agree that one should do both. What is more, in acting together we are always doing both, inasmuch as any common action embodies some vision of what it is best to do or to be. But the best way to persuade a skeptical world to aim at flourishing together is to show that shared ends are *both* unavoidable *and* contestable. Common ends mark the opening of discussion, not the close. They are common ground, not the special province of any single partisan camp. A formal grammar can put these ends in question in an evenhanded way, open to moral debate and empirical evidence, without loading the dice in favor of any particular moral or political view.

Skeptics about The Common Good, on the other hand, may find Team CG's race car too confining, or the components antiquated, or that the car is historically prone to bloody political accidents. There is not much that unites hard-left progressives with centrist social democrats or right-leaning classical liberals, but one thing they usually share is a critique of The Common Good as a substantive political ideal, with its whiff of the premodern.[18] I want to reintroduce these critics to a grammar of common action that is neither particularly political nor especially substantive, which can enhance their own analysis of economic institutions. The opponents of Team CG should not acquiesce to the idea that by rejecting a certain traditional vision of The Common Good, they oppose the very idea of common goods. Rightly understood, the disputed issue that divides them from Team CG is not *whether* to promote common ends, which are inescapable, but *which ones*. Ignoring common ends where they really arise is as unjust as it is shortsighted. Citizens of differing political or intellectual persuasions should all be able to agree, on consideration of the legal and social reality, that our economic order demands serious attention to common goods beyond private gain.

The main goal of this book is to map the lineaments of solidarity in two domains, the firm and the market. Different camps will presumably disagree, on account of their wider normative disagreements, about what true justice demands in each domain—who deserves which goods, and why. There would be nothing amiss about finding progressives, socialists, and libertarians (or, within the academy, Rawlsians, utilitarians, and Foucauldians) all couching their own disparate visions in terms of common goods. My proposed grammar of common action does not answer the substantive questions that divide them. "Proper grammar" indicates only *how* to argue clearly and coherently, not *what* to argue.[19] Just as we could all use the language of human rights without agreeing on a specific list of such rights, so there are many "grammatically correct" conclusions concerning the firm and the market. But I contend at least this much: every viable option respecting the basic social and legal realities of the firm and the market should analyze them, at least partially, under the rubric of common action. This is not the end of the story, but it offers a fresh, less distorting place to begin for a world saturated by the rhetoric of private gain.

EXCHANGE VERSUS COMMON ACTION

In order to see the distinctiveness of common goods more vividly, it is useful to think about the contrasting cases where they are absent. For the Aristotelian pluralist, outside of collaborative contexts where some irreducible and morally transformative "we" is at stake, the grammar of common action simply does not apply. Absent some emergency, Team A's coach is not responsible for Team B's common goods, any more than the mail carrier shares in my family's thriving or struggles. I see nothing troubling or stingy about this. There is no moral duty to seek solidarity with everyone in everything. The basic rule of a grammar of common goods is conditional: *if* one engages in common action, then one is answerable to the full scope of the resulting common ends and to the persons who share them.[20] Otherwise, private goods prevail. In the context of this book, the paradigmatic example of voluntary interaction that does *not* aim at a common good is market exchange.

What is a market? In its concrete historical meaning, "a market is a meeting place for the purpose of barter or buying and selling."[21] Today we speak of physical marketplaces, like a supermarket, and of abstractions like the "used-car market." These different types of markets all center on the readiness of some group of buyers and sellers to enter into a particular kind of exchange relation.[22] For Adam Smith and his heirs, the elemental character of market exchange boils down to a three-word slogan: Strangers Selling Stuff. What is distinctive about a paradigmatic market relation is its focus on the item or service at hand, not on the persons involved. Whether the transaction takes place depends overwhelmingly on the quality of the benefit and its price. As I walk the bazaar, it doesn't matter to me whether I buy from Maria or Jose, only whether I get a good deal. The social standing or status of the parties is largely irrelevant. They may be fellow members of a fraternal club, or even superior and subordinate in some organization, but on the market they meet, so to speak, as strangers and equals. Neither do power and authority determine the outcome of the exchange. In order to minimize their influence, market relations presuppose legal freedom as well as the existence of other, similar buyers and sellers, so that each party has an effective "exit option" both de jure and de facto.[23] As a starting point, we may say that a market relation is a free exchange in which price alone, or nearly so, determines if the transaction takes place, and not authority or social position.[24]

It is important not to confuse market relations in the sense of "Strangers Selling Stuff" with the much broader notion of "the free market," which often serves as a shorthand for the entire liberal economy of production, consumption, and trade.[25] The key difference is that free citizens often form organizations whose members do not stand in market relations to one another, such as the family farm or, as I shall show in chapter 1, the business firm. Farms and firms may be involved in many different markets—in raw materials, labor, retail, and so on— but they are not constituted internally by market relations inasmuch as they employ social mechanisms of authority and solidarity, not price signals.[26] They are in the market, but not of the market.

This clarification is not an arbitrary bit of linguistic hygiene; understanding what is and is not price-centered exchange is crucial for concretely locating common action and its ends within our commercial world. In practice, prices generally map the limits of common action, because the aim of an impersonal market exchange is not a common good shared by the merchants. It is true that a market bargain will be freely consummated only if each party judges it to their advantage. But, contrary to appearances, this mutual benefit is not an end held in common, only "a sum of private goods that happen to be interdependent."[27] Typically, buyers and sellers in an arm's-length transaction are not trying to pursue some goal together, but to get a good deal for themselves. This mutual disinterest does not imply that the market is a morality-free zone. It only looks that way (to some) because the governing norms of exchange are designed to ensure equality in private gains and prevent collusion. But in so doing, they rule out merchant solidarity as well, almost by accident. In a corporate merger or real-estate purchase, if bankers or regulators suspect some "community of interest" such as insider trading, they are apt to cry foul. Reasonably so, since sale prices among family or friends will likely not reflect fair market value. Where common ends are at stake, as among friends, there are relational goods to consider in addition to the strict value of the item changing hands. "Strangers Selling Stuff" are far more likely to bargain at the market price, just because they share no common goods.

This book's basic strategy for identifying the frontiers of common action in the firm and the market is to map the contours of price-centered exchange. Where prices are actually coordinating a complex set of social interactions, I will presume that common goods are absent, and legitimately so.[28] But only there. To the extent that coordination in the firm or market depends on common action beyond price, the "economic" analysis of private goods is insufficient, both practically and normatively. There is more going on, and we cannot understand either the social mechanisms or the goods or evils at stake without a "political" framing that uses the grammar of common goods to parse contested claims about power and justice.

For example, if the business firm were a nexus of market contracts, as supposed by Milton Friedman and the Chicago school of economics, there would be nothing wrong with the pursuit of private gain as the firm's supreme goal. What else *could* it pursue? But in fact a corporate firm is a type of common action, and a community governed on the pretense of serving purely private ends is something more pernicious. The shareholder-value corporation is not just another corner of the market; it is an "imperial oligarchy"[29] that unjustly empowers financial interests at the expense of the workers, local communities, and other citizens who have a multidimensional human interest in the firm, and in not seeing its common life instrumentalized for the sake of profit (of outsiders, no less).

Prices are never the whole story, even about the market itself, which has always been a politically constructed space. My goal in this book, then, is to identify and illuminate those dimensions of common action that cannot be explained by prices or justified by the rhetoric of private goods. If even market exchange cannot be fully assessed without adverting to common action and its ends, much less can we understand the flourishing of business in the cramped language of private goods, either in a hierarchical firm or in a dispersed global company. Working from this basic insight, parts 1 and 2 of the book follow a similar pattern. I begin each part by showing the inadequacy of influential views that focus on private goods alone, and then I move toward a fuller picture of the moral architecture of the firm and the market as sites of solidarity in their own right. The grammar of common goods gives us a rigorous language for articulating the pervasive sense of being caught up, in the very act of working or trading, in human projects that go beyond individual choices and interests.

The rhetoric of coordinated self-interest is especially inapt in the business firm, and the failure to recognize a pluralism of common goods is especially damaging there. Chapter 1 critiques one of the monuments of this reductive approach, the Chicago-school theory of the firm as a nexus of market contracts. With enviable elegance, the theory enshrines the pursuit of profit and wards off political meddling. But the legal and social reality belies this neat picture. In fact, firms gain a productivity advantage precisely because they do *not* operate internally through contracts, but through cooperation under authority. Much of this authority derives from a grant of state power, not from the property rights of stockholders, who do not own the corporation (in fact, no one does). Yet the leading critics of the Chicago theory have not gone far enough, because they still construe the decent firm without adverting to any intrinsically shared ends. The just goals of state-backed, morally formative collaboration could not possibly be couched in the reductive language of private gain, no matter how well the wealth may be shared.

In order to correct the myopic focus on private goods, chapter 2 develops the conceptual grammar of Aristotelian pluralism, drawing constructively on Charles Taylor, Alasdair MacIntyre, the English pluralists, and Aristotle himself. Common goods are fundamental ingredients of cooperative action, which we ignore at the price of injustice. Persons acting together form an emergent community, a morally formative solidarity that is oriented to its own set of irreducibly social ends—which may range from friendship to shared practice to legal order. Particular common ends—for example, of family or workplace—must be evaluated for consistency with broader normative standards: those of the polity (on account of its ubiquitous influence) and of the person (whose flourishing is the ultimate point).

Chapter 3 applies this normative grammar by constructing a theory of the corporate firm as a public/private entity, drawing on stakeholder theory and recent Aristotelian thought. Internally, the business firm is a community of work with its own proper common ends. I develop a typology for ordering profit, power, practice, and productivity as aspects of the overall flourishing of the firm. The primary members who share this complex good *as common* are its workers, whose claims therefore take precedence over investors or other community stakeholders. Because the corporate form rests on a grant of state power, however, corporate firms incur a fiduciary duty toward political common projects beyond the generic mandate to follow the law. We can only avoid the oligarchic shareholder-value corporation by orienting the culture and institutions of business to something other than a short-term, socially narrow, and morally reductive vision of its own flourishing.

If the hierarchical firm was the key problem of yesterday, the challenge of tomorrow is to pursue just solidarity in dispersed, global companies that do not fit inherited categories of who counts and why. Chapter 4 turns to gig-economy giant Uber to illustrate the need for a grammar of common action at the tech frontier. Like other "fissured" brands,[30] Uber specializes in profitable retail and coordination work while farming out any actual transport to a highly supervised network of market suppliers. Are common goods still relevant? I argue that Uber and its drivers are indeed engaged in a mode of formative common action, though the standard category of "employment" does not adequately capture their shared project. A better moral/legal language for Uber must be keyed to the common goods of tech-enabled collaboration, which is something quite different from competitive market exchange. On the other side of the ledger, market networks featuring less oversight and control than Uber's would be better conceived in transactional terms, not as actual or potential sites of solidarity in their own right.

Part 2 moves beyond the firm to consider the price system itself: How can an economy ordered in large part by the market, the zone of individualism par excellence, reliably promote (or, for that matter, damage) any common ends? The chapters of this part each challenge one pillar of the pervasive commonsense view that (A) politics is a form of common action, but (B) markets are not, so (C) they have no regular relation to one another. This is clearly too simple, since every stable democracy makes extensive use of markets, and a longer historical perspective shows a regular, cyclical relation between markets and political equality. Chapter 5 engages the tradition of liberal economics, especially the "spontaneous" approach of Friedrich Hayek, as an entrée to understanding markets as a distinctive form of social order. Hayek argues that the Invisible Hand of market competition leads to private benefits for all, precisely because the price system is an order of divergent private purposes, not a zone of common action. Hayek's stylized individualism does capture the nature and the appeal of many impersonal markets, such as online commerce or international commodities exchange, but it cannot explain the market's political frame. Markets have always been a matter of political construction and regulation, so Hayek's stark division between common ends and the individualistic market could never be more than half true.

Chapter 6 turns to the thought of Karl Polanyi for a more complex political picture of how markets relate to common action and its ends. On Polanyi's "instituted" model, though market exchange may be thin and impersonal, it is embedded in and dependent upon thicker common action in civil society or politics. The overall patterns of markets, though usually not their particular outcomes, are the product of common action embodying some broad vision of common goods. A liberal market economy remains a moral economy, albeit a somewhat paradoxical one, so it should be evaluated in terms of shared, embodied ideals of flourishing individuals and societies, not maximizing private gain. Despite his critical insights, Polanyi draws an overly bleak picture of the market as a ravenous juggernaut that brooks no compromise, and he leaps to the unwarranted (and likely nonviable) conclusion that a market system must be rejected entirely in order to secure essential common goods.

For a theoretical resolution to the politics-market discontinuity, chapter 7 turns to the Italian tradition of civil economy, which reenvisions market exchange as a sphere of mutual assistance rather than disinterest. For Enlightenment luminary Antonio Genovesi and his contemporary disciples, the market is (or at least could be) a sphere of common action and even fraternity. In principle, concern for a variety of common goods can be factored into market prices as a "social coefficient," somewhat as we already see where wages are swayed by collective bargaining and in relational industries of care and education. Market prices reflecting reciprocity could themselves be an instrument of solidarity without sacrificing the dynamism of decentralized decision-making. But the civil ideal is no panacea. Absent an ecosystem of virtuous citizens and mature institutions, the risks of politicizing exchange would be liable to outweigh the social benefits of a civil market. Since none of the redactions of the market treated in chapters 5, 6, and 7 definitively covers all markets or bests its rival views, I will conclude part 2 by suggesting a pluralistic approach to markets, and the book as a whole by glancing at a truly pluralist political economy that might take better account of all our common goods.

PART 1

DOING BUSINESS

A parable: Suppose an inquisitive alien arrives in our solar system, equipped with a scanner that can detect different kinds of social order—politics and family, love and war, and so on. In this remarkable telescope, price-centered market relations appear as thin red lines. Businesses like Honda, Amazon, and the corner grocery show up as solid green fields. Our interstellar tourist settles into Earth orbit and peers down, eager to observe the free-market economies she has read so much about in her guide to the galaxy. Imagine her surprise when she sees how the green patches dominate the scene below. There is indeed a spidery network of red market lines connecting the businesses, but a great deal more of earthlings' time and decisions are wrapped up in green than in red. Peering closely into an individual green organization, she notes that it is not held together primarily by the red lines of prices, but by pale blue curves of authority and cooperation. Some of the blue curves stretch between firms, and others connect them to the government. Disappointed at the seeming unimportance of the red lines of market prices, she writes a letter of complaint to the editors of the *Aliens' Guide to Earth*, asking them not to raise false hopes of spotting that elusive creature, the market economy. She suggests a new term for the next edition of the guidebook: "Wouldn't 'organizational economy' be more appropriate?"[1]

Nobel Prize–winning economist Herbert Simon, the originator of this parable, is quite right to suggest that the business organization has a strong claim to be the dominant form of economic order today. The decisions, leaders, and brands of the great corporations—Google, J.P. Morgan, Toyota, Walmart, and their peers—loom large in both private and public life.[2] Their great and growing importance is enough on its own to warrant careful attention in any political theory of the economy. But there is another reason why this book begins with business corporations as the first step in a larger argument that morally formative common projects already pervade the market economy: they present the most straightforward and obvious case.

I do not mean to suggest that the solidarities underlying business are obvious to every observer—far from it. Without an adequate moral vocabulary for thinking about the social realities of business, it is all too tempting to think of corporations solely as vehicles for making money, or more generally for promoting private goods. Chapter 1 will challenge the widespread conception of business as a visible instrument of the invisible hand by critiquing its most rigorous expression in the Chicago school of law and economics. Despite its elegance, the Chicago model of the firm as a market badly distorts the legal and social mechanisms by which businesses actually run. A more adequate view of the firm depends on a sturdier conceptual framework that is not founded on individualistic concepts tailored to market exchange. Chapter 2 will pull back from the business firm in particular to develop the general grammar of common action and common goods that is so often lacking, which can illuminate what a private-good approach leaves dark in the business corporation (and also, in part 2 of the book, in the market).

Chapter 3 returns to business as a specific social domain, using this conceptual grammar to rearticulate the business firm as a morally formative collaboration in its own right that is also constitutively dependent on larger communities and their ends. Because the traditional corporate firm is built around cooperation under authority and embedded in politics, it can be rightly understood only in terms of common action and ends. The same framework is also indispensable for the growing problem of fissured work, exemplified by gig-economy titan Uber, which has forsaken collaboration within the firm in favor of market-based outsourcing, as a way to boost profits while maintaining high levels of control. Existing legal and moral frameworks have only begun to confront this troubling development, but chapter 4 suggests that market constellations combining prices and power, like Uber's driver network, are themselves forms of common action stretching beyond the firm. Like any other community, their moral architecture bends toward irreducibly shared ends, albeit in a rather unstable way. The hierarchical corporation is only one of the many kinds of irreducibly social, morally formative common action that pervade the market economy as we know it, but for now it remains the most important kind.

The overall goal of part 1 is to reimagine what businesses are all about, by articulating their nature and goals with a conceptual vocabulary that is all too often reserved for politics, the grammar of common goods. One large contention of this book is that solidarity around shared ends arises wherever persons act together and that action in common must be evaluated in terms of goods held in common. Business firms are no exception. Despite the widespread opinion that business is oriented solely or primarily to private goods, or is itself a kind of market, the private-good imaginary is at its weakest when it tries to explain the commercial corporation. Businesses do not the fit into a market model, for they draw on too many human motivations that are absent from typical market exchange: trust, loyalty, shared practice. Classical economists from Adam Smith to Karl Marx to Friedrich Hayek were right to recognize a categorical difference between corporations and the market.[3] The bluntest way to express the normative distinction is to note that businesses aim at common goods, while markets do not. This simplified divide is not wholly adequate for a case such as Uber, where common action bleeds over into market exchange, and part 2 of the book will problematize it further by treating the market directly. Still, if even price-guided market relations sometimes demand to be conceived in terms of common ends, a fortiori should we think of business firms in this way, not just as an ideal, but in order to understand our imperfect world. To do justice to the solidarities that arise even in the hard-nosed world of business, we must learn to pay attention to common action and its goods.

CHAPTER ONE

NO PROFIT WITHOUT HONOR

In January 2008, the venerable department store Sears, Roebuck & Co. transformed its inner workings in a bid to mirror the larger competitive environment. The various divisions of the company—such as appliances, tools, IT, and HR—were split into more than thirty separate entities, which each had their own leadership and balance sheet. The changes were instigated by Sears' new chairman, hedge fund manager Eddie Lampert, who thought that running Sears as if it were a marketplace would improve "visibility and accountability" and ultimately deliver new efficiencies thanks to the invisible hand of price-centered competition. What resulted instead was that the various divisions began to use outside contractors rather than sharing costs, fight one another for space in ads and on shelves, and prioritize their unit's own profit at the expense of the larger bottom line. Sears declared bankruptcy in 2018, after 126 years in operation.[1]

Though Sears' "warring tribes" approach turned out a spectacular failure, Lampert's experiment was only an unusually audacious and thoroughgoing application of three ideas that have much broader currency, concerning the moral architecture of commerce. The most basic of these, shared almost universally today, is that the ultimate goal of business is to make money. If Sears' methods of pursuing profits went wrong, at least its heart was in the right place. Since practicality must also ask, "Profit for whom?," the second influential idea tells us that businesses should be judged primarily by the prosperity of stockholders in particular (as opposed to, e.g., workers, local communities, or the GDP). Stock markets certainly took notice of Lampert's bold plan: Sears' stock price initially jumped when the metamorphosis was announced, only to plummet as losses, dysfunction, and store closures mounted. Third and most specifically, Sears' reorganization scheme reflected the theory of the firm championed by the Chicago school of law and economics, which holds that a business organization is a "nexus of contracts" fueled by self-interested competition. Splitting Sears into rival units was a bid to enact a vision of the firm as a kind of market, an ideal that has proven influential not only in courts and classrooms but also in boardrooms and business culture.

The project of this first chapter is to call all three of these big ideas into question. My specific thesis is a critical one: any theory of the firm as solely a creature of market trading and private ends could not possibly be right. The Chicago school theory of the firm is the most cogent and influential such theory, and the main interlocutors of this chapter will be its proponents and critics. Both Chicago's "nexus of contracts" model of the firm and the broader doctrine of shareholder primacy have been frequently critiqued by scholars and reformers. But the revisions seldom go deep enough. Many theorists rightly recognize that the corporate firm is not a market owned by investors, but still hold that its raison d'être is profit or prosperity.[2] This position incoherently separates the overall point of business from the questions of what kind of social thing it is and whom it should serve. The three big ideas stand or fall together. If the business firm is not a market and is not oriented to stockholder returns, then its proper goals cannot be reduced to aggregated private goods of any sort, however well the wealth may be spread.

As I will show, the corporate firm turns out to be not just another mode of private exchange but rather a form of state-backed, character-forming cooperation under authority that inescapably aims at common goals. It is in the market, but not of the market. It is a creature of political action and collaborative work as well as prices and contracts. To attend only to the individual interests at play in the life of a firm is unjustly to ignore the irreducibly shared goods and evils that are active in any functioning business. The mechanisms and human consequences of enterprise always include irreducibly social goods (or evils) that could not be written down into a market contract. More broadly, it is not only the case that we *should* not have businesses oriented exclusively to the private profit of their shareholders, though this is true enough. In a real sense, we *do not* have such businesses, and never have. Business pulls us, often unwittingly, into common projects answering profound questions of how to live together. Wealth and private goods are never more than half the story.

The greatest merit of the Chicago theory is that its claims about what a business is *for* follow closely on a lucid (if mistaken) model of what a firm *is*. Conversely, the best way to show the shortcomings of Chicago's normative orientation to aggregate goods is to highlight those aspects of business as we know it that are distorted by imagining the firm as a market: the need for authority, the role of ownership, and the place of investors, workers, and the state. To see what part these play in actual firms is to set the stage for a constructive reimagining of the firm as a form of community, to be developed in chapter 3. I will structure the present chapter's critical arguments around four essential questions that should be asked of any human project: *What is the nature and goal of the endeavor? Who counts, and on what basis? How can their common goal be justly furthered? How does it relate to broader common projects?*

THE CHICAGO-STYLE CORPORATION

Aside from Milton Friedman, most of the key players in the Chicago school of law and economics are not household names, but this has not stopped their view of the firm from exerting tremendous influence in shaping public policy and the "common sense" of business. There is a political side to the story, involving money and strategic institution-building,[3] but there are also good intellectual reasons to begin in Chicago: the theory combines scattered truisms (not all of which, I hasten to add, are true) about the corporation into a powerful and elegant theory. The core of the Chicago theory is the audacious claim that the business firm is not a form of cooperative endeavor, as it appears to be, but rather a kind of market. Building on this basic premise, Chicago scholars have built a theory that is far more coherent than most competing accounts, which caters both to moral concerns about liberal rights and to economic concerns about wealth and practical viability. Although constant scholarly bombardment over five decades has compelled renovations in some wings of the Chicago edifice, the foundation remains mostly intact. Any theory built on a similar market logic will end up with substantially similar conclusions about the constitution, control, ends, and proper role of the business corporation.

The Chicago theory of the corporation arose in response to the "managerialism" that prevailed in midcentury America.[4] It was widely acknowledged that leaders of giant corporations such as General Electric and Ford Motor Company had great power and little accountability. The impotence or apathy of stockholders implied a "separation of ownership and control," as Berle and Means wrote in 1932 in the book that *Time* magazine called the "economic bible" of the New Deal.[5] This separation left an alarmingly large amount of human and physical capital in the hands of managers, who made up a potential oligarchy in the midst of a democracy. De facto control over this industrial power would depend on the fickle virtue of the managers themselves or on government regulation of the corporation as a quasi-public institution. This managerial dilemma prompted both increased regulation and moralized ideas of business leadership. The goal of postwar Chicago thinkers was to outflank managerialism—both the perceived threat to freedom and the case for public intervention into the economy— by radically reenvisioning the corporation as something other than a power structure of some persons over others.

According to the Chicago view, the essence of a corporation is to be found in the contractual agreements of private individuals. Here is a summary from Jensen and Meckling's seminal 1976 treatment, one of the most cited articles on corporate governance:

> The private corporation or firm is simply one form of *legal fiction which serves as a nexus for a set of contracting relationships* [among individuals]. . . . It makes little or no sense to try to distinguish those things which are "inside" the firm (or any other organization) from those things that are "outside" of it. There is in a very real sense only a multitude of complex relationships (i.e., contracts) between the legal fiction (the firm) and the owners of labor, material and capital inputs and the consumers of outputs.[6]

The layman might well object that suppliers or customers have a rather different relation to a business firm and to one another than do its managers and employees. But Alchian and Demsetz, another pair of influential Chicago thinkers, pugnaciously retort: "This is delusion. The firm . . . has no power of fiat, no authority, no disciplinary action any different in the slightest degree from ordinary market contracting between any two people."[7] They assert that the relations of owners, managers, and workers are fundamentally akin to a customer buying goods at a retail shop or to any other market contract, in that all are voluntary arrangements that any party can "exit" if unhappy. Obviously, the details of the arrangement will vary as one considers executives, line workers, machinery, real estate, or customers. But they are all variations, played in a market key, on the single great theme of private contracts.

The most important contract within the large corporation, on the Chicago view, is made between the shareholders and the managers. In a small business where a proprietor also acts as the day-to-day manager, she can do as she likes with the firm she owns—hire and fire, change strategy, fold up shop, and so on. But when the corporation is sold to dispersed stockholders, a problematic "separation of ownership and control" does indeed arise. As Milton Friedman writes, "in a free-enterprise, private-property system, a corporate executive is an employee of the owners of the business. He has a direct responsibility to his employers."[8] This raises the tough technical problem of how to arrange things so that the hands-on executive (the managers or board of directors) will do what the mostly passive owners (the stockholders) want, since all are presumed to be self-seeking rather than altruistic or cooperative. Much of the scholarship on business governance is devoted to this question. On the Chicago view, structures of corporate organization such as earnings calls, stockholder voting, and hostile takeover rules, which have proven themselves in the jungle of market competition, should be understood as evolved solutions to this principal-agent problem. The "market for control" will eliminate any ineffective or inefficient ways to align managers' actions with stockholders' wishes.[9] Despite its technical difficulty, the problem of fiduciary governance is not considered a serious moral problem, because the normative basis of the manager's role is the same as that of the small businessman—they both rest on the nearly untrammeled rights of owners to do what they want with their property.

Managers of a firm, then, have a fiduciary duty to serve the purposes of the owners.[10] What are those purposes? Absent any directive to the contrary, managers should presume that their stockholders are in market for the same reason as any other merchant: "to make as much money as possible while conforming to their basic rules of society," as Friedman puts it. Or, in Michael Jensen's less homely terms, managers should aim "to increase the total long-term market value of the firm."[11] Pursuing other goals than making money would break the terms of the manager's contract with the owners or would privilege those owners who value these particular goals while effectively stealing from the others. Friedman and other Chicago scholars are realistic enough to acknowledge that the manager should not always admit that these are the priorities she is following. In many cases it may be advisable or even necessary to support good causes or local communities, as a way of gaining goodwill or offsetting scandals. But the prudent manager must remember that the appearance of good citizenship is only a "noble lie" that covers over the collective self-interest of stockholders, whose rights give such expenditures their real moral and practical warrant. Looming in the background, ready to punish any managerial missteps, is the discipline of the market, whereby shareholders and other market actors will tell the firm, by means of prices, just where it stands and how well it is serving them and by extension society as a whole.

The great influence of the Chicago view of the corporation, which I have sketched all too briefly here, reflects real intellectual merits. The theory admirably succeeds in making the corporation intelligible and attractive to the discourse of enlightened self-interest. Merchants will invest or trade their own property with firms only when and so long as it suits their own pursuit of a bargain, and not otherwise. If the firm is no more than a corner of the market, it can be easily assimilated to core democratic values of freedom and equality, far from the stigma associated with hierarchical power (which might call forth state interference).

Moreover, the Chicago school coherently connects its empirical description of the business firm with a set of normative claims about justice and flourishing in business. If the corporation is nothing more than a market, then it is oriented to the aggregated private goods of the merchants, and there is no place for invoking the thicker standards of a formative moral project such as a sports team or family (or, in a negative valence, a criminal gang). The converse claim is yet more important: if, as most people seem to agree, *the* central goal of the business corporation is to make money, this would be justifiable only in a market-like social form. As I shall argue throughout this book, all (and only) forms of common action are oriented to common ends. If the corporation is legitimately oriented to an aggregate of private ends rather than any unified common end, then it must be a noncommunity—that is, a market. There is a compelling mutual reinforcement between the purposes and the form of the firm on this view.

Despite its clarity and coherence, the Chicago theory of business enterprise has one signal disadvantage: it's wrong. It badly mistakes the social and legal reality of the corporate firm. The firm is not just a nexus of contracts and is not owned or otherwise rightfully controlled by shareholders. It has its own internal common ends and, especially under the corporate form, a heightened responsibility to wider public concerns, neither of which are captured by financial returns. The allegedly hardheaded description of the corporation as a kind of market fails to capture what is distinctive about it, even from the point of view of material productivity. Because the Chicago theory misdescribes *what the firm actually is*, the impressive coherence between its descriptive and normative wings renders its conclusions about justice and flourishing problematic, if not totally unfounded. Its coherence does imply, however, that we cannot build a better theory by cherry-picking the best parts of the Chicago approach. An alternative theory of equal elegance or explanatory power would have to build on nonmarket foundations. In my view, this will mean dealing with the corporate business firm under the rubric of common goods.

FIRM VERSUS CORPORATION

An adequate theory of business enterprise must draw a clear distinction between two closely related terms: "firm" and "corporation."[12] The French jurist Jean-Philippe Robé has written, in a widely-cited article, that these often-conflated words "correspond . . . to totally different concepts: a corporation is a legal instrument, with a separate legal personality, which is used to legally structure the firm; a firm is an organized economic activity, corporations being used to legally structure most firms of some significance. . . . Firms are structured *using* corporations; they are **not** corporations."[13] Not all scholarly or legal usage observes this, or any, distinction between the terms, but precision demands it. Conflating the terms leads to foggy arguments and what Max Radin called "the endless problem of corporate personality."[14] Properly distinguished, "firm" is the more important and more general concept for economists and those who care about the actual workings of the business world, but "corporation" has a much longer intellectual history, going back to Roman law.

Virtually anything we would call a "business" can be classified among the "combination[s] of assets and people that we call firms," aside from a single person working alone.[15] Billy and Suzie's front-yard lemonade stand would be a firm, as would the Quantum Mechanics auto shop around the corner, and likewise such gigantic concerns as Microsoft or Honda. In essence, a firm is an order of common action for business purposes, or simply a "business association." Ontologically speaking, the firm stands on the same plane as familial, religious, or civic associations. This notion of the firm is so broad, however, that business law does not recognize "firms" as such, much as the Olympic Games do not recognize "athletes" as such but only pole vaulters, swimmers, or skiers. What the law recognizes are firms classified by governance or tax structure: sole proprietorships, S corporations, LLCs, and other categories familiar to accountants.

Suppose I hire my friend Peter to help me bake and sell my famous tarts. In practice and in social reality we will have formed a firm, which we christen Pie in the Sky Co. Yet in legal terms whoever transacts with the bakery, as a sole proprietorship, is only dealing with me myself, operating under a business mask. Later on, when Peter joins on as a full business partner, we could arrange jointly to own all the equipment and recipes, sign contracts in which we are each obligated, and jointly bear the legal rights and responsibilities of Pie in the Sky. His deeper involvement would transform Pie in the Sky into a general partnership. Legally, our firm would now be seen as multiple persons acting together but severally responsible for the undertaking. As a further step, if Pie in the Sky grew so big that it needed more capital than Peter and I or any small group of partners could conveniently supply, we would be well advised to govern the firm by means of a corporation.

The corporate form is a legal device that creates a separate legal person to enjoy all the rights and responsibilities that the proprietor or partners enjoyed in the earlier stages. In the *Dartmouth College* case, Chief Justice

John Marshall articulated the classical understanding of the corporation as a legal fiction: "A corporation is an artificial being, invisible, intangible, and existing only in contemplation of law. Being the mere creature of law, it possesses only those properties which the charter of its creation confers upon it. These are such as are supposed best calculated to effect the object for which it was created. Among the most important are immortality and, if the expression may be allowed, individuality."[16] Strange to say, the Pie in the Sky corporate entity is really best thought of as a separate person: call him "Charles." ("Charles is an artificial being, invisible, intangible . . .") On account of his unusual parentage ("the mere creature of law"), Charles is doomed to remain a "perpetual minor" who can only act through his guardians, the corporate board of directors,[17] even though he has supplanted Peter and me as the owner of Pie in the Sky's goods and signer of its contracts. As David Ciepley points out, the corporate form has nothing specifically to do with commerce or making money; it is rather a "governance technology" that was used to organize religious bodies, universities and even settlement colonies for long centuries before being widely applied in business.[18] In other words, Charles-the-corporation could have been a cleric or a scholar, but it just so happens that he currently has charge of a bakery.

Whatever his line of work, "Charles" would have enjoyed the three central rights of any corporation: "(1) the right to own property, make contracts, and sue and be sued, as a unitary entity . . . (2) the right to centralized management of this property; and (3) the right to establish and enforce rules within its jurisdiction *beyond* those of the laws of the land."[19] Governing by means of a corporation greatly facilitates the running of any large-scale, long-term endeavor, since debts and lines of authority are no longer dependent on the constancy (or lucidity, or survival) of particular natural persons.[20] Monasteries used the privilege of corporate immortality and legal individuality to amass and manage large quantities of wealth in the Middle Ages, no less than the railroads of the Gilded Age or the tech giants of today.

It is important to stress that the advantages of the corporate form could not be achieved by *any* scheme of private contracts, so its reliance on public authority is more than a mere convenience or an "off the rack set of contractual arrangements"; it is essential.[21] For this reason, up to the mid-nineteenth century corporations were relatively few in number, chartered expressly by legislatures as "quasi-public entities created by governments to serve a public good."[22] With the advent of general incorporation laws, however, virtually any business firm that underwent a few administrative formalities could create a corporation enjoying a fourth privilege: "(4) the right to turn this governing authority and property to the pursuit of private profit."[23] The modern business corporation was born, and the way was opened for "Charles" and his peers to seek their fortunes on the market.

AUTHORITY WITHIN THE MARKET

The descriptive core of the Chicago theory is the claim that the firm is a nexus of contracts, on which basis the firm can be defended along the same lines as the market. Underlying this assertion are two obvious truths: that the firm is a player in the market and that virtually all its key resources are bought, rented, or employed by means of contracts. Nonetheless, this foundational idea is by far the weakest plank in the Chicago platform, because it denies any role for authority in the firm—that is, for anyone telling anyone else what to do. In the memorable image of Alchian and Demsetz, standard-bearers of the Chicago theory, the relations between manager and employee are substantially analogous to those between customer and grocer. On its face, the idea is implausible, if not ridiculous. Yes, there may be an "exit" option in both cases, but the customer is not entitled to boss anyone around, while the boss, by definition, is.[24] Because of the central role of the entrepreneur/manager as a coordinator, the firm is a fundamentally different mode of economic order from the price-centered market, even if it can be explained in terms of market motivations. The inability of the Chicago school to admit this fundamental difference has given rise to a rival school of thought within economics, the transaction cost approach. The central contention of transaction cost economics (TCE) is that the firm is an authority structure, not a market, but it can beat the market at its own game when conditions are right. Although the partisans of TCE do not sufficiently draw out the normative implications of their richer picture, they lay the groundwork for replacing the reductive view of firms as types of market.

In his classic article of 1937, "The Nature of the Firm," Ronald Coase asked why the authority structure of the firm would arise within the world of the market, populated by merchants seeking to do well for themselves.[25] His answer, which would launch the TCE school some decades later, was that it is sometimes simply cheaper to coordinate projects through the authoritative direction of the entrepreneur than by the price-mechanism of the market. In the real world, though not in the canonical economistic model, there is an ongoing cost (in time, attention, taxes, etc.) to finding and contracting for goods on the market. These "transaction costs" mean that it is sometimes simply easier to gather a variety of human and capital resources under the direction of the entrepreneur. As Charles Lindblom puts it, "Once established, any single exercise of authority is costless, or nearly so."[26] By lowering transaction costs, the firm can gain a leg up on the open market.

One important advantage of the firm's authority structure is that it facilitates cooperation over time, since not every contingency can be foreseen and written into a contract. Perhaps Pie in the Sky would like to hire Julia, an inventive baker, without being quite sure about what the firm will ask her to do next year. Uncertainty makes this future decision "noncontractable," and it will be easier simply to ask Julia to accept the manager's authority to make the decision when the time comes. Alchian and Demsetz redescribe this apparent authority within a business as a continual "renegotiation of contracts on terms that must be acceptable to both parties."[27] That, however, is precisely what is *not* going on in the firm. As Robé puts it, "The employment contract *avoids* having to renegotiate all the time . . . on the details of how discrete tasks will be performed,"[28] which would be tiresome and time-consuming. A single negotiation whereby some factor of production "agrees to obey the directions of an entrepreneur *within certain limits*" can then serve for a time period during which a host of burdensome spot contracts might otherwise be required, as Coase points out.[29] Later TCE theories emphasize that firms also permit greater "relationship-specific investment" (in worker training, in specialized equipment) that would be quite costly for either party to duplicate using generic market exchange. From the fact that the firm owns material assets that specialists need to do their best work, it gains "a power of fiat which differs from ordinary market contracting."[30] On the other side, workers have expertise that the firm may need, so they have leverage of their own within the firm that they would not have elsewhere.

This transaction-cost theory also provides an elegant explanation of the boundaries of firms—that is, of what does (or should) take place within a firm and what does (or should) not. For the Chicago theory, this is a senseless question, because the firm is considered to be as large as the relevant market contracts. It may become, "if the chain of contracts is allowed to spread, as big as the whole economy. . . . Thus, it is futile to press the issue of what is or is not a firm."[31] On the TCE view, by contrast, "the distinguishing mark of the firm is the supersession of the price mechanism" in favor of the direction of the entrepreneur.[32] The firm has a principled boundary: its "organized economic activity" extends to all those actions that are directly ordered through authority, rather than by price. Some interactions thus take place "inside" firms, and some "outside" on the open market (chapter 4 will consider gray areas where it is unclear if power or price is in the driver's seat). This principle helps to explain why not all economic activities are ordered within firms, much less within a single giant centrally planned organization. As firms grow larger, the costs of bureaucracy increase, and so does the tendency for fallible managers to err. Beyond some threshold size it will be cheaper or easier to arrange matters by the price mechanism of the open market, despite the transaction costs.[33]

Coase's seminal account focuses on managerial authority, but political theorist Abraham Singer has insightfully filled out the TCE picture of why firms can outcompete the open market.[34] Anyone who has worked within a business, or cracked open a management textbook, knows that firms are not a simple extension of the entrepreneur's wishes (no doubt many frustrated bosses wish they were!). A good leader does not micromanage everything under her control; she builds up a team culture of shared vision and practice, which ideally add up to what Singer calls "norm-governed productivity." Workers within a business firm are keyed to following not only managers' orders but also, and perhaps more importantly, social scripts that they regard as legitimate "rules of the game" for the firm as a social space, as distinct from the family or the gym. The details will differ from industry to industry, or firm to firm, but most workers will tend to defer to certain officers, share information with some team members and not others, trust colleagues more than competitors, and so on. Why? In general, that is "just what you do" at work. If pressed, one could justify such actions in terms of playing a role well, and so contributing to the overall flourishing of the enterprise, but usually explicit justification is not called for.

The firm as a "norm-governed" setting is replete with implicit and explicit reasons for compliance—both claims of moral legitimacy and incentives of gain—and so it is likely to be a powerful force for the formation of character. To borrow a formulation of John Neville Figgis, firms are able to "limit and develop your life, make you do, or refrain from doing, what otherwise you would not. . . . More than that, they penetrate your imagination and your thought, and alter not only what you do but what you want to do."[35] One key advantage of a firm vis-à-vis the market is that it can shape its members' desires and skills in a way that the market cannot, and can call forth loyalty and initiative beyond what is contractually enforceable. Moral authority and formative power are standard features of almost any community—we find them also in families, schools, teams, and so on. By highlighting the contribution of thicker sociality to the firm's competitive advantage, Singer adds an important economic rationale to the descriptive claim that the firm is a genuine order of cooperative action. Even when considering only material productivity, merchants have good reasons for gathering to work in common. But there is something more to consider.

The TCE school lacks a grammar for articulating shared goods, so it misunderstands the normative implications of (correctly) describing the firm as a form of common action, rather than a market. On the TCE view, because firms arise on account of the self-interest of merchants, they are no more than "the cost-saving devices of transacting parties."[36] As Singer puts it, "The firm exists in order to produce things more efficiently relative to the market."[37] The point of the firm, on this perspective, is nothing more than efficient coordination of private interest. Unfortunately, TCE's teleological claim about the firm underrates the fundamental difference between common action and market exchange. The firm only outdoes the market by incurring a moral burden. Its "efficiency advantages" derive from the normative structure of its common action, since they trade on the trust and loyalty and shared culture that arise in human communion. This means that the economic advantages of collaborating in a firm can be justly enjoyed only as common achievements—that is, as something good "for us"—and not as private benefits, even though they may also serve the individual interest of each member considered separately. The firm's moral scripts and claims of legitimacy rest on relations of solidarity that demand to be treated as goods or values in themselves.

This is a normative demand, but failing to meet it will ultimately vitiate the very material benefits on which TCE concentrates. If I suspect you of instrumentalizing our every interaction, I will not trust you, and our collaboration will suffer. In TCE's reductive language, transaction costs will rise. Only by subordinating economic calculation within its internal moral framework can the firm gain the economic advantages that it actually enjoys relative to the market. Even if every member of Pie in the Sky were motivated only by private gain, "rational self-interest" would still give each of us good reason to act *as if* we cared about our work relations and about the firm as a whole as forms of solidarity valued in themselves. The massive hypocrisy required to pull this off should be enough to show that such a firm is not flourishing, not achieving its normative raison d'être.

In actuality, I doubt that any sizable firm could build on such shabby personal purposes successfully enough to enjoy benefits of ostensibly ethical cooperation for any length of time. Its moral culture would simply fall apart. Community pays, in other words, but it comes at a price: private gain or "efficiency" must be demoted to a conditional or instrumental goal, in service of some morally weightier common end. It may be true that economic efficiency is the "implicit morality of the market" that explains why firms arise in all market systems.[38] But such a reductive ethical goal does not fully determine the ends of the firm itself; it is checked at the door along with the price mechanism. Anticipating the grammar of common action to be sketched in the next chapter, I can restate the large claim here as follows: if the firm is constituted as a community and not a market, it can only be justified in terms of common goods, and not, as TCE supposes, in terms of the private ends that guide merchants in market exchange.

THE ABSENCE OF OWNERS

Chicago's second foundational claim is that legitimate control of the firm derives from the rights of ownership—which are assumed to lie with the proprietor, partners, or, in the case of large corporate firms, the stockholders. When this claim is yoked to the idea of the firm as a nexus of contracts, the resulting theoretical picture shows an intricate corner of the market, where merchants make free exchanges of property for the sake of their private interests. I have already critiqued the first leg of the Chicago stool, bolstering commonsense objections with insights from TCE to show that any firm is much more than a nexus of market contracts. This second claim of the foundational role of ownership is better supported by law and scholarship, as well as everyday rules of thumb. It is quite true that in a "free-enterprise, private property" system, as Friedman calls it, there is a central and vital role for ownership, which is to be understood as a virtually unlimited right of persons over things. Yet the role of ownership in the business corporation cannot be what Chicago makes it out to be, since stockholders of the corporation are *not* its owners, as many critical appraisals in business ethics, political science, and corporate law have argued.[39] Indeed, one of the main functions of the corporate form is to *remove* claims of sovereign, arbitrary control over assets that have been enlisted into large shared enterprises, in favor of more qualified claims. "Because no natural persons own corporate assets, legitimate control of these assets not only might, but must, derive from something other than ownership of them."[40] What is true of the corporation is also true, in a qualified way, of firms in the broader sense. Even where legal control rests with a natural person, whom we are apt to call a "business owner," proprietors or partners do not have full rights of ownership over their firms. A moral community of persons cannot be owned, in a moral sense, any more than a legal person can be owned in a legal sense. Neither for corporate enterprises in particular nor for business firms in general can the rights of legitimate control derive from ownership alone.

The idea of "owning a corporation" predates the ideology of stockholder primacy by centuries. It is reflected already in the formation of the British East India Company in the 1600s and is repeated even by New Dealers such as Berle and Means, whose larger agenda is to emphasize the corporation's broad social duties.[41] Analytically, the main feature of corporate governance supporting the idea of stockholders as owners is that they seem to be "residual claimants," as owners typically are. Stockholders are paid last (e.g., in distributing revenue or in bankruptcy), claiming what is left over after the corporation's contractual obligations are discharged. Analogously, if I choose to sell my house, I get whatever may be left of the sale price after paying off the mortgage balance, a mechanic's lien, and outstanding taxes. Chicago theorists argue that assigning tradable ownership rights to shareholders, who have a contractually unprotected risk in the corporation's decision-making, turns out to be an efficient way of bringing market discipline to bear on it.[42] It is also a great piece of PR for drawing in investors: Own a piece of Tesla—own a brighter future! According to Anglo-American folk wisdom, if anyone owns the corporation, it is the stockholders.

But no one does. Despite the historical endurance and rhetorical appeal of the idea of shareholders as owners, it does not stand up to sustained scrutiny. A. M. Honoré famously set out the bundle of claims included in ownership, which include the right to use, to exclude others from using, to claim residual value, and to sell or bequeath, and the liability to seizure for harmful use.[43] Stockholders have none of these rights over the corporation or its assets, only over their shares of stock. When Peter and I were general partners in Pie in the Sky, we were joint owners of the business property, and we could do with it as we saw fit. When we incorporated the bakery, all our rights and responsibilities as owners passed to Charles, the "corporate person," and we became mere stockholders. Supposing we sell a few shares to others, they have no right to use, sell, or exclude others from using what is now property of the corporation. If the board of directors hires on a chief executive baker, she may have practical control of the recipes and the ovens, but she does not own them any more than the stockholders do, and she is obliged to use them for Charles's purposes and not her own.

No more do stockholders own the corporation itself. As a legal person, it, or rather "he," cannot be owned; "he" is an owner. Owning "Charles" would be an unusual form of legal slavery that would extinguish his legal personhood, such that his rights and duties would pass through to the stockholders. This would obviate most of the business advantages of the corporate form, such as two-way limited liability (by which neither corporation nor investors are responsible for the other's actions) and asset lock-in (by which real assets are made the permanent property of the corporation in return for equity shares). Charles gains his business advantages—such as the ability to attract financing and acquire specialized capital at a lower risk for all concerned—precisely by removing ownership from the hands of any natural persons and vesting it in a legally defined corporate person that cannot die, abscond from justice, or otherwise depart from the procedures laid down by the law.

The fictitious personality underlying the business corporation makes it particularly clear that shareholders own only a financial instrument; legally, no one owns the corporation. A qualified version of the same argument can be made of firms in general. Suppose that I decided to run Pie in the Sky as a sole proprietorship. Since I decline to incorporate the bakery, all the rights and duties that could have been given to "Charles" (or shared with Peter in a partnership) remain with me. In law, the firm is construed as just me myself, operating under another name—all profits and assets and contracts, all debts and torts, attach to me personally. As a matter of accounting hygiene, my CPA might urge me to keep my personal and business affairs separate, but at bottom everything that would have been owned by the corporation is owned by me. But as we have seen already, a firm is more than contracts and more than assets. Contracts are a way of bringing in both people and capital goods into an order of common action under authority. In this case, practical authority would rest with me because I own the ovens and recipes that the bakery needs. But I do not own the "organized economic activity" that is the firm itself, because I own neither the people who are carrying out that activity nor the moral culture of "norm-based productivity" that is essential to the success of the bakery.

The fact of my arbitrary power over necessary tools of the firm gives me sufficient control over the bakery that I could be said to "own" it for most practical purposes. Nonetheless, if we ask not *whether* I control the firm, but *how* I should exercise this control, the fact that I do not have full arbitrary power over the collaboration should alert me to the fact that there are shared goods at stake that could well be at variance with my own private interests. Suppose that I get a lucrative, one-time buyout offer from a big corporate chain, at a moment when my lead baker and her team are close to perfecting a recipe for the elusive persimmon tart and when we recently launched a training program for at-risk youth. Shared goods of this kind are clearly part of what it has meant for us to be a good bakery. Because they could be imperiled by the take-over, they constitute some kind of moral counterweight to my proprietor's right to sell, which is legally absolute. Consideration for such goods may not rule out my selling altogether, but my obligations to the flourishing of the bakery would give me reason in justice to accept less money in order to preserve shared goods (e.g., by negotiating with the big chain or finding a more sympathetic but less deep-pocketed buyer). More generally, fidelity to the common goals of the firm is what elevates my raw power of ownership into legitimate authority that can provide principled (as opposed to merely strategic) reasons for the bakery's members to comply with my directives. In this context it might be well for the "owner" of the firm to think of it not as a piece of property but as a kind of friendship, a better metaphor for tuning our ears to the demands of goods held in common.

The role of ownership differs, therefore, in corporations and in other sorts of firms. Shareholders own neither corporations nor their assets in any meaningful sense, and so cannot invoke owners' rights to claim that the corporation should be run in their interest alone. In an unincorporated firm, the proprietor or partners do legally own its property and personally bear all the rights and duties of that ownership.[44] Nonetheless, owning assets and signing contracts does not make them owners of an order of common action; it only gives them power within the community of the firm (and a concomitant responsibility to its shared goods).

If this nonownership is true of firms in general, it must also be true of corporate firms in particular. A corporation, and a fortiori its stockholders or board, also does not own the firm that it governs. Therefore "Charles" also has responsibilities beyond his own purposes as a corporate person (whatever those may be), just as the small business owner ought to look beyond her private purposes. To borrow terms from Aristotle, any firm is a "community of the free," not a despotic property relation such as one finds between master and slave. Since the arbitrary purposes of an owner cannot rightly govern the firm, which is not owned by anyone, the moral authority of the firm must be established by giving reasons to free persons, reasons that should rest primarily on an appeal to the goods that they hold in common.

MEMBERS AND ENDS

The grand upshot of the Chicago school theory is a broad perspective on what business enterprises are *for*.[45] Granted, the matter is approached so obliquely through the mechanisms of property and contract that important

Chicago thinkers can feign the same indifference to the teleology of the firm that Friedrich Hayek will show toward the market (see chapter 5), which does not seem to be "for" anything in particular, except coordinating private interests. In a seminal Chicago text, Easterbrook and Fischel ask themselves, "What is the goal of the corporation? Is it profit, and for whom? . . . Our response to such questions is: who cares?"[46] Milton Friedman, a savvier apologist, recognizes that a great number of people do care, and that a public shrug is not an effective bid for political legitimacy. He argues directly that the point of the business firm is, usually, to "increase its profits." The importance of making money is an old chestnut, of course, at least as old as Aristotle. What was scandalously new in Friedman's 1970 argument was that financial returns could be, and usually were, the *only* point of a business, to which all other moral, environmental, and social concerns could be justly and safely subordinated. A half-century later, the idea is familiar to the point of cliché.

This notion of profit as the ultimate end stands and falls together with the closely related idea of stockholder primacy. The twin ideas are answers to two linked questions about the corporate firm: *What is its point or end?* and *Whose participation is constitutive?* It is Chicago's reductive answer to the "Who?" question that leaves "value maximization" as the unqualified answer to the question "What for?" If stockholders were the primary or only members of the corporation, then their purely financial interests would indeed largely determine its proper ends in the direction of profit. This account would also settle at a stroke the last of the three central questions that should be asked about any human endeavor: *How can benefits and burdens be justly shared in the achieving of its ends?* Profits would be fairly distributed on the basis of ownership stake, and all other claims would be subject to the (nondistributive) justice of contracts.[47]

Taken together, these three Chicago theses form an elegant and powerful vision of the business enterprise and its goals, both for intellectuals in search of parsimony and for managers interested in a single "scorecard" by which to evaluate performance.[48] As a bonus, focusing on stockholders also neatly sidelines normative deliberation about common ends—the contestable principles and morally charged goals shared by members of a community—in favor of technical metrics or judicial rules. Despite its wide influence, however, the Chicago case for the priority of profit has a serious flaw: stockholders have a very weak and perhaps nonexistent claim on membership. If they are not the primary members of the corporate firm, then their financial interests cannot justly prevail, and the claim of profit above all is without foundation.

Nonetheless, the flawed idea of stockholders as dominant members has worked its way deeply into the theory and practice of business. The entire countermovement of social enterprise has arisen to combat the standard "C corporation" and its supposed focus on stockholders. But far from challenging the Chicago view of the business firm, the "B corp" and its "triple bottom line" actually confirm Chicago's premises and evidence its dominance. In the first place, Chicago scholars such as Easterbrook and Fischel argue that it has always been entirely up to the signers of the "corporate contract" to stipulate what ends a business will serve. Profit is only a default option, not a requirement, and they would say that B corps are free to aim at broader goals so long as they are explicit about it. In addition, the existence of a separate corporate form with an explicit focus on wider ends seems to confirm the common belief that the standard corporation is oriented to stockholders and profit alone.[49]

This belief finds additional support in two key features of corporate governance: fiduciary duties and the stockholder franchise. Day-to-day control belongs to the corporate officers, but the officers are hired by the board of directors and the board is elected by the stockholders. Even though they are several layers removed from the activity of the business, the stockholders seem to be the essential "audience" that the directors and officers need to please, to whom they are linked by fiduciary duties. Unlike employees, suppliers, creditors, or customers, the stockholders in a corporation have signed no explicit contract securing their interest in a financial return, and likewise no agreement specifying what they will do with their shares. Dividends are paid at the discretion of the board, according to their fiduciary duties of loyalty and care, if and when there is money in the treasury after contracts are honored. Stockholders' exposure to the free action of the corporation bespeaks the risks of membership, in much the same way that children, as members of a family, may get treated to a vacation only if anything is left over once all the bills are paid.

Considered more broadly, however, the analogy between stockholding and other social roles is too faint to support the claim that stockholders are members of the corporation in any substantial sense. As I will discuss in the next chapter, a "member" of any community is someone who joins in a common project and so participates in its emergent ends. Running backs, schoolteachers, and platoon sergeants are all members in this sense. Common ends are always something good (or evil) "for us," so they are available only to the participants in some common project who can speak of what "we do together." Only the members of a sports team can really experience their team's victory (or loss) as something "we did together" and benefit (or suffer) from the collaboration as an end in itself, as a form of solidarity. If I placed a bet on the team, I may be cheered by the win, but I will not thereby share in the team's common goods. All and only those persons who share in some common goal *as common* should be regarded as the members of a given community.

Stockholders do not share in any common projects in this way, and therefore they are not members. There is seldom interaction, much less solidarity, either among stockholders or between them and the firms whose shares they own. If the returns are not to their liking, they can "exit" by selling their shares. At bottom, the stockholders have price-centered market relations with the firm, relations that are not forms of common action and so do not unite merchants as the members of any distinct community. It is true that shareholders' interests are aligned with the firm's, so they share risk and may toast the same successful outcome. Nonetheless, the good to which they aspire is only another variant of mutual benefit, a "sum of private goods that happen to be interdependent,"[50] since what is valued on each side has nothing to do with any social relation valued in itself. This abstract argument jibes well with personal experience. To be a member of some community is to participate in a moral order that is a source (in some degree) of identity, fellowship, and character formation. Stockholding does none of this. Like many passive investors, I myself have only the faintest idea of what stocks I own at any given time, since my savings are invested by a mutual fund, and they define nothing about me except the size of my 401(k).

David Ciepley has made a cogent historical-legal case for an even stronger claim: not only are the stockholders not members of the business corporation; it has no members at all, properly speaking.[51] Up to the early-modern period, a guild, university, or town might have been organized as a "member corporation" or *universitas personarum*, which accorded legal personality directly to an association of persons. Its legal form was quite unlike the business corporation as we know it, in three key ways. The members (1_a) collectively controlled the membership (they could admit or eject members) and (2_a) used a one-man-one-vote system of majority rule in order to (3_a) erect internal laws to govern their own conduct within an association or trade. The member corporation operated in every way like a "little republic," as Blackstone put it, and was an important model in the early-modern development of constitutional democracy.[52]

The business corporation departs from the member corporation model on all three of these crucial points. (1_b) The right to vote is attached to freely tradable shares of stock, so membership is not collectively controlled. (2_b) Control is apportioned on a one-share-one-vote basis (and some shares may have more votes, or none), so the personal equality of stockholders is irrelevant. (3_b) The stockholders do not vote to govern themselves, but rather to govern another group—a firm. Unlike in republics large and small, the human relations and conduct of the shareholders are a very minor concern in the business corporation—this is the whole point of limited liability.

What takes center stage is the use of property, and so Ciepley argues that the true legal ancestor of the business corporation is not found in the medieval guild, much less the early-modern republic, but rather in the "property corporation," the *universitas rerum*. This legal device is unknown in common law, but it persists in civil law forms such as the German *Stiftung*, wherein some heap of property is granted legal personality by the state. Unlike a guild, it has no members and therefore no right of self-government, but only appointed officers who are bound to use the property for some stipulated (public and/or charitable) purpose.

Ciepley's revisionist understanding of the stockholders and the corporation returns us to the teleological questions that began this section: *what* ends, and *whose* ends, is the corporation meant to serve? The common ends of any association are authorized, at least in part, by the characteristic interests of its members. If the corporation as such has no members, then its ends cannot be authorized in this way, either by stockholders or anyone else. Surprisingly, then, Ciepley pulls almost the same intellectual move with respect to the corporation as the Chicago school did with respect to the firm, albeit on stronger juridical grounds. His *universitas rerum* model empties the business corporation of any intrinsic normative content or teleology, such that it must derive its proper ends from elsewhere, from outside. Chicago did much the same, with the difference being that for the Chicago school these external ends seep into the firm through "horizontal" market contracting, reflecting the individual economic interests of its putative owner-members, the stockholders. By contrast, if the business corporation is a "property corporation" then its derived ends are essentially governmental, in that they correspond to the creation and use of hierarchical authority. This authority-focused account comports well with the transaction-cost theory of the firm as a nonmarket cooperation structure. The "vertical" dimension emphasized by Ciepley and TCE is itself the best argument for the need to analyze the corporation in terms of common goods, since cooperation under authority cannot be evaluated by private goods alone.

THE CORPORATION AND THE COMMON

Having examined the Chicago theory of what firms are in themselves, I turn lastly to the question of where they fit into the wider political world. For policymakers, citizens, and other onlookers, this is where the rubber hits the road. The Chicago approach has gained much of its public influence thanks to its clear and forceful view of business's social role. The whole "nexus of contracts" theory is designed to recast the business organization as nothing more than an intricate form of market exchange, voluntarily undertaken by assumedly self-interested merchants, for their private benefit. If the firm is simply a permutation of the market, then it occupies basically the same place in the larger political world as any other market. (What exactly that place is will be the main question of part 2 of this book.) At first glance, any market is a space of relative freedom, equality, and mutual benefit among individual actors, where arbitrary power is at a minimum. These general features are tailor-made to allay the fears of concerned citizens and to defray the need for, and the effectiveness of, government interventions. Chicago's theory of the firm as an innocuous, price-disciplined market will naturally tend to deflect attention to other, more consequential political actors.

Yet no theory of business within the political order can be fully and finally neutral in its political implications. Chicago's account of the firm as a market will inescapably favor the interests of some over others, as would any alternative account. To get a clearer sense of the political valences, it will be useful to recall categories developed in the Progressive-era debate over giant firms like Standard Oil and US Steel. The Supreme Court's 1886 reaffirmation of corporations as legal persons kicked off a decades-long quarrel that eventually coalesced around three rival views of the corporate business firm: as an "aggregate" of private persons, as a "real entity" with a social life of its own, and as a state-granted "concession."[53] The "aggregate" position is, in essence, the Chicago view, while its critics merit brief comment:

- *Real Entity*: The first fin de siècle critique insisted that the collaborative work at the heart of the business corporation makes it more than a mere aggregate of individuals or a market. It has a social density and life of its own arising from human cooperation, with all the communal goods and evils this might entail. This view is recapitulated by many of Chicago's critics today, including political philosophers such as Elizabeth Anderson, Isabelle Ferraras, and Abraham Singer.[54] Bolstered by the insights of transaction cost economics, they regard businesses as islands of private power in the midst of the market economy. The key analogy for locating the firm politically, therefore, is not a comparison with the market, but with other civic associations (families, clubs, churches, trade unions), which all can and should be brought before the bar of liberal norms of justice.
- *Concession*: The second vein of critique regarded the business corporation as a delegation of public authority rather than an island of private power. Inasmuch as the corporate legal vehicle is a concession granted by the state, the business corporation is a public/private hybrid that stands on a different plane from either market exchange or private associations. It is more akin to the IRS than to a church or hobby club. This view is represented today by scholars of corporation law such as David Ciepley, William Bratton, and Lynn Stout.[55] On their view, what is politically decisive about business corporations is not that they are *similar* to states and should be held accountable in similar ways, but that they are in a sense *appendages* of the state, and thus expressions of the shared project of citizens.

This three-cornered dispute may seem abstract, but the prolonged Progressive-era discussion highlighted its real-world stakes. Each theory caters to one important constituency of business as we know it: investors, workers, and citizens at large. The aggregate view, which focuses on contracting individuals, prioritizes those interested primarily in divisible private goods—namely, stockholders and other investors. The "real entity" view, by contrast, draws our attention to the internal dynamics of the firm (as distinct from the corporation) with its shared ends and moral culture, thus forwarding the interests of those immersed in the firm—namely, workers. And the concession view, by its focus on the state-granted corporate form, highlights the "public" interest of the sponsoring state and its citizens.

Which of these three views should we choose? If possible, all of them. It is telling that the historical debate in the 1930s ultimately failed to conclude. None of the three rivals could gain a decisive advantage over the other two, and today's corporation law weaves pragmatically back in forth between them.[56] The fundamental reason for the stalemate is that each of the three views latches onto one key part of the picture, a nugget of truth that could not be sensibly denied. The social reality of any corporate firm weaves together several kinds of human relations with distinct moral structures:[57] Every firm needs resources drawn from the market, so the aggregate idea cannot be eliminated. Yet there is more to the story than "horizontal" contracting. The concession and real-entity views disagree about the source of the extra "vertical" dimension: does it descend from the state or arise from below through ordinary human collaboration? The social facts would suggest, "Both." So debate about outward-facing justice in business has to account for multiple sources and rival patterns.

The "concession" tradition emphasizes that the corporation is what Ciepley calls a "franchise government," deriving its authority and its ends "from above," in a grant of state power for public ends. The foundation of the authority of any corporation (for-profit or nonprofit) rests in a legal charter that establishes its board and specifies its constitutive purposes. This charter imparts to a corporation, such as "Charles" from Pie in the Sky, the authority over assets and people that the board is to exercise on "his" behalf. The corporate charter functions as a "higher law" within a corporation, setting its general framework and basic roles much as its historical descendent, the written constitution, does for a political community. The (dis)analogies between firm and state are instructive.[58] As members of a republic, citizens have the right, real but difficult to exercise, to amend the higher law of the constitution, usually in view of an "even-higher" law of human rights or natural justice. But stockholders and directors, who are not members, do not have any such right in the corporation. Neither one is legally empowered to alter the basic ends and powers set out in the charter; the authority they exercise is legitimized only by faithfulness to it. There is no "living Constitution" in the corporate context, which makes sense if the corporation is a heap of property having only what Maitland calls "fictitious life."[59]

This idea of charter-derived authority helps to make sense of two puzzling features of corporate legal structure: the stockholder's customary right to elect the board of directors and the fiduciary relations between them. Normally, the stockholder franchise is seen as a way of holding the board responsible to its fiduciary duties toward the stockholders and their goals. But if the legitimate ends of the corporation are unalterably given in the charter, then the situation is reversed. The stockholders' goals are no longer primary or ultimate. It is not that the corporation has a duty to voting stockholders; it is *they* who have a duty to *it*. Unlike citizens, stockholders can legitimately sell their votes by selling their shares. But if they choose to vote and so exercise "voice" rather than "exit," they have an obligation to elect directors who will, if I may, "protect and defend the (corporate) constitution," rather as citizens do in the political realm.

Unfortunately, the charters of today's business corporations do not live up to the central role that the corporate form assigns to them, in terms of establishing authoritative ends. Down to the mid-nineteenth century, corporate charters were extended only for reasons of putative public interest—to build a canal or a turnpike (or to colonize foreign lands or monopolize trade with the Far East). These goals were directly stated in the corporate charter, and an *ultra vires* lawsuit could be brought against a corporation that exceeded its legal mandate. With the advent of general incorporation laws in the later nineteenth century, however, corporations were permitted to broaden their constitutive goals to "any legal purpose." In practice, this usually meant "making money." The mechanisms of corporate law effectively abandoned the idea that corporate privileges were to be granted in return for specific public benefit, much strengthening the impression of the corporation as a private market form. Even so, concession theorists insist that the corporate form remains a type of "franchise government" that still derives its power from the state. This leaves the anomalous situation of public authority wielded for apparently private ends. In terms of top-down political guidance, then, today's business corporation is effectively adrift, like a naval ship cut off from its admiral. In the absence of official orders, it is apt to turn its considerable firepower to piracy.

Nonetheless, it seems right to hold that even today's corporations, just because they still wield state-backed authority over persons in a firm, have a heightened responsibility toward implied public ends such as "establishing justice" or "promoting the general welfare." The ever-shifting discourse of "corporate social responsibility" (CSR), which is as old as the modern business corporation itself, has always emphasized the corporation's direct obligation to The Common Good in some wide, vague sense. It is true, of course, that virtually every individual or group in the polity—citizens, resident aliens, even foreign visitors— has some obligation or other in the same vein, whether to obey the law, pay taxes, help out in a crisis, and so on. Without a special argument to the contrary (such as Milton Friedman attempts), one should assume that the business enterprise has duties of good citizenship just like any other civil association.

The corporate firm is a special case. In view of its state-granted legal form, its public duties are twofold. Not only is it a member of the polity; the polity is a "member" of it. The corporate form gifted by the state enhances the collaborative work of a firm, so one of the essential "internal" contributors to corporate firms is the public. The state "invests" in every corporation, so to speak, but what it invests is a legal vehicle rather than money. The return owed on this investment, plausibly, is not taxes but a vision of the corporate purpose that is sensitive to the broader concerns of citizens. Any firm under the corporate form continues to be a kind of public-private hybrid that is intrinsically oriented to the political community and its ends in a deeper way than private persons or associations are.[60] It cannot be "what it actually is" without internalizing public ends in some way. Summing up this line of argument, the concession tradition identifies a vector by which the corporate firm is oriented beyond aggregate private goods, though it is a lamentably vague one. Without a detailed legal mandate for each corporation, it is unclear what, if anything, these public-facing duties actually entail. One old and damning critique of CSR-talk is that it has never had any real teeth.[61]

In current practice, the authority of the business corporation is not publicly chartered "for" any goal in particular, except for governing a firm. The firm itself, then, is the best place to seek concrete, authoritative ends for the corporation. As we have seen, the economic point of granting corporate privileges is to facilitate the acquisition and management of property and people so that a firm can do business at large scale and in the long term. Presumably, a firm is enlarged in this way, pumped up on corporate steroids, so that it can better achieve whatever its ends are. The corporate form returns us, therefore, to a fundamental teleological question: What is a firm for?

If a firm were just a nexus of market contracts, then its public and private goals would reduce to an aggregate of private interests, such as shareholder value. But the firm is an order of cooperative action under authority that is qualitatively different from a market in its goals as much as in its constitution. The ends of the firm involve making money, undeniably, but also a great deal more: excellent products, effective leadership, shared practice, and a healthy moral culture of "norm-governed productivity." It will be the task of the next two chapters first to develop a grammar for thinking about justice regarding divisible and shared goods, and then to apply that new vocabulary to the firm. For present purposes, the point is that any firm counts as a "real entity" with normatively weighty ends of its own.

What all firms have in common, no matter how much they otherwise differ, is that they aim at irreducibly social ends beyond a mere aggregate of private goods. It has been decades since the corporate form was released into the wild, so to speak, with no specific political mandate. Even so, the fact that a business corporation exercises authority over a firm means that it retains a built-in responsibility, obscurely present in its current legal structure, to promote the flourishing of the firm in a just fashion. This shared end, which is common to the members of the firm, marks off a second, more promisingly concrete sense in which the corporate firm ought to serve common goods beyond profit. Its primary public contribution is to become a flourishing version of itself.

PILES OF MONEY

A corporation, essentially, is a pile of money to which a number of people have sold their moral allegiance.

—Wendell Berry

The economist Abba Lerner once observed that "an economic transaction is a solved political problem."[62] Market exchange takes place only after the basic political question of legitimate power has been answered in favor of the owners of property, who may do (almost) whatever they like with it. If the firm could be shown to be, or even coherently theorized as, a series of market transactions, then moral and political concerns might be tabled in favor of technical questions of how to make it work better. The promise of the Chicago theory lies in this kind of reduction: stockholders own the firm, and they sign market contracts with directors, workers, and capital to accomplish their financial goals. Chicago's intellectual influence is not surprising, since it fits into a broader imaginary of a normatively neutral economy as a space of private gain, and its contract-centered theory has powerfully shaped the public conception of what businesses are for. Yet simply changing one's mind does not alter the underlying social and legal realities of corporate business to bring them in line with its imputed market teleology, and therein lies the problem. An actual business firm is not just a nexus of contracts, and stockholders are not owners or members of corporations.

Corporate firms are sites of publicly empowered, morally formative cooperation under authority. They extract, sometimes grudgingly, the "moral allegiance" of persons in their power. This practical authority of the firm, which transaction-cost economists correctly see as essential to its productivity, cannot be justified on the stockholders-and-profits picture, so Chicago scholars generally deny the very existence of authority in business. The Chicago approach tries to bend the nonmarket reality of the corporation to conform with its alleged pecuniary ends, buying theoretical coherence at the price of misdescribing how the firm actually works. Admitting that the firm is wholly unlike a typical market exchange would open the door to a swarm of uncomfortable moral and political questions that the economic transaction model was supposed to foreclose: *Who has a legitimate claim on the firm's shared project, and how should we understand its goals in light of these claims?* There are various legitimate answers to these questions, multiple ways to institutionalize the business firm so as justly to respect its moral architecture. The current corporate settlement, skewered in Wendell Berry's aperçu,[63] is not one of them.

A pile of money does not deserve anyone's moral allegiance. A corporate officer, as an agent of such a pile, faces two live normative options. First, she might operate strictly in the world of the impersonal contract, where allegiance is neither asked nor given, and thereby bring the reality of her undertaking in line with pecuniary goals. All market, no firm. As we will see in chapter 4, platform businesses such as Uber are moving (albeit incompletely) in this direction. Secondly, she might put the pile into the service of some cooperative project and so subordinate it to common ends that legitimately call forth deeper commitments. There are good economic reasons to choose the latter, as Ronald Coase and the transaction-cost school argue, which is why hierarchical corporate firms are such a robust aspect of market systems. What is not a live option, normatively speaking, is to claim authority over a firm and yet proceed as if growing the pile were a justifiable source of legitimate commands.

As I will discuss further in the next chapter, legitimate authority in any social order can be exercised only with respect to goods shared in common, and not simply for the furtherance of private divisible goods.[64] Why so? Authority is legitimate power exercised within an order of common action, and within such an order there is always something more than private goods at stake: there are questions of status, honor, shared practice, friendship, and, importantly, distributive justice. How could a firm's leader claim allegiance without respecting and promoting these goals, which cannot be analyzed as concatenations of divisible individual goods? The power to direct the members *as members* can be well founded only through attention and fidelity to these essentially common goods, by which the members will flourish *as members*. It is because such goods cannot be achieved through mere market contracting that authority is required in the firm, and they justify its use as well.

The Chicago theory of the firm is an ingenious and elegant theory of how businesses work, clear enough for the manager and rigorous enough for the theorist. One can scarcely imagine a more coherent or plausible justification of business in the terms of coordinated self-interest. But any private-good account of the firm is bound to fall apart upon closer scrutiny of the legal and social reality. The internal relations of the firm are not merely a matter of contract, but rather of open-ended collaboration guided by a shared moral culture. No one, least of all stockholders, owns the corporation and its assets, nor the human activity that constitutes the firm. Nor can we deduce the point of the corporate firm from the financial interests of stockholders, since they are not members. Legally and morally, the owners of equity shares should be beholden to the full flourishing of the firm, and not the reverse.

Workers, investors, and citizens all deserve better than Chicago's reductive view of the goals and workings of business. It is a fearful thing to fall into the hands of an executive who is thinking only of private goods. Anyone who calculates whether the firm is more valuable as a going concern or as a pile of capital assets, as the Chicago school supposes that stockholders and managers alike constantly do, is apt to ignore and therefore to wreck the common action of the firm and the larger tissue of human concerns that it evokes. Successful leaders know this intuitively, even when their public rhetoric suggests otherwise. A working, flourishing firm is a communal project, not a market.

Ideally, this basic affirmation would suffice to show the primacy of common goods over divisible private goods in business. But the modern social imaginary of the economy is so saturated with the logic of private exchange that it is hard to avoid slipping into a reflexive atomism about the goals of business (as TCE ultimately does) even once we admit that the firm is a cooperative endeavor. The next step, then, is to lay down a strong and clear distinction between the private goods of individuals and the irreducibly social goods they share in common action. Chapter 2 will sketch a general grammar of common action as categorically distinct from transactional exchange, drawing on examples from politics and civil society. Chapter 3 will then deploy the framework of "Aristotelian pluralism" to rearticulate the business firm as a mode of morally formative cooperation around common ends, without ignoring the role of money and competition. For those who actively participate in the business enterprise, the stuff of their collaboration cannot even be described, much less evaluated, in the morally reductive language of self-interest and profit maximization. Citizens, too, who underwrite the corporate form in all its guises, have a constitutive interest in businesses that wield their authority with a full sense of the human concerns at stake.

CHAPTER TWO

HOW TO THINK ABOUT COMMON GOODS

The basic problem of a nexus-of-contracts approach to political economy is a lack of vision. It fails to see how there could be anything at stake beyond the private goals of individuals. Such a restricted perspective will inevitably misunderstand even the most collaborative or political dimensions of an institution as matters of coordinated self-interest. The business firm as a human reality is much more than this, in its ends as well as its constitution. It cannot be evaluated or even properly described in terms of privately held purposes that make no reference to, and remain unchanged by, inherently collaborative goals. Those who join a business are drawn into a morally formative solidarity, in which the members' actions, motivations, and even identities are to be conformed to the shared project. Individuals and their pocketbooks are only half the story, and a firm cannot flourish in justice without taking its common life fully into account on its own terms. As Sears Roebuck's abortive metamorphosis illustrates, the reductive view of the firm as a kind of market leads inescapably to modes of failure and injustice that it cannot even recognize.

In order to correct the moral myopia that sees only private goods, this chapter develops a conceptual grammar for analyzing common goods, which I call "Aristotelian pluralism." Its central claim: every form of common action is to be reckoned as an end in itself, a mode of solidarity built around internally shared goods of its own. The compound label indicates some of the rival views I reject. Against atomistic versions of pluralism, I argue that human communities are legitimately oriented first to shared goals that are not reducible to (aggregated) individual goods. Against the Aristotelian monist, who yearns for a homogenous society dedicated to a single political project of virtue, I insist on the legitimate multiplicity of common goods. Where and how the grammar of common action may apply in human affairs is not a question that can be settled a priori from the armchair of the philosopher (or the dictator). It should be approached with a pluralist appreciation for the character of various communities, including business firms, which may or may not fit together neatly within a political order.

Here, in a nutshell, is the best way to think about common goods: the members of any community share a good in common, which is to flourish together in justice as whatever kind of community they form—firm, school, family, polity, and so on.[1] The good held in common by participants in a school is to be an excellent school, and the common good of soldiers in an army is to be a flourishing army; neither goal can be finally reduced to anything nonsocial such as teachers' pay or soldiers' strength. More generally, wherever there is common action, there are ends that cannot be reduced to individual goals or benefits, so they must be measured by the good held in common. These common ends are not a matter of arbitrary individual choice, but are built into the social reality of the community. We get at the common goods of a given social order by asking three key questions about its normative social ontology —To what ends is it characteristically oriented? Who participates in them? How could their shared ends be justly achieved? To ignore common ends does not remove their normative pull; it only ensures that they will not be shared justly. In any community, the primary allegiance of members as members is to their common good, so they should pursue personal interest only to the extent of a just share in the common burdens and benefits.

In order to flesh out Aristotelian pluralism, this chapter will first explore the meaning of essentially common ends, illustrated in the domains of politics and friendship. I will then show that shared ends of this kind are built into the social reality of any community in any domain, such that we should adopt a teleological realism as a general view of social life. If the grammar of common action is of such broad applicability, however, we have to ask afresh about its normative weight, since not every community makes equal (or any) moral demands on its members. The moral gravity of common ends can be shown either by top-down deductive theory or, more promisingly, by relying on the normativity built into everyday social roles backed by a modest view of natural obligation. To demonstrate the social reality and moral weight of common ends, as I try to do in this chapter, is to state the case for Aristotelian pluralism as the best way to think about common goods. Upon this foundation, the ensuing chapters will build up a fresh, nonreductive account of the moral architecture of the firm and the market, as they should be and as they already are.

Readers primarily interested in applied thinking about firms and markets can skim over large parts of this chapter, the longest and most abstract in the book, provided they are willing to take my word for it that the key claims of Aristotelian pluralism are defensible. I would recommend they read the upcoming section, which gives the intuitive sense of what common goods are all about, and then the middle section on "hard cases." Alternatively, those pressed for time might first consult my supercompact summary of the common-action framework written for a general magazine audience,[2] and then dip into sections of this chapter as needed for more depth.

"WHAT FRIENDS HAVE IS COMMON"

In the spring of 1979, the citizens of Aalborg, Denmark considered a plan to revamp their historical city center.[3] The key proposals were to close off several downtown thoroughfares to cars, converting a portion of one street, adjacent to a sixteenth-century castle, into a bus terminal. The plan had been devised by the town's technical department, composed largely of engineers and urban planners, who aimed to reduce the number of cars in the city center. But Aalborg's chamber of industry and commerce came out strongly against the project, arguing that downtown's businesses depended heavily on customers driving in by car. A political battle was joined that would engulf Denmark's third-largest urban area for more than a decade, in closed-door negotiations as well as public hearings and the local newspaper.[4] Ultimately, the chamber successfully kept downtown streets from being closed to cars, while the planners got a modified version of the bus station. The Aalborg Project seems to be a paradigmatic example of the desirable sort of political conflict. Various groups deployed reasoned civil discourse, rather than insults or physical force, in a matter of shared concern. But were they in fact displaying the traditional virtue of citizens, concern for their common good?

As described, we don't yet know. There are two ways of understanding this or any political conflict, or perhaps two levels, depending on the kinds of goods that are at stake. The first and more obvious level regards the goods specific to the contending parties. The technical department was concerned with making the downtown more amenable to buses, bikes, and pedestrians. The chamber, by contrast, aimed to put kroner in the pockets of business, and so to attract and retain retailers in the city center. The initial proposal set these sectional interests at odds, and the final resolution managed to satisfy them both. At this level of analysis, do we see some good that both groups share? We may be seeing "smart politics" unfolding, but for all we have described so far, the two groups did not have any good in common. As Bent Flyvbjerg's book *Rationality and Power* makes clear, the final compromise satisfied the two sides by trading off their private interests at the expense of a diffuse third group, the residents of the city center. Even if all three groups had been satisfied, however, to consider only the horse-trading among separate interests is to rule out any appeal to a genuinely shared or common good.

A distinct concept of common good comes into view only when we look past conflicting private interests. In addressing the public, advocates and critics of the Aalborg Project would have appealed to something beyond "what the traffic engineers want" or "the needs of the business community." Citizens without a particular stake in either group would not be persuaded by these sectional appeals. But they might have been persuaded by the need for pedestrian mobility or downtown retail *as aspects of the overall flourishing of the city.* To put the case in this way is to make a genuine appeal to a common good, which is not a lineup of separate interests but rather a single end that can justly benefit all the parties involved. An order of justice among disparate individual or group interests is necessarily shared; if I consider that my own legitimate personal interests extend just to this point here, because this is the extent of my just share in a common endeavor, then I invoke a common good. The citizens of Aalborg shared an orientation to an excellent common life in the city, which involved a proper ordering of retail and traffic, and also education, housing, recreation . . . but we are getting ahead of ourselves. Complex political questions are the end of the story, not the beginning. Going straight for The Common Good in its grand, capital-letter version will not provide any new answers, much less new questions, about the stakes of life together. We need first to see the idea of common goods as a distinctive *kind* of moral aspiration.

At bottom, any theory of common goods is an attempt to articulate the aspects of human flourishing that transcend the individual (and to measure legitimate authority by them). Atomism, the idea that individuals are all that finally count, is wrong. Clearly, there are real goods that we experience as individuals—the unforgettable taste of a ripe mango, the thrill of summiting a mountain at dawn. But there are also goods that we can only achieve in common with others—a great ensemble performance of Bach's *Brandenburg Concerto No. 3*, deciphering a cellular protein in a biophysics lab. There is a categorical divide between these two types: private (or divisible) goods and common goods. To get this distinction right, though, we must look beyond whether many persons are involved or not. Some private or individual goods also require cooperation in a fairly strong sense.

The provision of what economists call "public goods"—defense, roads, education, GPS—is sometimes taken as the model of all political goals. Even Aristotle recognized that "people keep company for some advantage and to supply something contributing to their life."[5] Let's say that Citizens A, B, and C pay to maintain the dam upstream, and in return they each gain security from floods.[6] We have social cooperation here around a goal that, as a practical matter, is well beyond the capacities of any individual. Notice, however, that A, B, and C are not finally aiming at the same goal, but rather at a set of convergent individual goods. Each one is seeking her own security, which just happens to depend on the security of the others. The shared apparatus is a mere instrument, so the real goal in question here is contingently, not irreducibly, social. In principle, A, B, or C could each achieve the same goal of personal flood security on their own, by erecting huge sandbag walls around their house, or in some other nonsocial way. The point of the dam is best seen as an aggregate of private goods. Virtually any other public utility can be analyzed in the same way, so one could be forgiven for thinking that all the goods of political cooperation can be glossed on atomistic lines. If this were so, "The Common Good" could only name a certain kind of convergence among the goods or goals of individuals.

The atomistic point of view may tell us something about the average citizen's interest in defense or education, but it cannot explain what is at stake *within* the armies or schools that achieve these goods. Teachers and students do not pursue knowledge or civic formation as individual interests that happen to coincide. These goals are common in a stronger sense, because they are defined by a certain way of acting together. Alasdair MacIntyre underlines the distinction: "Public goods can be understood as goods to be achieved by individuals *qua* individuals, albeit only in cooperation with other individuals, and to be enjoyed by individuals *qua* individuals, while common goods are only to be enjoyed and achieved . . . by individuals *qua* members of various groups or *qua* participants in various activities."[7] As Charles Taylor puts it, a common good in the strict sense is something that is good "for us" rather than simply for me and for you. Taylor notes that such goods come in two flavors. "Mediately" common goods would be good for me alone but are different and better when they are "for us." For instance, "what raises a smile when I read it alone can put me in stitches mediated in the ritual of telling, which puts it in common space." There are also "immediately" common goods, "where what centrally matters to us is just that there are common actions and meanings."[8] This latter kind is simply inconceivable apart from a dialogical context: think of a free-flowing conversation or a ballroom dance. Yet both flavors require a "we" to be the concrete goods that they are.

Immediately common goods such as dancing are the clearest case of action aiming beyond individual goods. A successful dance is beneficial for each of the dancers, of course. If it were not, they would not willingly do it. The point is that it is good in a different sense than a public good, because it cannot be decomposed into individual goods, his and hers. There is no atomistic analysis of the foxtrot. What each dancer values is not just what she is doing, enabled by him, and vice versa, but rather what she and he are doing *together*. The dancers cannot conceive of the good they are aiming to achieve, an excellent tango, without thinking of their relation to their partner. One of the key aspects of a good dance is the communication between individuals, not because this allows them to realize some private objective more efficiently, but because their coordination is a large part of a good dance. It is something that only "we" can achieve. The unity of their action is logically linked to what is valued in the dance, so we have an irreducibly rather than contingently social good here. The relationship between the dancers itself is of value, and its flourishing is a genuinely shared good, a common good.

Aristotle has a name for the kind of cooperation that we see on the dance floor: friendship. The label highlights the mutual goodwill that is typical of dancers, and also that being together is itself a major part of what they value, as it is with friends. But Aristotle also famously classifies fellow sailors and even fellow citizens as friends. Sailors and citizens resemble personal friends only in an abstract way—in that their practice of reciprocity orients them to their relationship as a value in itself. As Danielle Allen puts it, they "establish functioning collaborations, and succeed at bringing the techniques of friendship to bear on rivalrous self-interest."[9] Friendship in this capacious sense can serve as an unlikely bridge for connecting niche pursuits like chamber music or dancing to the fraught world of politics, by seeing both in terms of their common goods. It is worth dwelling on Aristotle's arguments about friendship as a way of reimagining the normative stakes of various associations, a trajectory that will ultimately help us to think about political conflicts like Aalborg's as a question of common goods.

Even on a commonsense view, personal friendship is easy to see as a common good. Whoever is interested in a supposed friendship just for what she can get out of it—money or power or pleasure or whatever—is no true friend. This is also where Aristotle begins in defining friendship: "To a friend . . . you must wish goods for his own sake," and this must be reciprocated.[10] So far, we have mutual altruism, but real friendship is something more. It is something that "we" do and is good "for us." Friends must express their goodwill in some kind of common action, such as conversation, living together, or shared activities. "Lack of conversation has dissolved many a friendship,"[11] as Aristotle comments. Friendship is, then, a more ubiquitous case of what we saw in the esoteric example of ballroom dancing: a relation intended as a good in itself, as a common good.

Because he is focused on shared goods rather than affection or intimacy, Aristotle can acknowledge a broader lexical range for friendship than the modern term could bear. On his analysis, there are three ethical categories of friendship, and only the highest or noblest form involves friends who are in it simply for the sake of the other, as "another yourself."[12] One can also be a friend in two lower registers, to someone who is pleasant or useful, like a groupie or a business partner. Friends of utility "deal with each other in the expectation of receiving benefits,"[13] not with the other's good uppermost in mind. Their relationship will be more contentious and fragile than the nobler form, apt to end when its benefits run out. Yet Aristotle's insistence that such mundane relations are really kinds of friendship helps us to see that they do involve something beyond atomistic self-interest.[14]

With these wider possibilities in mind, we are in a position to better grasp Aristotle's famous claim that citizens and members of other communities are properly called friends. "For in every community [*koinōnia*] there seems to be some sort of justice, and some type of friendship also. At any rate, fellow-voyagers and fellow-soldiers are called friends, and so are members of other communities. And the extent of their community is the extent of their friendship, since it is also the extent of the justice found there. The proverb, 'What friends have is common' is correct, since friendship involves sharing [*koinōnia*]."[15] Unfortunately, Aristotle's surviving works do not develop a full-scale social theory around the suggestive triad of community-justice-friendship. Even so, it is clear that he closely links friendship with the reality of any *koinōnia*, which is Aristotle's "generic term for all social groups."[16] He portrays the link from both sides: communities (the social noun) involve friendship, and friendship involves community (the social activity). When we engage in common action and so form a community in Aristotle's sense, we are friends in respect of whatever it is that we share—a journey, a campaign, a performance.[17]

In order to accomplish something *together*, we must intend both the realization of that task and also the relationships that are constitutive of realizing our goal. Fellow soldiers, for instance, must act in concert in order to defeat their enemies. But in order to defeat their enemies *together*, they must also intend the order of the army that makes this possible: the chain of command, the arrangement of divisions, and the authority and honor and respect that prop them up. The army will fall apart if this order is not taken as a good in itself, at least provisionally.[18] The dimension of friendship is even clearer in the case of citizens. What citizens value is importantly, or even primarily, that they should be treated with respect and included in public deliberations and distributions, and so forth. To say that soldiers or citizens are friends is to say that their just and healthy mutual relations are something valued in themselves, not merely as an instrument to winning wars or passing laws. In other words, soldiers and citizens share a common good.

Friendship in its various forms has both a descriptive and a normative force. It is a factual matter whether you and I are friends (though, as Facebook reminds us, "It's complicated" is also an option). But this is a normatively significant social fact, because our friendship creates rights and responsibilities. If I am moving house, you will help carry furniture; if you have a newborn, I will bring you a meal. Friendship entails a thousand claims in justice subtler than these, but the price is worth paying since, as Aristotle observes, "having friends seems to be the greatest external good."[19] To be a friend is to bear this burden of justice. The same dual structure of facts and norms applies to friends in the larger sense of fellow members. What communities you belong to is, in large part, a fact about you, but it is a fact that makes claims on you. For the soldier, the citizen, or even the salsero, there are countless courtesies that are just part of being a "friend" in the relevant sense and so achieving some common good. These claims are never fully spelled out, though friends of utility are apt to demand more explicit conditions.[20]

Before we end our first detour into the arguments of Aristotle, it is worth noting that his vision of friendship is also key to his claim that human beings are intrinsically social. In order to achieve excellence, or perhaps even bare human identity, human beings need cooperation. Anyone who doesn't need others must be, as Aristotle puts it, either "a beast or a god."[21] The gist of this claim has been ably defended from any number of philosophical and empirical perspectives, from the traditional to the postmodern.[22] I will not mount another defense here, just a note of interpretation. The idea that the human being is a political animal (*zōon politikon*) is meant to convey more than the atomistic thesis that political authority is required for the enforcement of law and contracts, and so for the achievement of individual goods. Thomas Hobbes would agree with that.[23] To be a citizen is to share more than public goods; it is to be a friend in the sense of having some good in common with other citizens. To claim that the human being is a political animal is thus to claim that common goods are internally related to the human good. We can recognize the force of these arguments even without retaining the capacious meaning that the ancient Greeks gave to "friendship," which jars the modern ear. To avoid misunderstanding, I will refer to the friend-ly aspects of social membership, the dimension of sharing common goods, as "solidarity." Translated into these terms, Aristotle's claim is that humans need to stand in various kinds of solidarity with others, acting with them in relations valued in-themselves, not as a matter of convenience or expediency but as a condition of being human and living a flourishing life.[24] If this is correct, as I think it is, then the stakes for understanding common goods are high indeed.

TRADITIONS OF SOCIAL REALISM

Friendship is the paradigm case of a shared relation to a common good, and it was a commonplace of the ancient world that fellow sailors and fellow citizens were "friends" in some extended sense. But we moderns seldom act together in public with friendship uppermost in our minds, as the ancients did (or at least told themselves they should). In Aalborg, the debate over the downtown was finally settled by the exercise of power, not by an appeal to solidarity. In a world of vast bureaucracies, populated by consumers, clients, and job seekers, The Common Good as a political ideal seems like a call to nostalgia or revolution. But, to take our cue again from Aristotle, our convictions about ourselves are not the whole story. There is more here than meets the eye. The notion of common goods is not an exhortation to an unreachable standard of public spiritedness, and its relation with common life remains as close and as contested as it ever was. To see this, we will have to think about common goods in a deeper way, not just as relations that we particularly value and affirm but as essential constituents of acting together with others.

My aim in this section is to show that common goods are built into the fabric of social reality. By acting together, we create communities that are oriented to something beyond our private interests, to irreducibly social goods that we can enjoy only through membership. An orientation to common goods is not a special feature of homogenous or intimate communities, nor yet of public-spirited or political ones. Rather, on this neo-Aristotelian view, common goods are a universal feature of any order of common action—that is, any community. The common good is more than an ethical appeal; it is first a linchpin of a sensible and realist social ontology. We cannot understand the communities that surround and penetrate our lives if we do not understand the goals and goods to which they are ordered.

The social theory that I will sketch here is built on two main claims. The first and more generic one, which I will call "social realism," is the idea that there is such a thing as a community, emergent but distinct from a crowd of individuals. This realist approach takes on an Aristotelian flavor if we acknowledge a second claim, that distinctly social things must be oriented to distinctly social ends. Those social ends, which are present and active in your life and mine, are the grist for normative deliberation about the common good. There is then no reason to wonder or worry about the relevance of the notion of common goods in industrialized, democratic modernity. The realities to which the idea refers are still with us, even if unnamed or unacknowledged, wherever persons act together so as to contribute something to human flourishing.

We must first consider the notion that communities are real things in their own right, an idea that I will call "social realism." Without this idea as a conceptual background, Aristotelian or republican claims about communities and common goods are, or at least sound very like, sheer nonsense. Social realism is an old and venerable theory, and today it is regaining some of the scholarly currency it lost in the twentieth century.[25] F. W. Maitland gave a classic statement of social realism in a 1903 lecture:

> When a body of twenty or two thousand, or two hundred thousand men bind themselves together to act in a particular way for some common purpose, they create a body, which by no fiction of law, but by the very nature of things, differs from the individuals of whom it is constituted.[26]

In a mysterious but pervasive process, interacting persons can form something new, a group that is "more than the sum of its parts." When this happens, there are "$n + 1$"[27] agents to take account of, the *n* interacting persons and the distinct social entity they compose. This possibility is familiar to us from the innumerable words we have for collective agents, from general terms like "community" or "society" to more specific ones such as "family," "club," or "team." Almost equally familiar, however, is the atomistic interpretation that such words are just useful fictions. For the atomist, any apparent social agent is finally nothing but the individuals who compose it, and when rigor is required we can reduce any truths about the group to truths about its members as individuals. The Chicago school theory, which redescribes the business firm as a set of individualized market contracts, is a paradigmatic case of atomistic thinking.

The social realist would retort that we have words for social entities for the same reason that we have words for dogs: because they are real things! That is, these words pick out a distinct item in the world, a unity that cannot be analyzed or dissolved into its constituent members without loss. It is no accident, then, that the "nexus of contracts" theory of the firm fails; it was bound to fail because the reduction it aspires to cannot be successfully done. It is true that social unities are far harder to perceive than a physically connected natural unity like a dog. But just as those who describe dogs as nothing but a heap of individual cells will miss important facts about canine biology and health, so the atomist who sees communities as nothing but individual persons will fail to see the human realities that ensue on ordered interaction. That, at any rate, is the central claim of social realists, which I will develop by looking at two twentieth-century schools of thought: English political pluralism and critical realism.

Social realism is first an ontological thesis, a description of how things really are in the world, but its normative implications were clear to the English political pluralists. Inspired by the legal historians Otto von Gierke and F. W. Maitland, the pluralists flourished in England from roughly 1900 to 1930, linked to a political movement with the arresting name of "guild socialism."[28] Though their practical efficacy was limited, the pluralists had a deep influence on the "real entity" theory of the corporation, which I mentioned in the last chapter. Premodern legal history may seem an unusual wellspring for a movement focused on questions of social ontology, until one recalls that the law has always needed an implicit and often an explicit idea of what various communities are, in order to perform its practical tasks. The pluralists' project was to vindicate the associations of civil society (whether religious, economic, recreational, etc.) against absolute theories of sovereignty. "Our concern," wrote John Neville Figgis, a leading pluralist, "is not with individual but rather with corporate liberty."[29] On a Hobbesian conception, no civil association could have any existence apart from the dictate of the omnicompetent state. "Into its nostrils the State must breathe the breath of a fictitious life, for otherwise it would be no animated body but individualistic dust."[30] The troubling implication of this conception was that associations, unlike individuals, could not enjoy a principled immunity from state interference. What the state had given, the state could take away. The pluralists' strategy for opposing the absolutist threat to civil associations was to espouse a social realism.

The normative center of the pluralists' realism was the claim that communities have a life and dignity proper to them, which made them real players in the moral and political order. "If the law allows men to form permanently organized groups," writes Maitland, "those groups will be for common opinion right-and-duty-bearing units; and if the law-giver will not openly treat them as such he will misrepresent, or, as the French say, he will 'denature the facts.'"[31] Note that Maitland is not claiming that groups should be treated *as if* they had rights and duties but that in fact they do. Law and political action should recognize, not create, the status of groups as "moral persons." Figgis writes that "a society of men bound together for a permanent interest inevitably acts with that unity and sense of direction which we attribute to personality."[32] The idea of the moral reality of groups enables Figgis to give a bracing restatement of the claim that the human being is a political animal. Human "personality as a fact never grows up except within one or more social unions. . . . There is an interpenetration of his life with that of the society, and his personality is constantly being changed by this fellowship."[33] One can scarcely define a person, much less understand her, without reference to the associations of which she is a part: "All these groups and unions have their effect, and limit and develop your life, make you do, or refrain from doing, what otherwise you would not, and in so far prevent you being a free and untrammeled citizen of the state. More than that, they penetrate your imagination and your thought, and alter not only what you do but what you want to do."[34]

The upshot of this account, for the pluralists, is that the state does not have an unrestricted title to interfere in the affairs of civil associations in the name of individual rights or other political goals. The life of the group itself must also be taken into consideration, since participation may be a constitutive aspect of its members' own identity or flourishing. In Maitland's terms, there are "n + 1" persons to be considered, and the extra one is the group itself.

In retrospect, the pluralists' emphasis on the "personality" of groups was a rhetorical mistake. Its main problem is that it tries to explain something quite familiar (the reality of associations) in terms of something more elusive (the idea of personality). For jurists, a person is simply something that bears legal agency or responsibility, but when one is "talking English, not law,"[35] personhood means a great deal more than that. The narrow and broad meanings are apt to bleed into one another. This was evident in the US Supreme Court's 2010 ruling in *Citizens United* that corporations, as legal persons, should therefore enjoy speech rights similar to those of natural persons.[36] It should come as no surprise, then, that when pressed to explain how "moral persons" work, some pluralists reverted to broader and vaguer analogies of personality, to the point of claiming groups to be "psychic organisms."[37] This is a much stronger claim than is necessary to secure the integrity of the civil associations that the English pluralists cared about, or in general to found a workable social realism.

To shore up the foundations of social realism, I turn to a more recent school of thought in the philosophy of social science, known as "critical realism." The central figure is Anglo-Indian philosopher Roy Bhaskar (1944–2014). Unlike English political pluralism, critical realism has not been moored to any overt political project. Taking its bearings from natural science, it aims to rescue social theory from both of two reductive approaches: an atomism that reduces everything to individuals and a collectivism that reduces everything to society.

Critical realism is premised on three key concepts from the philosophy of natural science: (1) ontological stratification, (2) emergence, and (3) downward causation. What the success of the sciences shows, Bhaskar argues, is that the world is stratified into irreducible levels. The division between physics and biology, for instance, is not arbitrary but corresponds to real levels of reality. This layered view of the world rules out a reductionist picture (sometimes called "Nothing Buttery") which would hold that a giraffe is *nothing but* a collection of tissues, which are *nothing but* collections of cells, which are *nothing but* . . . and so on, down to particle physics. The levels of reality are ordered to one another by emergence: entities at a "lower" level interact to generate/sustain a more complex entity, without losing integrity at their own level.[38] One oxygen and two hydrogen atoms combine to constitute a water molecule—the molecule is emergent from them, but also rooted in them (if they disappeared, so would it). We know that the "higher" level is distinct from the "lower" from the fact that the higher has sui generis powers that are irreducible to the powers of the lower level. Important among these emergent powers is the ability of the higher level to act back upon the lower, which Bhaskar calls "downward causation." So, although it may be true that my liver can be described in terms of chemistry, its chemistry will change based on sociobiological facts such as sickness or age.[39]

Critical realism applies this general model to human society in order to claim that social things are emergently real. Communities and other social phenomena exist in their own right, at a different ontological level than the persons who are their members. It is not the case that a family, sports team, corporation, polity, or what have you is *nothing but* a collection of individuals with their traits and beliefs. Rather, in coming together as a team or a family the members jointly generate an emergent thing, which exists in a specifically social way. Of course, the traits and beliefs of the individuals matter, because every emergent layer is rooted in the strata "below" it, which sustain it. When you watch a soccer team at play, you might want to take account of any of these various levels. There is not only a sociology or strategy of soccer, but also a psychology, a biology, and a physics of soccer (all of which Real Madrid or Manchester United tries to master). The key point here is that the team itself is irreducibly real, because the "persistent relations"[40] of its members have generated an emergently new thing at the level of the social.

For Bhaskar and the critical realists, we know that social entities are real not because of any "personality" they may have, but because they are causally efficacious in the world. Suppose I am a player on a professional soccer team. The relations of player-to-coach or owner-to-employee are essential for motivating me to act in certain ways. The coach gains a set of emergent powers from her position in the team, which enable her to make me play or ride the bench, undertake a certain training regimen, change my diet, and so on. On the other hand, my own conduct and that of my fellow players affects the reality of the team—whether we win or lose, please our fans, build a new stadium, and so on. Thus we see downward causation at work in the context of an ("upwardly") emergent social reality. It is both convenient and precise to refer to the actions and powers of "the team itself," which plays an irreducible explanatory and causal role, and thus constitutes a reality in its own right.

Because social realities emerge from the interactions of conscious persons, not physical parts, the analogy between social and natural composition ought not to be pressed too far. Social phenomena depend on intentional action, and their emergent powers are mediated by the ideas and desires that go into personal agency. My coach cannot "make me" play a new soccer position in the same sense that I can make my hand write this sentence.[41] She can draw on her role in the team to give me strong *reasons* to comply, but she cannot determine what my response will be. Persons in social contexts remain the authors of their own actions.[42] To claim that social things are emergently real, then, does not deny the integrity or agency of the persons who constitute them.

The overall point of any social realism is that social things exist in their own right. We can talk or theorize about them without any intellectual embarrassment. A strict atomism is descriptively false, and we will miss important dimensions of the human world if we consider only individuals and their qualities. Although it is mainly an empirical idea, social emergence is not morally innocent, as we already saw hinted in the pluralist vision. The apparently normative idea of common goods is at the heart of an Aristotelian version of social realism.[43]

ARISTOTELIAN REALISM

The distinctive claim of an Aristotelian social realism, as I will defend it, is that common goods are essential to the emergence of communities, and thus to social reality more generally. I take my bearings from the main line of twentieth-century Aristotelian thought, which is often understood only as a moral philosophy and has gotten too little attention as a serious social ontology. The French neo-Thomist Yves Simon is especially clear on the centrality of common goods to the reality of social things. He writes, "Every community is relative to a good to be sought and enjoyed in common."[44] This is not a contingent regularity, as though it were a happy coincidence that persons in every community should happen to be seeking the same thing. Rather, this is a matter of definition, of what a community really is. Part of what it is for a community to exist is for persons to have a good in common. Simon explains, "The members of a community—family, factory, football team, army, state, church . . .—are engaged in a common action whose object is qualitatively different from a sum of interdependent goods."[45] A community is nothing other than an order of common action, as Simon suggests here, so his point can be put concisely: *Every instance of common action is a locus of common goods.* The inverse claim holds as well: as Simon himself puts it in the same passage, "Where there is no common action, there is no common good." Since common goods ensue on common action, and only there, common good is a basic principle of social ontology. Translated into the language of real emergence, the core of an Aristotelian social realism can be stated as follows: a real community emerges if and only if persons engage in common action around a common good.

The idea that communities are defined by common goods has strong intuitive appeal for many familiar examples. Let us return to my hypothetical soccer team. What are the goods that provide us with reasons for acting together?[46] Players and coach may all have individual interests in getting fit or making money or seeing the world. But what defines us as a team is, as a starting point, our shared goal of winning games. We cannot plausibly describe winning as a sum of interdependent private goods. True, you win if and only if your teammates win as well. Yet it is backward to say that the soccer team wins because its individual members won, as if some could win and some lose on a given day. Rather, each member won because the team won. It is the team that wins at soccer in exactly the same sense that the individual wins in singles tennis, so the record books charge the victory to the group, not the members. The goal of victory is available to each player only as a common good, which can be participated in but not cashed out to individuals considered separately.

Suppose that my fellow players and I are a trifle less superficial, in that we care about playing excellent soccer as well as winning. Playing well together is also more than a sum of individual goods. According to a familiar sports trope, a team full of star athletes who are fractious or selfish will often play worse than a team of lesser specimens who play well together. Team quality is certainly not a matter of adding up individual talents or performances, because excellent soccer requires each player to take account of what his teammates are doing. As we saw above, whenever one's relation to others is a constituent ingredient in the good in question, as it is with great soccer, we are dealing with relations of solidarity around some common good. So in respect of both outcomes (winning) and activity (team play), the team aims at a common good beyond a mere aggregate of private goods.

Every kind of community can be conceived on analogous lines to the soccer team. Russell Hittinger's summary could apply to any community: "Wherever there are plural rational agents, aiming at common ends, through united action, and *where the unity is one of the intrinsic goods aimed at*, we have a [community]—something distinct in dignity."[47] The potential complexity of a community's good, which we glimpsed already in the tension between winning and playing well, is made explicit here. The object of a given common action is not best thought of as a single monolithic goal, but rather as composed of two different kinds of common goods.

Let us borrow a different example from Yves Simon—a shoe factory. What is its shared goal? At first glance, it may seem that "great shoes" sums up the common objective of the community. Yet this misses something crucial, because it fails to respect the fact that social agents are constituted by interacting persons. A fuller statement of their common object is necessarily complex: something like "working well together so as to produce great shoes." The factory workers do not have a good in common simply by looking at the same goal or objective—namely, the shoes—but rather by aiming at some good *together*, such that their coordination with one another in solidarity is part of what they value. So it is not only the shoes produced that constitute the common good of the cobblers, but also the good relations of solidarity within their social order. That these dimensions are separate we can see by considering two ways that a shoe concern could fail. First, it might create mediocre shoes, failing to achieve its extrinsic goods or goals. But it could also fail to flourish, even if it produced great shoes, on account of misogyny or tyranny or fraud, or from any number of other specifically social dysfunctions.[48] The common good animating a given community can be complex, with two distinct dimensions of value, which are intertwined but do not collapse into each other.

Drawing on Aristotle's *Metaphysics*, medieval commentators developed a vocabulary for this dual order (*duplex ordo*) of common goods.[49] That dimension of the group's flourishing that is outside the group itself, such as victory or fine shoes, is known as its "extrinsic common good." The good condition of the social order itself (which will involve justice, friendship, coordination and communication, etc. among the members) is its "intrinsic common good." This latter kind of good, which is necessarily social, is more fundamental to the existence and flourishing of any community, because it allows persons to continue acting *together.* As Hittinger emphasizes, only where "unity is one of the intrinsic goods aimed at" do we find a real social entity. What makes any nonsocial objective into a common goal is its being pursued together, as the object of common action. A good like beautiful shoes, unlike friendship, is not necessarily social, so it must be "made common," by being taken as an end of action in common. In Charles Taylor's terms, such extrinsic goods are "mediately common" because they could be pursued by individuals alone (perhaps not very efficiently), but they are different when they are "for us." Recall Taylor's example of a good joke: amusing in private, hilarious in company. But even where extrinsic goods may be lacking, as in the earlier paradigms of friendship or dancing, the intrinsic common good of the members still provides a good reason to act together. A community does not need to have objectives that are as clearly specified as those of the soccer team in order to have a common good. Whenever persons choose to act *together*, whether for some great project or simply to be in company, they aim at something "qualitatively different from a sum of interdependent goods."

The converse of this claim also holds good: "Where there is no common action, there is no common good." Not every sort of peaceful interaction is common action forming a community, as we have already begun to notice in the case of arm's-length market exchange. Yves Simon presses the point further by analyzing tricky cases of apparent cooperation without any properly common goods, drawing on Roman law categories. The clearest legal analogue of an emergent social entity is the *universitas* (corporation), a unitary legal actor distinct from any natural person. But some types of cooperation use a different legal form, the *societas* (akin to a general partnership), which involves colleagues acting together but separately responsible for the consequences. This individualization of legal responsibility has echoes in the social realm. Imagine that you and I launch a start-up business in which I am a silent investor and you are the working entrepreneur. Our arrangement leads to profits that we can divvy up. The mutually agreed-on goal would seem to make this an instance of common good, but in fact it is not. Shared profit, as the goal of this interaction, is only "a sum of private interests that happen to be interdependent."[50] The motivating reasons for action are my bottom line and yours, not any good that is properly and irreducibly "ours." It is not the salience of money that makes this a pure case of *societas*, but rather the absence of common action or deliberation. As Simon puts it, "Each action is traceable to some partner. . . . None is traceable to the partnership itself."[51] Since there is no common action, and the partnership can be managed by contracts concerning individual goods, there is no basis for the partners to hold a good in common.[52] Common goods do not result from the mere convergence of private interests. They arise only when common action generates solidarity around a set of shared ends.

The model under development here applies a characteristically Aristotelian line of teleological thinking to social realism. Every particular thing has a form, which makes it the kind of thing it is, and an end or a *telos* to which it is oriented. The end or telos of any thing is just to be a flourishing version of itself, an excellent whatever-it-is, and "the good" for that thing is to realize its end. But the form and the end of each thing are woven together, so we cannot properly understand what that thing is unless we know something about its telos or its good.[53] Living things are the clearest examples of this. The end or telos of an acorn, which has a biological form, is to grow into a mature, healthy, reproducing tree. Having such an end, and pressing toward it, is just part of what it is to be an oak tree. It is written into the DNA of the acorn in a quite literal sense.

We should understand social entities in an analogous way. A community also has a distinct social form and a corresponding social end or telos. Consider an art museum. The average citizen has no problem telling apart an art museum from a fast-food restaurant in terms of its physical layout, its norms of conduct, likely opening hours, and so on. Generally speaking, we know what the form of an art museum is, and we also have a sense of its end or telos, which centers on collecting, preserving, and displaying works of art. A great museum does this really well. Aiming for such a goal is "written into the DNA" of any art museum, now in a metaphorical sense. As a social thing, the museum must have a properly social good, which is shared in by those who participate in the life of the museum (as artists, curators, patrons, etc.). The members have a stake in the flourishing of their joint project, so its telos is a common end. Even skeptics about biological ends should find social teleology persuasive, in that human action is undeniably goal oriented. It is the purposiveness of personal actions that gives social realities their own emergent ends, which are distinct from individuals' purposes but which act back upon individuals in "downward" fashion. The idea of common goods helps us to take account of this dynamic of social reality.

HARD CASES: SELF-INTEREST, CONFLICT, EVIL

The upshot of a teleological social view is that every community is oriented to some common good as its end. Where we do not find common goods, we are not dealing with emergent social realities. But these universalizing claims could well be accused of serious naïveté about the human world. If we look at modern workplaces, for instance, the goods of common action seem to pale in significance next to profit, pleasure, and power. A naïve version of the theory could easily fall into a fatal dilemma, either denying that such communities exist in their own right or seeing the common good as a tacked-on normative concern that floats above the imperfect social reality that we find. Either way, common goods would not be built into social reality in the strong sense that I have claimed. Aristotelian realism needs to be toughened up in order to deal with social forms that are amorphous, contested, or corrupt.

> *(1) The Challenge of Self-Interest: Restaurant owners found a local tourism board that meets quarterly to advertise the region's charms, in order to drum up business for its members.*

The tourism board looks like an instance of common action around a goal that is nothing more than an aggregate of private goods, even if that isn't mentioned in their billboards. If you asked the members what would make their project a success, each would probably mention first its effects on their customer traffic, a private good. Still, there is something more going on here, because the restaurateurs have chosen to enhance their own bottom lines through common action. Consider the two main ways in which the project could fail. Obviously, if it fails to drum up business, it will likely fold. But the tourism board also needs to succeed as a social order, with a thin but not negligible kind of solidarity. It might also fold if participants fail to respect each other in deliberation, to discharge whatever offices they may have taken up, to distribute the group's benefits and burdens justly, and so forth. Even if the marketing side works, the collaboration may become too bothersome to sustain. In the jargon I introduced earlier, even though the group is focused on the private interests of the business owners as an "extrinsic common good," it has an "intrinsic common good" in the relations of the members who comprise the common action. If the owners fail to achieve this latter good, their private interest in customers will cease to be a common end of action and will lapse back into a merely private interest. So long as the association holds together, however, it aims at a common good in addition to merely convergent private goods. A neo-Aristotelian account of emergent community can accommodate a rather large degree of private interest as a possible object of common action, so long as one recognizes that private satisfactions are never the whole story.

> *(2) The Challenge of Disagreement: The electrician's trade union is sharply split between two candidates to lead the local IBEW branch, of whom one advocates compromise with management, while the other supports prompt resort to strikes. After the election, the backers of the losing candidate recurrently threaten to walk out and form a rival union.*

The fractious trade union looks like an instance of a single community that does not have any common goal or telos; what counts as excellence or success in the eyes of the hawks is repudiated as faltering and failure by the doves. If we assume that social emergence requires "some shared conception of the point of continuing co-operation,"[54] then a union without consensus seems to have neither social unity nor a common good. But this assumption is faulty, since it is the very point of social realism to deny that the features of a social form can be simply reduced to the ideas or desires of individuals. In this light, the common good of a community is best understood as an emergent feature of the social entity itself, which is rooted in, but also distinct from, the actions or beliefs of its members. In speaking of common goods, we refer to what is socially real, to the potential for promoting flourishing that a community really has, rather than to individual theories or aims that may mistake its reality. If the telos and so the common good of a community are built into its nature as a social thing, then they are as robust in the face of conflict as the community itself.

Common good theorists influenced by Thomas Aquinas tend to emphasize the affirmation of goods as the "glue" of social reality. Aristotle and the tradition of critical realism leave more room for power and social conflict, so that individuals' intentions are only *one element* of societal emergence. As Roy Bhaskar puts it, social forms "do not exist independently of the conceptions that the agents possess of what they are doing in their activity."[55] When they join in common action, persons act on reasons, but these reasons may rest on errors or a lack of insight, and they importantly depend upon power relations or material resources as well as upon ideas about what would be best. It may be the case that relatively few members of the IBEW affirm it as good, or do not wish it to change, but that powerful others are in a position to punish dissent. The fact that cooperation is motivated by the distribution of power rather than wholehearted affirmation does not fundamentally alter what is socially achieved, even if it makes the achievement more precarious. Similarly, Aristotle's regimes for The Common Good endure more because of power than consensus: "The multitude that wants the regime [must be] stronger than the multitude that does not."[56]

Social unity is not (necessarily) fellow feeling or an identity of aims, but the unity of shared social order. The "common end," likewise, is best taken as the emergent goal of the society, as that telos toward which the society itself really tends, which can be taken in more specific or more generic terms. The participants do not need to share a detailed conception of their community's flourishing, only a vaguer notion of what it is they are doing together. All the members of the fractious union do have a general sense of what the point of the IBEW is, as opposed to a bridge club or a church. In accusing their opponents of unjust or unwise union policy, they appeal implicitly to the generic goals of any trade union. But the backers of the losing candidate also clearly recognize that if they continue to support the union, they will further a specific vision of its common end with which they disagree in some measure. It is true, of course, that disagreement can deepen to the point that even the most basic character of a community is in dispute. This will likely put an end to all common action through exit or even war, as the case may be.

> *(3) The Challenge of Moral Corruption: The members of a homeowners' association agree upon a scheme to exclude members of racial minorities from buying homes in their jurisdiction. (Consider also the Mafia, the slave plantation, etc.)*

The redlining HOA, the slave plantation, and the Mafia look like cases of community that are not "relative to a common good," because their shared ends are intrinsically unjust. However much the members may enjoy consensus, social order, and even mutual affection, theirs can only be a solidarity in evil. These cases show that it is one thing to say that a community exists, and quite another to say that it is, or aims to be, (morally) good.

Such (hopefully rare) perversions should not be the center of any social ontology, but they still pose a serious challenge to the universality of common goods. One dead-end response is to maintain that no moral evil can be the end of a genuine community, so these communities do not in fact exist. Another nonstarter is the notion that each is a deformed version of some decent enterprise—as though the Mafia were a misguided mutual aid group, or the slave plantation a wayward cotton farm. For they plainly do exist, and are just as plainly corrupt to the core. The best response to the challenge of moral corruption, in my view, is to bite the bullet and acknowledge that some communities are oriented to evil ends.

This admission compels a careful restatement of the central claim of Aristotelian realism, but not a rejection of the whole approach. The objection about corrupt social ends is really just a special case of a general worry about Aristotle's foundational claim that "every craft and every investigation, and likewise every action and decision, seems to aim at some good," which opens the *Nicomachean Ethics*.[57] His claim is obviously meant to cover unwise or evil actions. To explain how it is possible to do evil under the "guise of the good," one must distinguish between two senses of the word *good*: what the agent takes as a good (the formal sense) and what is really good (the substantive sense).[58] Like an individual agent's action, an order of common action is oriented to apparent moral goods that may turn out to be otherwise. From the perspective of the (dominant parties within the) community as it happens to be, its shared end will seem good and desirable. Even though the HOA or the Mafia is flawed in a larger sense that ought to take priority, there must be something good about them or they would simply fall apart. As Plato famously observed, there is justice among thieves.

It is the common good in this formal sense, a social end that is taken as good, that is built into every community without exception. Of course, the term "common good" usually connotes substantive rather than formal worth. For the sake of clarity, then, the central claim of Aristotelian realism should be restated in terms of a thinner kind of emergent goal: every community is relative to a common end. This restatement drains away some of the normative pull of common action, because mere common ends do not deserve allegiance just as such. But this, I think, is a virtue of the theory rather than a vice. We cannot and should not unrestrictedly promote all the common ends that we are confronted with. They may be morally bad, misunderstood, or not worth prioritizing. It requires further argument in a normative key to conclude that some case of common action is genuinely good and deserving of support.

COSMOS AND COMMUNITY

The distinctive claim of Aristotelian social realism is that communities are real agents in the political world, defined by emergent common ends. These ends are what give specificity and social texture to the common action of members—a school aims to educate, an army to defend, an art museum to collect art, and so forth. But this largely descriptive insight does not show why various communities *deserve* allegiance or support. Roughly speaking, it shows in what way their ends are *common*, but not why they are *good*. Any practical appeal to common goods, such as the disputants in Aalborg might have made, invokes a morally substantive ideal, not a mere shared goal. On the Aristotelian pluralist account, only when common ends are normatively compelling as reasons for action are they genuine common goods.

As a descriptive matter, every community is oriented to some embodied vision of its own flourishing. Normatively, every community is oriented to true flourishing in justice—where justice entails both the members' due participation in its benefits and burdens and also consistency with broader moral and political concerns. To realize common ends in justice is a genuine common good, an emergent social goal with real moral appeal. For Aristotle, only some political regimes aim at The Common Good, and so deserve unqualified support, because only some regimes are just to their members. The others should be reformed. Deeply corrupt forms of common action, such as the Mafia or the slave plantation, have no common good at all because they are defined by unjust ends, so they call for resistance rather than reform.

What is the ultimate source of the moral gravity of common goods? Over a long intellectual history, common goods have been anchored in two main ways: by derivation from unchanging human nature or by close analysis of actual communities. With some unfairness to two nuanced thinkers, I will associate the first, metaphysical approach with Thomas Aquinas, and the second, inductive approach with Aristotle himself. These approaches share three key features. Both wield the idea of common goods as a tool for framing political conflict as disagreement about shared ends. Furthermore, both rely on the metaphor of part and whole.[59] As the Aristotelian maxim has it, "The whole precedes the part," so to identify the good of the whole is a promising way to transcend sheer opposition among the parts. Finally, common goods are something participated in and shareable—like the good atmosphere at a party—rather than individually possessed and zero-sum— like the wine being served.

If the idea of The Common Good is associated with a totalizing or theocratic approach to politics, this is likely due to the first approach, the metaphysical-deductive. Its standard-bearer is Thomas Aquinas,[60] and it also owes a good deal to the Christian Neoplatonism of Augustine. The main idea here is to argue from some profound principle of goodness that precedes human choice. A deep anchor for The Common Good is typically developed in one of two modes: via human nature or the cosmos as a whole.[61] The first mode relies on the idea that whatever has the same kind of nature has the same kind of good. Here it is the human species that is the "whole," and the good of the whole is the orientation that individuals have to the same goal, usually seen as a virtuous life and/or eternal salvation.[62] This sort of abstract good is common by "predication," just as the color turquoise is common to turquoise things, or winning elections is the common goal of politicians even when they are pitted against each other.

Notice that The Common Good in this sense has little prospect of bringing people together, because it is unchangingly true of individuals, no matter what they do. But human flourishing also points to a second sort of totality, namely the ordered system of the cosmos itself. This "whole" of which individuals are "parts" is not an abstract species but the concrete, if immeasurably vast, order of the universe. The idea here is something like the Great Chain of Being.[63] Like soldiers ordered into place by their commanders, human beings have been assigned a place in the world by "nature and Nature's God," which gives them a teleological part to play. In the medieval metaphysic, The Common Good of the universe is a single ordered value that includes every last aspect of human flourishing, so there is finally no distinction between the goods of the individual, of the human community, and of the cosmos. From the diverse starting points of human nature and cosmic order, these two approaches converge to a theological point since, as Saint Augustine writes, "the common good of them all [is] God Himself, and His eternity, truth, and love."[64]

There are considerable philosophical advantages to the metaphysical approach. It reduces normative conflict, because The Common Good in its grandest sense will coordinate every particular good in a vast cosmic peace.[65] A deductive outlook simply posits an a priori norm for human cooperation rather than trying to foist a common goal onto apparently conflicting individual ends. But its practical downsides may be just as great, since a goal that is simply posited or shared in a metaphysical sense can do little to generate solidarity around practical issues. Both the foundational claims and their concrete implications are endlessly contestable—and if this was true in ancient or medieval context it is doubly true today. A liberal-democratic outlook is particularly inhospitable to philosophers' claims that fly in the face of widespread conviction or lived experiences.

Fortunately, Aristotle's own approach to common goods depends less on endlessly contestable philosophical questions, and more on the practical exigencies of acting together, where disagreement cannot go on forever. As Yves Simon puts it, "In common action alone does concrete existence, with all its determinateness, with its character of totality, its location in time, and its contingency, tend to procure unity among men."[66] A biologist at heart, Aristotle employs an inductive method in his account of the human world, beginning with the particulars of actually existing communities and their presuppositions. Whereas the metaphysical method reasons down from the broadest statements about goodness in the universe, the inductive asks what shared undertakings are already underway and what would make them good.

But was Aristotle really such an inductive reasoner about The Common Good? A typical reading of Aristotle's political thought places him squarely in the first, metaphysical, camp. He famously argues that the goal of the city is living well and that true happiness is defined by virtue, so the best possible city is one arranged according to the principles of virtue. On the traditional reading, in a word, virtue is The Common Good. If the basic content of The Common Good were given in human nature, then that content would be mainly an object for speculative, not practical, debate. This reading of Aristotle is mistaken, as I have argued at length elsewhere, because it runs together political ideas that he kept separate: virtue or happiness on the one hand, and common goods on the other.[67] Even though Aristotle does conceive the human being as the "political animal," he never even mentions the term "common good" in the books of his *Politics* that deal with true virtue and happiness. The notion of common good, by contrast, takes center stage in a down-to-earth discussion about the types of regime, which canvasses practical questions such as the role of border walls and whether children with only one citizen parent should count as citizens.[68] The role of common goods in this discussion is to distinguish decent or "correct" (*orthos*) political regimes from corrupt or "defective" (*parekbasis*) ones. For Aristotle, the idea of common good is a lower standard than true human flourishing or *eudaimonia*, but it is still a standard of justice.

How does this lower standard work, if it is not hooked to the highest human goods? The "correct" regimes serve the common goods of their citizens by corresponding to "what the city actually is."[69] A Greek city-state (or for the neo-Aristotelian, any political community) is essentially a partnership among free citizens that is self-sufficient in respect of living well. The regimes in the common good reflect this reality by honoring the contributions of all the citizens to the city's broad project. The problem with "defective" regimes catering to the ruling class is not that they fail to promote true happiness, but that they are not really cities worth the name. "For they are despotic, but the city is a community of the free."[70] Any city, given what cities really are, ought to share its benefits with all its citizens. "For either it must be denied that the persons sharing [in the regime] are citizens, or they must participate in its advantages."[71] What Aristotle's common goods look to first, then, is not any metaphysical feature of human nature but rather to an "empirical" account of what politics is about, which he draws from widespread understandings and practices of contemporary cities. Of course, this account of politics is inherently normative, in that everyone involved understands that cities and citizens must stand in certain relations with one another, in order to be the kind of things that they are.

The hallmark of an inductive account of common goods is to begin looking for normative sources of solidarity among the common endeavors that are already afoot. We do not have to begin with high metaphysics, because we find in normal human affairs a set of built-in ends and norms that can make for far-reaching immanent critique.[72] Still, an emphasis on ongoing communities does not imply that an inductive account of common goods can be metaphysically innocent. We still need to be able to speak about the raison d'être of this community or the flourishing of that relationship, and these are more than merely empirical claims. But the philosophical footprint here is quite modest, since one can start, as Aristotle does, with widely shared ideas that are essential to making one's way through the human world.

THE PRIORITY OF ENDS OVER PURPOSES

An inductive approach to common goods draws its immediate moral force from the normativity built into a social role, such as the citizen or the business colleague. But as Aristotle himself observes, the virtues of the good human being and the good citizen rarely coincide. So one can always ask: What good reason do I have to respect the norms of citizenship (or the common ends of a business) in the first place? A classical answer to this fundamental question might run on the following lines: human flourishing requires politics, and politics in turn requires norms of citizenship, so every human agent has good reason to respect norms of citizenship.[73] But general claims about the good life could not show why *this particular polity* deserves my allegiance as a citizen. Still less could they prove anything about a business firm, which does not occupy a unique or essential place in human affairs. The moral gravity of such voluntary associations is easier to see if we reframe the classical, eudaimonistic answer in a modern, juridical way. That is, rather than appealing to the good life as a whole, we should focus on the finer-grained moral obligations binding voluntary communities and their members together.[74] Why, then, does any community with its common ends impose obligations in justice upon its members?

The most straightforward answer to this juridical question rests on a modest formulation of natural law, though one might also argue for the obligating force of common ends from a republican version of consent theory.[75] Robert Sokolowski, drawing on the work of Francis Slade, gives an unusual but penetrating formulation of the key idea: "Natural law is the ontological priority of ends over purposes."[76] He elaborates this distinction in the following way: "An end, a *telos*, belongs to a thing in itself, while a purpose arises only when there are human beings. Purposes are intentions, something we wish for and are deliberating about or acting to achieve."[77] What the natural law enjoins, in this highly general sense, is that when we deal with something—be it a rare orchid, a sharp knife, a child, a recipe—we take account of its characteristic ends, which may not align with our plans and wishes. Sokolowski goes on, "We must have a sense that our purposes must be measured by the way things are, which means that they must be measured by the way things should be. The distinction between purpose and end has to dawn on us, and when it does dawn on us we experience the pressure and the attraction of the way things have to be. We encounter 'the natural law.'"[78]

The notion that built-in ends should measure our purposes can be applied to common action just as readily as to plants or tools, since any community is built around emergent ends. Social realities ought to be approached as the kind of things they are, especially by those in a position of authority: we should not deal with a school as if it were a sports club, nor a business as if it were a piggy bank. When we mistake or willfully misconstrue the nature of some community, we will distribute its goods unjustly, erode its basis for public support, and generally wreck the common enterprise. Nor can we justly deal with some community as though it were only a group of individuals pursuing their own separate interests. The vice of "heedlessness," as Alasdair MacIntyre has called it, ignores the specifically common dimensions of acting together.[79] One should remember that, in J. N. Figgis's phrase, common action will "alter not only what you do but what you want to do."[80] A community is not composed of untrammeled individuals, but of members. To be deprived of the goods of common action is potentially to be cut off from a major piece of one's identity. Jonathan Lear poignantly illustrates such a loss in his meditation on the "cultural death" of the Crow Indians in the nineteenth century.[81]

The point of prioritizing ends over purposes is to show that common ends, in their full scope, make a real claim in justice, and so they may not be overlooked by whoever engages in common action. We owe something in justice to those from whom we receive; if we receive something strictly common, then we owe something to the community. This is not a call to unthinking communalism, for the priority of ends over purposes can pull in two directions, opposition as well as support. The language of common good is firstly a way to legitimate the actions of authority, and in this register it lends itself to patriotic exhortations: Rally around the Common Good! But as we saw briefly above, Aristotle's *Politics* presses the idea of common goods into the service of an immanent critique of the prevailing Greek regimes. In his argument, the purposes or ideologies of democrats and oligarchs neglect either the rich or the free poor as members of the city. Their limited interpretations of who counts should be reformed in light of a full empirical account of the common ends of the polity. But common goods have an even more critical register. The priority of ends implies that there is no way to excuse cooperation with deeply perverse social forms, since their common ends are necessarily repellent. I ought not to work as an accountant, say, for the Mafia or the slave plantation, even if my own tasks, goals, and personal convictions seem innocent. The common ends that my role promotes are evil, and they take normative precedence.

Because Sokolowski's general formulation of natural law understands particular communities as sources of obligation in their own right, it licenses a principled pluralism in much the same sense that we saw with the English political pluralists above. All forms of common action, except the most depraved, deserve normative respect because they are potential sites of solidarity.

To use the classical vocabulary, they are forms of friendship, and friendship is a precious and powerful thing. Some solidarities may prove wicked or corrupting, but this is all the more reason to treat them as consequential features of our moral world. Justice demands that their members support or reform these common projects, not because of some authoritative imprimatur or a cosmic five-year plan, but because of the ends invested in them by common action. This metaphysically modest form of Aristotelian pluralism can help to map out the normative terrain of highly various social landscapes, including the modern economy with its corporate firms and markets.

SOMETHING IS ROTTEN IN THE STATE OF DENMARK

The priority of ends over purposes gives the best fundamental explanation, in my view, as to why the participants in an order of common action should (and generally do) prioritize their common ends as valuable in themselves. Yet there are many such ends, and only very seldom can a vibrant plurality of intrinsically valued forms of solidarity all be weighed equally. In my personal life, for instance, I must decide how to apportion my time and resources among the competing common ends of family, workplace, neighborhood, religious congregation, sports club, and so forth. As MacIntyre puts it, "Each individual as an independent practical reasoner has to answer the question of what place it is best that each of those goods should have in her or his life."[82]

Nor are individuals' decisions made in a vacuum; they are powerfully affected by the prevailing political order, which favors some shared projects with public power or cultural prestige, and burdens others with scorn, taxes, or legal impediments. Thanks to the ubiquity of such political influence, inquiry into the limited common goods shared in private associations leads naturally to the more capacious goals of the political community. Like members of any other community, citizens explicitly or implicitly ask one another, *Who are we to become?* But unlike with teammates or colleagues, the answer that citizens forge by their common action affects every corner of human life. If vague political rhetoric about The Common Good refers to anything, it is to an architectonic project of this kind. For the Aristotelian, a broad scope for politics is legitimate because it is inevitable—as characteristic of contemporary liberal republics as it was of ancient city-states or absolutist Baroque kingdoms. The prospect of a definitive moral goal for the sweeping project of politics is what most entices traditional theorists of The Common Good, and what most troubles their liberal critics.

A grammar of common action could not settle their dispute on its own, but would greatly enrich it. Both sides of the debate can (and I think should) subscribe to Aristotelian pluralism as a way of clarifying the most fruitful division between proponents and liberal critics of The Common Good. Cast in its most jaundiced light, their wide-bore debate presents two unappealing political choices: an alienating individualism that eats away at all forms of human communion versus a stifling, top-down nostalgia that subjects all human affairs to a single, homogenizing purpose. But political liberals need not be atomists any more than traditionalists need to be political monists. Rather, liberals could retain their inclination to equality and self-determination while cheerfully acknowledging that both politics and civic associations are morally formative modes of common action. Likewise, the traditionalist could admit that citizens can and do pursue a shared moral life precisely in the political order *among* diverse communities, without subsuming all human goods into a monolithic public project. The fruitful debate between these camps, in my view, is not about *whether* citizens share a morally formative project (since they obviously do), but about the subsequent questions: *what form* this project should take, *who* justly rules, and *which* dimensions are to be settled by political authority or left to lower-level forms of common action.

This book deliberately stops short of tackling these political questions head-on, for two reasons. First, I am interested primarily in a grammar for articulating the moral architecture of common ends in a clear and rigorous way. This is admittedly much less than the full-blown normative theory that traditional partisans of The Common Good would like. But it is challenging enough, both to the fuzzy thinking that often travels under their banner and also to the idiom of private goods to which their critics often default. Second, it is fitting for a pluralist to approach questions of political economy through the prism of the firm and the market as normative institutions in their own right. Parts 1 and 2 invoke politics and its ends only to the (sometimes large) extent that they bear on the firm and the market, which are my main focus. In the book's conclusion, I will briefly turn the grammar of Aristotelian pluralism onto politics proper. Before embarking on this longer journey, however, let us first return to the conflict over the downtown traffic regime in Aalborg. The (relatively) discrete cast of characters and issues involved in a municipality simplifies, at least somewhat, the task of pinpointing their common goods. The citizens of Aalborg did not need to resolve every dilemma of Danish civil rights or of global justice in order to reach an authoritative judgment on the shape of their streets.

There is no one method for evaluating a scenario like Aalborg's in terms of common goods, but Aristotle models a general, three-step blueprint. The first step is to determine the character of the partnership and its chief goal. The second is to identify the main constituent groups or interests, the contributors to the partnership. The third step combines these two elements in an inquiry about justice: How can the common goal be furthered in a way that incorporates the just claims of these key members? Flourishing together with justice—this is the common goal (or The Common Good) that deserves the support of citizens.

In the case of Aalborg, the social stage is the city itself, a regional center with maritime connections lying on the flatlands of North Jutland. A municipality within a liberal state is not a sovereign political community, but it does wield nearly total authority over its own road system. The ends of a city are not morally in doubt, but that does not mean they are clear—articulating them is a key part of any contest. All the parties to the Aalborg Project seem to agree on the importance of a flourishing downtown as against the pressure of suburban sprawl. They likewise agree that environmental concerns, nonautomotive traffic, and a flourishing commercial base, in some order, are the main pieces of the downtown puzzle. In Flyvbjerg's recounting, the prime movers are clearly identifiable: they are initially the technical department (TD, the town's official planners), and the local chamber of industry and commerce (CIC). A group of bicycle-riding Social Democrats emerge briefly with a compromise plan after the initial antagonists deadlock. The audience for the debate is the holders of authority: the city council and the inhabitants of the downtown area and the city at large. Notice how quickly the parties multiply, even in this stripped-down account. And what does justice require? Ay, there's the rub.

We might start by asking which of the various parties are concerned in good faith with their common good, but this turns out to be an unhelpful question. Only once the city's common good has been authoritatively located could the question of good faith be resolved, so it does not help in the seeking. While the search is on, the most egregious self-interest can be painted as concern for some aspect of the common good in which one happens, just coincidentally, to have a stake. At the outset, then, the question of good faith amounts to a question about rhetorical skill at dressing up one's own concerns in civic garb. According to Flyvbjerg, the CIC single-mindedly pursued the interest of the business community with scant regard for the facts, which seems to merit condemnation. Yet thriving commerce both was and was acknowledged to be a key piece of the downtown puzzle. Any community's good does involve legitimate advantages for the members, who should each enjoy their just share. The real question is, How much does each member deserve in justice? This can hardly be settled ex ante. Even morally upright businesspersons, in their private capacity, could hardly know just how far the interests of the city's businesses were to be rightly promoted or favored. It is the point of public deliberation among citizens qua holders of authority to hear and weigh the interests of the relevant parties and lay down an authoritative order for their common good.

As the advocates of various causes compete in the public arena, they bring into public view the ingredients of an authoritative decision: rationality and power. The rationally best result for Aalborg's citizens *as citizens* would have been the just achievement of the city's common good. They did not want downtown commerce to languish, but neither did they want a polluted or traffic-filled city center. The TD scheme seemed to have rational insight on its side, as evidenced by the national and international planning awards that it won. But in adversarial politics, the final result depends more on power than on rationality. The business community wielded practical muscle and just enough of the truth to hamstring the street-closing plan in favor of their car-driving customer base. Aristotle would not be surprised: "Even if finding out the truth where equality and justice are concerned is very difficult, achieving this is still easier than convincing those people of it who have the power to gain more for themselves."[83]

Interestingly, late in the game the businessmen of the CIC recognized that promoting their narrowly construed interests at the expense of the overall common action of the downtown was not a good idea even from a business perspective. Having successfully fought to keep some key downtown streets open to cars, they realized that the piecemeal traffic changes that resulted from their own power advantage actually made the retail environment worse. They tried to reverse course and close the streets, but by this point the incoherent compromise had crystallized as a political decision, to the ultimate detriment of the city. Flyvbjerg concludes, "The losers in the struggle over the Aalborg Projects are those citizens who live, work, walk, ride their bikes, drive their cars, and use public transportation in downtown Aalborg, that is, virtually all of the city's and the region's half-million inhabitants."[84] When a community fails to achieve its common goods, it is not a social abstraction that suffers, but rather the community's members, whose persistent relations make the common action what it is.

The case of the Aalborg Project illustrates why we need a moral grammar of common action. Aristotelian pluralism is firstly a mindset, an impulse to look beyond divisible private goods for the common ends that are built into any community and make first claim on the members. Such a lens could not have guaranteed civic success in a conflict like Aalborg's. But it might have better attuned the participants, going in, to the full scope of the goods they had at stake, and so moved them to chart a wiser course before it was too late. The CIC might have recognized that they had skin in the game not only as a (potentially aggrieved) interest group but also as members of the city whose own fortunes would rise or fall along with the common action as a whole.

A grammar of common goods points to normative realities beyond the individual, which we neglect at our peril. It was not primarily the moral failings of the CIC or their adversaries that accounted for the final shape of the common action in Aalborg, which was perhaps worse than inaction.[85] The explanation resides instead in the emergent features of the local regime—the arrangement of offices, the political culture, the balance of power. When such things are in good shape, even an imperfect moral community can achieve a common good. When they are not, common action will result in something else: in pervasive projects that have less than the full authority of justice and less than salutary consequences. This goes for the forms of common action in all their variety—for states, for cities, for civic associations, and, as we shall now investigate, for business firms.

CHAPTER THREE

WORK TOGETHER

In the summer of 2019, the CEOs of the Business Roundtable declared: "While each of our individual companies serves its own corporate purpose, we share a fundamental commitment to all of our stakeholders."[1] The press fanfare accompanying this pronouncement was meant to highlight a major change of course from the executives' previous allegiance to stockholders. In 1997, the same group had avowed that "the principal objective of a business enterprise is to generate economic returns to its owners."[2] The change is indeed stark, at least verbally. The adoption of the "stakeholder approach" in the boardrooms of America's leading corporations cements its status as the most prominent rival to the Chicago school's narrow focus on the stockholder. More broadly, the rhetorical about-face evinces a growing public desire for a mode of business that is conducted for the benefit of workers, customers, and communities as well as investors.

The desire for just and humane business firms is hard to square with the dominant imaginary of the market economy as a vast space of coordinated self-interest. This pervasive picture exiles the goods of common action to a foreign land called "politics," where for prosperity's sake it is hoped they will stay. As I argued in chapter 1, the private-good approach is downright catastrophic as a model of the business firm (part 2 will show that it doesn't quite fit the wider market either). Firms are not constituted by price-centered exchanges of private goods, but by common action around shared ends. To restrict a firm's telos to divisible individual goods is to distort the experiences and the normative claims of everyone whose life and livelihood is tangled up with a business. There is more at stake than money. No complex theories are needed to appreciate the critique; on-the-ground experience is enough. Little surprise, then, that practical movements toward a humane economy have gained most traction in respect of the firm, where the market imaginary is at its weakest.

Unfortunately, it is far from clear what concrete changes, if any, follow from the Business Roundtable's commitment to stakeholders over stockholders. The trade group's own history suggests that the shifting rhetoric mainly reflects diminished public confidence in big business after the financial crisis of 2008. The CEOs' profit-centered proclamation of 1997 followed a long period of business growth. The previous official statement, issued in 1981, had emphasized "responsibility to society," and it sounded a good deal like a calibrated response to the malaise of the 1970s.[3] As the decades pass, business practice has not seesawed back and forth in response to these apparent changes of heart.[4] But even if the new stance is sincerely taken, the discourse of serving stakeholders implies little more than a generalized desire think more broadly about the point of a business firm. Unless this impulse is articulated in a way that is concrete and compelling, it can hardly stand against cogent theories and institutional inertia that take it for granted that the goal of business is to make money, period. This work of articulation does require a robust theoretical apparatus, and the grammar of common action developed in chapter 2 gives us the concepts and distinctions that we need.

The task of this chapter is to outline the decisive contribution of the Aristotelian pluralist's logic of common action in clarifying and honing the broadly felt desire for better business. My positive approach to the common ends of the firm will be structured around the same essential questions that I used to analyze the Chicago corporation and the Aalborg Project. The first three apply to any sort of common action whatsoever: (1) *What is its point or goal?* (2) *Whose participation is constitutive?* (3) *How can they share justly in the common project?* The fourth question asks how a private association such as a firm fits into larger common goods, for example, of the state. Rigorously applying the grammar of common action yields an immanent critique of the firm, a fresh picture of the flourishing business that remains rooted in social reality as we find it.

Given the centrality of political life in most rhetoric about "The Common Good," it may seem that thinking about the business firm in terms of common goods is a recipe for a more politicized, publicly sensitive firm. A recipe, some might think, for a variant of socialism. On the pluralist account that I propose, something close to the opposite is the case. If the business firm is a form of common action, then it has a solidarity of its own that is oriented primarily to its own common ends. A business association "serves The Common Good" (in the broad, vague sense that one might hear on the hustings) primarily by becoming a flourishing version of itself as a social order, not by maximizing its profits, boosting GNP, reducing discrimination, or by any other external metric.

The needs of politics, or of whichever other stakeholder may press a legitimate claim against the firm, must be read through the ends that are built into the social reality of the business. In other words, public concerns about justice or culture or climate may affect *how* the firm legitimately pursues its ends, but they do not fundamentally alter *what* ends are instilled in the firm by the common action of its primary members. As I shall argue, those key members are the workers. The primacy of workers does not by itself entail any particular scheme of business governance, such as workplace democracy or cooperative ownership. But it does force us to consider the full range of goals that are built into the firm as an emergent social reality, among which the excellence of its core work takes pride of place. No single evaluative term can fully capture the human meaning of working together well (or, for that matter, badly). The flourishing of the firm will remain a contestable matter for its own workers as much as for the citizens who confront the task of integrating firms into a wider order of common action. The normative grammar of common goods provides a helpful compass for navigating this jungle of competing claims.

This chapter will sketch central theses about the business firm and its relation to politics that follow more or less directly when we apply an Aristotelian logic of common action. Reconceiving the firm as a form of solidarity demands profound changes to the structure and culture of business as we know it, all pointing beyond profit to the reality of the firm as a transformative moral project of shared work.[5] Of course, one need not share my common action framework in order to recognize that profit is only one dimension of a humane firm, even if an important one. The primary interlocutors in this chapter will be fellow travelers who share this broader premise, ranging from card-carrying Aristotelians to stakeholder management theorists to workplace democrats. If I can use the grammar of common goods to add insight to ongoing conversations about the humane business firm, the ambitions of the chapter will be achieved. I will not even pretend to trace all the organic outgrowths of culture or all the entailments of justice that might follow on a deeper vision of the firm as common action. My story is thus lacking its essential denouement, since turning toward common goods is not primarily a matter of personal virtue, but of just and capacious institutions that would help the business firm to embody something other than a short-term, socially narrow, and morally reductive vision of its own flourishing.

PUTTING PROFIT IN ORDER

The first thing to ask of any social form is *What is its point or end?* The question is best answered not by listing all the purposes that a given community may serve, but by homing in on its central and distinctive goals. A public school, for example, may function in some respects like a daycare service or an athletic club, but its primary common end is the instruction and formation of the young. All its other purposes are rightly subordinated to this goal. The business enterprise also serves a wide variety of social functions—for example, as a source of personal identity, a place to meet a spouse, a site for exercising democratic agency, or a vehicle of national pride. But we find similar functions in a university or a fraternal club as well. What distinguishes the firm as a social domain is some set of organizational features clustered around labor, commerce, and making money. Intuitively, we might define a generic business firm as "people working together to produce and sell goods or services at a profit." This is, I admit, as obvious as it is vague. Much of the appeal of the Chicago nexus-of-contracts theory lies in the clarity of its vision, by which the various dimensions of the firm are made auxiliary to the usefully precise goal of maximizing shareholder value. As I argued in chapter 1, the bottom line cannot be the last word, since the firm's moral structure can be had only at the price of subordinating profit as one aspect of a common project. What should be "maximized" is the firm's common good—its all-around flourishing as a community of "participatory productive work."[6] But the notion of a firm's common good will remain cripplingly fuzzy until we articulate more precisely what the reductive focus on profit leaves out, and also where profit fits in. A theory of the firm as a "business community" must steer clear of Chicago's exaggerated emphasis on private goods and also of the romantic temptation to leave money and the market entirely out of account. To do this with clarity and rigor, we need a more elaborate blueprint of any community's ends.

Consider some of the ways that a business might fail: through lack of needed capital, wasteful or unwise administration, low-quality products, or poor sales. These different ways to fail suggest, by way of contrast, that there are also several irreducible dimensions to the flourishing of the firm. I propose to analyze *the* overall common goal of a firm as the properly ordered achievement of multiple common ends, each of which might be thought of as *a* common goal. As a framework for articulating and ordering these dimensions, I will build on two distinctions that we have already encountered, concerning the kinds of goods that are involved in any common action.

1. Intrinsic versus Extrinsic Goods: Any community will aim at ends that bear on its social order in one of two ways. Some goals are *intrinsic* to the social order itself, because they are simply a certain quality of relations among the participants in the common action. The main common end of personal friends, as of ballroom dancers, is precisely that there be good relations between them: of love, trust, respect, artistic harmony, clear communication, and so on. Intrinsically common goods of some kind are essential to every case of common action without exception, since it is impossible to act *together* without considering the quality of relations among cooperators. On the other hand, common action may also aim at realizing some goal *extrinsic* to the common action, at some state of affairs in the world outside. The army aims at victory; the SPCA aims to end cruelty to animals; the cobblers' shop aims at fine shoes. Because extrinsically common ends are not simply a quality of social order, they must be "made common" by being taken as an end of common action. They could also be pursued, in principle, as private ends (e.g., you and I could each make shoes separately, or we could make them together). There is typically an order among these categories, with the intrinsic pointed toward the extrinsic, as Aristotle

notes early in the *Nicomachean Ethics*: "When there is an end beyond the action, the product is by nature better than the activity."[7] The soccer team takes the form that it does—the coach's authority, the players' teamwork in a 4-3-3 formation—in order to win games, just as the orchestra's social order is for the sake of great ensemble music.

2. Goods of Excellence and Effectiveness: Alasdair MacIntyre notes that we may engage in some practice in order to taste the very particular enjoyment available only to those who take part in it. Only connoisseurs of chess can truly grasp the brilliance of the grand masters; likewise with the appreciation of portrait painting or hot-rod engines. These are *goods of excellence*. What the uninitiated can readily appreciate, on the other hand, are the all-purpose goods of status, power, and money that the best chess players, mechanics, or painters may earn from their skilled achievement (but may not, as in the familiar trope of the starving genius). MacIntyre calls these broadly useful resources *goods of effectiveness*, and he notes that they are a central concern of those institutions, such as the chess club, the speed shop, or the *école des beaux arts*, on which communities of practice rely to sustain themselves. The goods of effectiveness are characteristically zero-sum and thus rivalrous, while the achievement of goods of excellence is typically "a good for the whole community who participate in the practice."[8] We may have all enjoyed a stimulating chess game (or political debate), but you won the prize money (or the nomination) and I did not. There is a normative order here as well: the point of the chess club with its tournaments and prizes is to facilitate the playing of good chess, not primarily to enrich the players, and much less the club officers. There is always a temptation to invert this priority, and MacIntyre famously argues that the virtues are just those dispositions that practitioners must have in order to resist the pressure to let the competitive goods of effectiveness trump common goods of excellence. Although MacIntyre's terminology is novel, at bottom he is reworking the classic Aristotelian distinction between merely instrumental goods and goods valued in-themselves.

Both the above distinctions purport to be exhaustive: *all* shared ends are either aspects of social order or not; *all* common goods are either tools

Table 3.1. Four Categories of Common Goods

—	Goods of Excellence	Goods of Effectiveness
Intrinsic to Social Relations	(C) Intrinsic goods of excellence *Cooperative work: "practice"*	(B) Intrinsic goods of effectiveness *Administration: "power"*
Extrinsic to Social Relations	(D) Extrinsic goods of excellence *Goods or services: "product"*	(A) Extrinsic goods of effectiveness *Material resources: "property"*

of effectiveness or excellences to be valued in themselves. Some Aristotelian scholars have written as though these were different names for the same division,[9] but further reflection shows that they carve up the terrain on different lines. Some goods of excellence (such as a soccer team's coordination) are a way of acting together well, while others (such as the throaty rumble of a custom V8) are evidently not. On the other hand, some achievements of a healthy social order (such as a well-oiled administration) are valuable in an instrumental or supporting sense, while others (such as a glorious corner-kick goal) are to be valued in themselves. Rather than conflating the two distinctions, then, we should lay them across one another, which yields a much more robust and potentially fruitful picture, captured in table 3.1.

This four-slot typology captures several intuitive dimensions on which common action can flourish or fail.[10] My imaginary bakery, Pie in the Sky Co., could languish on account of shortcomings in any one of the four categories—e.g., (A) lacking good ovens, (B) promoting the wrong people, (C) failures of baking technique or teamwork, or simply (D) making bad bread. Each dimension counts as an end that we seek together, and flourishing on any dimension thus counts as a good common to all the members of the firm. As a beginning, then, it is helpful to name Practice, Power, Property, and Products as qualitatively different kinds of common goal. On the other hand, members qua members are not committed to four separate categories of ends, but rather to the flourishing of the community as an emergent social whole. Each constituent common end is a compelling reason for cooperation only insofar as it is rightly ordered to the others, in much the same way as leisure and professional success are choiceworthy for me only to the extent that they fit into my life as a whole. A community's overall common good is not to be found in any one of these boxes, or as an aggregate of them, but in their *rightly ordered* joint achievement.[11]

I suggest that this right ordering traces a teleological path following the letters indicated, moving from the outside, from what is least common, inward to what is most common, and then back out.

(A) Extrinsic goods of effectiveness, or "property," are easily acquired from outside of common action—for example, from the market—and are easily detached for distribution into private hands. Goods of this kind appear at the border of common action because they can oscillate between private and common use, money easiest of all.[12] As such, they reflect only faintly the quality of the common action itself and are of largely instrumental value to it. Property can appear in common action as a means or an end. The capital in the treasury of Pie in the Sky is common qua resource insofar as it fuels a cooperative enterprise, and will need to be employed so as to further the shared project. On the far side of some collective accomplishment, divisible private resources can appear as common qua reward insofar as a shared conception of justice governs their distribution, again as a way of recognizing the priorities of the community and who has contributed most to them. But apart from these moments of common use, the resources themselves bear little stamp of the common project and easily pass into private control.

(B) "Power," on the other hand, can be created and used only within an order of common action. Because they depend essentially on the ongoing solidarity of members, intrinsic goods of effectiveness can seldom be instrumentalized in the unqualified way that money can. There is a morally formative aspect to hierarchical command or to bureaucratic rules, in that the affected behaviors are presented as praise- or blameworthy. Organizational schemes of reward and punishment help to define what it means to be a better or worse member (ergo a better or worse person). And the use of authority is tied to an implicit or explicit claim to serve a just order that is valued for itself. For example, excelling in HR is a good thing for an organization, but no one claims that "administration for administration's sake" might serve a common goal. Witness the frequent academic complaint that bureaucrats are taking over the mindset and budget of universities. Power points beyond itself.

(C) "Practice": the core dimension of any common good is excellence in the shared activity that makes a community the distinct kind of social thing it is. This core practice may involve scholarship and teaching (in a university) or baking (at Pie in the Sky) or playing soccer, building engines, making laws, and so on, along with all the incredibly various relations of collaboration, rivalry, respect, friendship, or mentoring that go into seeking such ends together. The goods at stake are apt to be highly particular, inaccessible to outsiders in the way that a nonphysicist cannot hope to grasp the elegance of a theory in quantum mechanics. If promoting such particularistic goods of excellence is the central point of the goods of effectiveness, then we have reason to doubt the pervasive idea that the power and money can be well managed by generic techniques of management or finance (rather than familiarity with the practice at hand), a notion that underlies the whole consulting industry.[13] Witness again the ill-advised project of enlisting corporate executives as university presidents, whose alleged expertise often fails to respect, and so to promote, the distinctive form and ends of a community pursuing knowledge.

(D) Ultimately, the proof is in the pudding—that is, in the "product." We cannot evaluate or even engage in common action without attending to the extrinsic ends that it aims to achieve. Producing great and affordable bread, or gaining wisdom or knowledge, is the best measure of the success of a bakery or a university, even if not the only one. It is perhaps surprising that these ultimate goals lie outside the community—customers can take the bread home and eat it, and alumni retain their knowledge after graduation. Although the good of a social thing (as of any other thing) is primarily to be a flourishing-version-of-itself, this flourishing is embodied in an important way in ends beyond its constitutive culture and social structure, whether in a material product or service, as in Pie in the Sky Co., or in a human excellence, as in the university.[14] This renders any common action amenable, in at least some degree, to evaluation from without, cutting against the particularity of its internal excellence.

Each of these four common goals poses a thorny challenge unto itself, but a community flourishes over time only by solving the even-thornier problem of ordering the four dimensions so as to promote the overall common end in just fashion. There is no merely technical answer to this essentially political question. Let us say that any reasoned distribution of power among rival claimants—choosing some over others and justifying the choice—involves small-*p* politics. Even in a business firm, the problem of right ordering takes on a political color, because each of the four dimensions is apt to be the focus of a specialized constituency. Those who focus on finance or sales in a business, for instance, will characteristically have a different take on questions of the firm's common good than HR personnel or core workers (e.g., How many financial reserves do we need? Long-term R&D? Investment in technology or in people?). Deciding between common goals is thus also choosing between persons, who need to be persuaded of the justice of any settlement. Justice requires that each constituency share common benefits in proportion to the contribution it has made to the emergent whole. This is a highly particular matter, and the theory sketched here offers only the most general guidance: each common goal (and associated constituency) matters to some degree, but the internal goods of excellence should take normative priority.

One enduring challenge is that the capacity to render authoritative judgment usually lies with those who wield institutional control over goods of effectiveness—such as corporate CEOs or university presidents—who may have little connection to the core practice. This helps to explain why institutional corruption usually tilts toward money or power, and not away. We are all tempted to overemphasize (whether sincerely or not) what is personally salient for us, so those who deal with goods of effectiveness are liable to overrate the importance of those goods. Aristotle comments, "Even if finding out the truth where equality and justice are concerned is very difficult, achieving this is still easier than convincing those people of it who have the power to gain more for themselves."[15] On Aristotle's account of the political regime, the best practical solution is to give the main constituencies a hand in ruling, so that multiple forms of collective self-interest may be mutually offsetting and thus track more closely the demands of common flourishing.

The notion of common goods as a right political ordering among different shared ends is not at all specific to business. Healthy universities or sports teams use goods of effectiveness as instruments to achieve their defining goods of excellence, just as does a healthy firm. Yet we can draw on this conceptual framework in order to distinguish business from other human endeavors (a notoriously tricky task) and pinpoint the role of profit.[16]

What gives some community a "business dimension," I would argue, is that some of its goods of excellence are sold for money, a good of effectiveness. This kind of exchange in itself is not unique to business firms either—universities and sports teams may also sell merchandise to raise funds (which might be the concern of the university's "business office"). What does distinguish the business enterprise is the central importance of this kind of sale and its proceeds for the common action at hand. A business firm does not sell products just so that it can keep the lights on; the proceeds from the sale are in some sense the point of the whole affair. At very least, the pecuniary motive is not incidental to a business firm in the way that a merchandising department is incidental to a university, which could perfectly well live off donations or its endowment without ceasing to be the kind of social thing it is. A "business" that does not aim at selling anything is not properly called a business.

The teleology of the business firm seems to complete a circle, moving from goods of excellence ("products"—category D) to terminate in easily distributable goods of effectiveness ("property"—category A). A business that cannot sell its products is a failing business by definition. And it will not survive if these sales do not, on the whole, turn a profit. Have we then taken a winding road back to where we began, to the Chicago school's focus on profit? Perhaps so, but now we "know the place for the first time," as T. S. Eliot put it. Even if a firm is an Aristotelian "friendship of utility," it is still a kind of friendship or solidarity. Making money as a mediately common goal of cooperative action is something quite different than money as a private good, since the personal and normative desirability of this profit is in part a reflection of common action and its irreducibly social goods.

Consider the difference between the first profit turned by your start-up business and winning the same amount of money in the lottery. Construed as purely private goods, they are identical. Yet the lottery prize tells us nothing about what we have done or should do together. The profit from the start-up, by contrast, derives from producing goods of excellence, which for the firm's members bear the stamp of a whole social order of cooperation. Even if they did not literally "make" money together, the products they sold are a concrete embodiment of their common action, and so the members can rightly regard the revenue as a good "for us." Viewed in this way, financial returns cannot be simply maximized at the expense of the other dimensions of common action. A business firm can seek to increase its profitability only insofar as this pursuit is consistent with justice and its flourishing as a social form. Money itself has no natural form or limits, as Aristotle observes, but the social form of the firm can make profit a common end and therefore impart a form and limit to money as an aspect of the firm's common good.

STAKEHOLDERS VERSUS MEMBERS

The public debate between shareholder and stakeholder teleologies, with which I began this chapter, is really about one of the essential questions for any social order: *Whose participation is constitutive?* The instinct to think broadly about these issues is a welcome change from the narrow focus on owners of stock that still dominates boardrooms, the financial pages of newspapers, and the Chicago theory of the firm. Stakeholder theory enjoins the opposite: include everyone who might be affected in any way. Throwing wide the doors of the firm does reopen essential questions that are scarcely even visible on a private-good model. Unfortunately, to include every stakeholder would be nearly as damaging and distorting as including none at all. Precise, practicable answers to the question *Who counts?* demand a rigorous set of distinctions drawn from reflection on the common action of business. It would be nice if *The Common Good*™ were an Aristotelian algorithm for satisfying every interested party—every stakeholder—unrestrictedly and simultaneously. Alas, it is not. If anything, the grammar of common action suggests that for a firm to please everyone is probably not possible and may not even be desirable. Once we apply the essential distinctions I have been developing—for example, private versus common goods, contractual exchange versus common action—it will be clear that only a subset of business stakeholders have a constitutive share in the common action of the firm. Since the firm is primarily an order of "participatory productive work," as Alejo Sison notes, I argue that those who determine its common good are, above all, its workers—those employees, directors, owners, or collaborators whose labor and cooperation constitute the firm as a social reality. The legitimate interests of other stakeholders in the firm should be understood either as matters of contract or as ends of communities other than the firm itself.

The idea of a business stakeholder is intentionally amorphous, in contrast to the legally ascertainable class of equity owners. Edward Freeman, whose work launched stakeholder theory in the business academy, defines the term as "any group or individual that can affect or is affected by the achievement of a corporation's purpose."[17] This is incredibly, even impossibly, broad, but in practice stakeholders are usually grouped into a more manageable set of categories. The 2019 Business Roundtable statement highlights customers, employees, suppliers, community, environment, and stockholders. Other lists include government and competitors as stakeholder groups. The variety of incommensurable interests represented by these disparate groups demonstrates, if nothing else, the intellectual difficulty of running a firm according to the stakeholder vision, which is "about creating as much value as possible for stakeholders, without resorting to trade-offs,"[18] as Freeman and his coauthors put it. Each stakeholder is essential, and each ought to be satisfied, somehow—it is up to the (heroic) manager to figure out how.

As Freeman and coauthors' downplaying of tradeoffs suggests, the stakeholder approach sees itself less as a rigorous theory of the flourishing of the firm, which would put various interests firmly in place, and more as a provocation for entrepreneurs and managers to imagine their enterprises in a more capacious way. At bottom, stakeholder ideas are meant to be practical or "managerial" rather than theoretically precise.[19] This makes for a studied vagueness about what, if anything, a stakeholder approach entails aside from breadth. The leading textbook on the approach is so ecumenical that it counts even Milton Friedman and Michael Jensen, Chicago champions of shareholder value, as proponents of an exotic variant of stakeholder theory: "After all, the only way to maximize value sustainably is to satisfy stakeholder interests."[20] But if the stakeholder approach can subsume even ostensible intellectual rivals who would vehemently object to being annexed in this way, it is perhaps best thought of as a perpetual postponement of the main issue, of who *primarily* constitutes the firm, in favor of keeping all the options open.

Alejo Sison and Joan Fontrodona have appropriated the stakeholder imaginary in their common-good theory of the business firm, arguing that various broad constituencies can be seen as "citizens" of a shared order of virtue-enhancing work, and thus as proper participants in the firm's common good. Stockholders participate in the firm, they argue, by investing their "accumulated or capitalized work," while clients enjoy a firm's products more when they mix in their own work, as in IKEA's some-assembly-required furniture.[21] Similarly, governments have a direct interest in too-big-to-fail firms like Samsung in Korea, and governments also provide a background of justice for all businesses. Thanks to this variety of constituencies in the firm, and their incommensurable interests, Sison and Fontrodona conclude that justice in light of the firm's common good does not require any particular scheme of corporate governance. I am sympathetic to their conclusion, which I will discuss in the next section, but not because the firm's constituents are impossibly diverse. The stakeholder approach on its own is an inadequate foundation for understanding the common ends of the firm, since it conflates having an interest in the firm with participating in its common action.

In the early 1960s, the term "stakeholder" was first coined at the Stanford Research Institute to mean "those groups without whose support the organization would cease to exist."[22] The definition stands in interesting contradiction to Aristotle's notion of membership. He comments that "not everyone without whom a city could not be is to be regarded as a citizen of it."[23] Any kind of association, from a marriage to an empire, depends in some way on a huge constellation of persons and institutions other than itself. Similarly, everyone who deals directly or indirectly with a business firm has some kind of stake in its flourishing or failure. But not all these persons or groups are members of the association, because they do not share in its common good *as common*, as an end of their common action. Its enemies or competitors do not share in it as "good" either.

A firm like Pie in the Sky, for instance, may buy its flour primarily from a single miller, such that the bakery and the miller have an obvious stake in one another's success or at least survival. But even if Pie in the Sky is its miller's biggest and best client, the miller is not a member of the bakery or a sharer in its common good, just because price-centered market exchanges are not a form of common action.[24] The miller remains outside the firm. Of course, this frontier will be breached if the bakery buys the miller's operation and brings him into the firm (or if the miller actively helps the bakery with its recipes), in which case we are dealing (temporarily) with a single order of common action, rather than separate communities related by contract. By failing to distinguish between those who share a common good *as common* and those who have some other kind of stake in an association, Sison and Fontrodona run roughshod over just those distinctions that need to be made if we are to understand the firm in terms of its own distinctive common good.

Who among the firm's many stakeholders deserves to be considered as a sharer in its common goods? Not all those who affect it or are affected by it, but only that subset who find themselves under its authority or who otherwise participate in its common action. We can rule out those stakeholder categories that relate to the firm primarily by means of market prices: clients, suppliers, competitors, and stockholders. Of the nonmarket stakeholders, one category has the strongest and most obvious claim to be constitutive members of the firm: its workers. The market does provide a means of entry and exit for most workers in a firm, whether they are employees or owner-managers. But the internal world of the firm is a space of authority and common action, of "norm-governed productivity" and not of prices, as we saw in chapter 1. Within that space, the intrinsic and extrinsic common goods of the firm can be compelling reasons for action for workers, quite apart from their ratable market value.

Whereas stockholders are primarily interested in profit, and regulators in compliance, workers have a built-in interest in realizing the full scope of the common good of the firm, on all four of the dimensions analyzed in the previous section. They have a stake in profitability and compliance, certainly, but not at the price of excluding or instrumentalizing their own excellence as a productive team. Even when a worker concentrates on a single dimension of the firm's common action, such as finance or sales, her main allegiance is due not to her own department in itself, but to the flourishing of the firm as a whole. At the end of chapter 2, I noted how the businessmen of Aalborg, Denmark, came to regret their own advocacy for narrow retail interests at the expense of the overall flourishing of the downtown. By pushing their just claims too far, they ultimately harmed even their own narrowly construed interest in customer traffic. In a similar way, the constitutive interest of workers, as members of a firm, is directed toward the rightly ordered achievement of its various common goods as dimensions of a unified social order.

By privileging workers in this way, I am not denying that other stakeholders may be crucial to the success of a firm, only that their interests are not constitutive of its common good in the way that workers' interests are. To misuse an Aristotelian distinction, workers are essential to the common action of the firm, whereas other stakeholders are accidental. Stockholders are an unusual case of nonmember stakeholders who seem to be "within" the corporate firm itself. They own an open-ended financial claim (and a right of control) that lingers throughout the life of the firm, even when the initial cash infusion from the firm's sale of equity shares is a distant memory. Even so, the owners of contractually unprotected equity stock are not members of the firm, except insofar as they participate in its common life, which most do not. Such participation would generally require taking up an active role, such as director, officer, or employee (or even voter), though Jean-Philippe Robé notes that a corporation's "controlling shareholder owes [legal] duties similar to the ones owed by directors" even if he has no formal office or role. Ownership is a kind of power, and the majority owner cannot rightfully decline to use his. "He becomes part of the 'team' because of his monitoring position."[25] It remains true that other passive, financially oriented stockholders are nonmembers, so their interests are not constitutive of the firm's purposes, even if it does owe them something in justice (much as it owes something to every exchange partner). Normally, the stockholder must rely on the impersonal discipline of the market to vindicate her claims. Her primary means of redress is to sell her share and so exit through the same market-shaped door by which she came in. Unless stockholders become workers in some way, they cannot claim to share in, much less to define, the common goods of the firm.

DEMOCRACY AND OTHER WORKPLACE REGIMES

For many normative thinkers, the solution to the challenge of the business firm is the same as the solution to other besetting problems: more democracy.[26] Isabelle Ferreras and Hélène Landemore have recently reiterated the most intuitive argument: firms are analogous to states, and so, "if democracy is the only legitimate form of government in the state, it should also be the only legitimate form of governance in the firm."[27] By my lights, the proponents of workplace democracy are pushing for an institutionally specific answer to the third essential question for any social order: *how to promote the common end in light of the just claims of its constitutive members.* This chapter's larger argument makes clear that firms are indeed like states in a crucial respect: both are kinds of common action under authority, normatively oriented to the common goods of their members. Regarding the governance of the firm, though, less follows from this similarity than democratic theorists would like.

The hard edge of my normative commitment to workers' common action is a negative one: it rules out financialized, shareholder-oriented models of the firm as unjust. Workplace democrats would certainly agree with this critical judgment. The positive dimension of a common-action theory of the firm, however, is more open ended than they allow. Aristotle argued that a decent form of democracy is one way to govern a city in the common good, but not the only way. We should think of firms in the same way. As there are multiple decent political regimes, so there are multiple legitimate ways to govern the firm, which could each respect its multidimensional moral architecture and the constitutive interests of its primary members. If workplace democracy is decent rule by the many, there could also be decent rule by the one or the few. This normative latitude opens up a path toward common goods in those many firms in which worker control is not (yet) practicable.[28] On the other hand, decent rule by the one or the few is attractive mainly in small or medium-sized firms. The most feasible and fitting way to govern the large corporate firm justly and well, taking another leaf from Aristotle's book, might employ a "mixed regime" with egalitarian and hierarchical elements, which splits power among various constituencies.

Aristotle's seminal arguments in the *Politics*, which launched the whole tradition of thinking about The Common Good, were chiefly intended to distinguish "defective" or corrupt forms of government from "correct" or decent ones.[29] The problem with tyranny, oligarchy, or "bad democracy" is primarily that they fail to distribute benefits and burdens justly in light of the what the city "actually is," namely a partnership among free citizens of various classes. These defective regimes cater only to whoever happens to wield power—respectively the tyrant, the rich, and the poor—rather than accounting for the varied contributions of multiple member-groups to a functioning polis. The correct regimes of kingship, aristocracy, and polity, by contrast, do not treat any citizens as masters who could legitimately exploit others. A decent political regime embodies the truth that all the city's members make *some* contribution, and so in justice deserve *some* share in the city's advantages, but some citizens make a greater contribution, and so deserve more. In Aristotle's ideal regime, one or a few rulers of great wisdom and virtue would hold the levers of power, justly apportioning benefits and burdens to various citizens according to the nuances of each situation, without being tied down by legal accountability. Aristotle admits that this scheme is impractical and potentially dangerous, since one will seldom find persons who actually have, and are politically acknowledged to have, this degree of wisdom and virtue. As a more feasible option, he recommends a mixed regime under the rule of law, in which the rich and the free poor share power and acknowledge one another's just claims, and so serve The Common Good despite average levels of human goodness.

We can apply Aristotle's regime critique by analogy to today's corporate firm by asking again, *Who rules, and on what grounds?* David Ciepley notes that the current shareholder-primacy system can be thought of as an "imperial oligarchy."[30] A market orientation combines with the "one-dollar-one-vote" system of the stockholder franchise to enshrine money as the dominant principle, much as it was in the classical oligarchy. Strangely enough, thanks to the interposition of property rights, the persons whom this arrangement primarily benefits are not even members of the community, as Greek oligarchs would have been. Stockholders are more like a conquering power extracting tribute through compliant local lords (corporate officers), whence the epithet "imperial." In a final bit of irony, most of the stockholders who buy their way in through the stock market do not actually contribute capital to the undertaking.[31] Their primacy thus epitomizes the symbolic—as opposed to grubbily practical—importance of money as the alleged point of the whole enterprise. The problem is that these narrow pecuniary terms do not do justice to what the firm is and could be as a shared moral project. Insofar as the shareholder-value firm is governed on the pretense that it is a pile of money, it is a "defective" kind of corporate governance.

Where worker self-rule could be made to work, it would be an apt way to replace the corrupting focus on shareholders with a "decent" business regime serving the common goods of the firm. As Aristotle observes, the distribution of power and offices is one of the primary ways that the moral telos of a social order, its vision of its own excellence, is visibly embodied.[32] Workplace democracy would be a very effective icon of the firm's fundamental social reality as an order of common action. Scarcely anyone could mistake the worker-controlled firm for a market structure or a heap of property. The workers as a class, as members of the firm, have an interest in the full scope of its just flourishing, and so in ruling they would have compelling normative reasons not to magnify one dimension (such as short-term profitability) at the expense of their other common goods. On the other hand, workers are a heterogenous group, and they face all the perplexities, collective action problems, and conflicting visions that confront any political association. Worker control is no silver bullet, then, but for many businesses it could mark a promising way to institutionalize the firm's commitment to its own common goods.

"Promising" is not the same as "mandatory." Theorists such as Landemore and Ferreras, Robert Dahl, and Michael Walzer overstate the case for worker control when they argue that it is the only live option, normatively speaking.[33] Workplace democracy is not a strict requirement of justice, for the simple reason that participating in the governance of the firm is not the same as participating in its common good. It is certainly conceivable that heroically ethical leaders might direct the firm to its true common ends even where workers have no direct hand in governing. (More than conceivable, this is certainly the case in many conventionally run firms!) This comes as good news for the many firms where workers have little real prospect of self-government and for those scholars who argue that worker co-ops in many industries cannot compete with traditionally run firms.[34] The common good of the firm offers such industries a more attainable normative goal, achievable without a democratic revolution in the economy. On the other hand, as James Madison points out, "enlightened statesmen will not always be at the helm."[35] It is not obviously easier to forge a virtuous class of executives than it is to transform the institutions of business, especially where the prevailing order is itself a morally corrupting force. Firms that do not directly embody the common ends of workers in the institutional distribution of power will place a heavy, and sometimes impossible, moral and intellectual burden on their leaders.

Drawing on Aristotle's regime analysis, we can classify business regimes according to the number of owners, since property rights are (usually taken to be) the backstop of power in the firm. A sole proprietorship has one ruler, a partnership has few, and a worker-owned firm has many. Aristotle notes that a political monarch will either rule for self-interest, and so be a tyrant, or rule for The Common Good as a wise king or queen. As the "owner" of a firm (in the qualified sense discussed in the chapter 1), a sole proprietor faces an analogous choice. She can foster the common ends of the firm, and so enjoy legitimate authority within it, or else wield the power of ownership in her own interest as a small-scale despot. Even for the sincere proprietor, it is a hard thing to discern and then do what the common project requires, when one has the power to do otherwise with impunity. Aristotle thought almost no one had the wisdom and virtue that a truly good monarch needs. The bar for running a small firm well is not as high, which is why good business owners are not as hard to find as philosopher-kings. Still, steering a firm toward common goods is not a task to be done from the armchair or the spreadsheet, especially in the absence of a simple metric of success. Doing it well will require the owners to engage in some kind of democratic consultation, both to learn from those workers in close contact with various dimensions of the firm's common action and also to convince those workers of the justice of authoritative decisions. This is a demand both of practical efficacy and also of the firm's normative structure. Whether they acknowledge it or not, the owners of small hierarchical firms bear a heavy moral responsibility for the common goods of their workers, a burden they can put down only by abdicating the "throne" of ownership.

The situation in the large corporate firm is otherwise. Though the corporation is customarily treated as though it has many owners (its stockholders), as a matter of legal fact it has none. A corporate firm, therefore, is not a specific kind of business regime, because the corporate form as such does not assign power to anyone, and certainly not to today's "imperial oligarchs"—that is, the stockholders. Properly speaking, the corporate form is an invitation to distribute power to one, few, or many on a basis *other than* ownership. And a good thing too. The advantage of incorporation is the capacity to get big, but size entails both larger temptations to govern unjustly and a harder task of integrating disparate worker interests and the pressures of multiplying markets.

Acknowledging the difficulty of ruling well amid heavy crosswinds, Aristotle argued that the most practical political regime would share power among the various contending parties, thus moderating the human tendency to exaggerate one's own side. An example of such a mixed regime in business governance is the German system of codetermination for firms of more than five hundred (with a higher standard at two thousand) workers, in which one-third (one-half) of the board of directors is elected by workers, and the remainder by stockholders. The Aristotelian echoes are not accidental, since *Mitbestimmung* was instituted after World War II by Christian Democrats strongly influenced by Roman Catholic ideas.[36] By extending power to the main contending groups in the firm—labor and capital—this mode of mixed governance both reflects the social reality of the firm as a mode of economic common action and also makes it more likely that the internal politics of the firm will eventuate in decisions that track its manifold common goods.

The best arguments for worker control are thus practical considerations rather than moral requirements, which makes a weaker kind of defense than the most ardent proponents of workplace democracy would like. In considering different types of worker self-governance, prudential concerns about attracting investment or about decision-making costs can be legitimately weighed against greater agency or self-development for workers. On the other hand, in some circumstances it may be impossible to steer a large corporate firm toward common ends without adopting some form of worker control, such as Germany's codetermination. In such cases, justice would indeed require an institutional shift, since the firm's primary normative end is its common good, which is shared primarily by its workers. But we should also acknowledge, following the arguments of Abraham Singer, that the competitive survival of the firm sets an upper limit on how far or how fast such changes should go.[37] As Aristotle comments, "Justice is not destructive of the city."[38] Nonetheless, the demands of the firm's common good are not a normative luxury that can be put off indefinitely. A firm that is viable only at the price of serious injustice may be better off closing up shop, since it is cut off from the good that makes its common life worth living.[39]

BEYOND THE FIRM

I have argued that we should see the business firm as a form of solidarity that is primarily oriented to the complex good shared by its workers as participants in its common action. Taken to extremes, this inward-looking approach would end in a reformulated version of Friedman's solipsism: "The social responsibility of business is to increase its own common good." If the internal flourishing of the firm looms too large, it will obscure the relation of business to the broad questions of The Common Good in matters such as justice, culture, and climate. On the other hand, if we magnify the claims of nonmembers until they come to define business success, as stakeholder theory does, we will render ourselves totally inarticulate about the firm's raison d'être as a distinct social form. A firm that was only a "nexus of stakes" would have no moral density, no normative inside and outside, and thus no principled defense against market or state. Neither extreme yields an adequate response to the fourth essential question, which asks how the firm fits into larger common projects. The upcoming chapter on the "Uber problem" will explore the firm's location within market-based constellations; in this section I ask how business relates to wider projects of a more political character.

Aristotelian pluralism balances a foundational focus on worker solidarity against the just claims of nonmembers, in two ways. First, every firm has contractual relations at private law, but these will fall under my later analysis of the market in part 2, so I will not dwell on them here. More pertinently, like any other civil association, the firm itself should be seen as a member of geographic and political communities, with the benefits and burdens that come from this membership. But these latter duties will remain frequently inoperative in a world without a vibrant institutional ecology of common action beyond the firm.

This invocation of The Common Good in the grand political sense invites us to reflect briefly on the proper role of public ends in any private association. It would be a mistake to think of citizens' shared goals as dominating every detail of private life. For the Aristotelian pluralist, The Common Good of the political community makes more modest, though still real, claims on its members. As Yves Simon argues, citizens who are not acting in a public capacity should look first to their own particular (private or common) goods. A society where they did not would be "like a dead world."[40] Yet this does not render The Common Good entirely irrelevant to private actors. Politics and law do set a framework for private action and association, and the virtuous citizen steadily intends (only) the *form* of The Common Good in all she does. That is, she wishes for the success of the community, whatever it may consist in, and she is ready to respond if called upon. But as a private actor she has no way of knowing in concrete terms what overall political success looks like or what it demands of her, so she attends firstly and rightly to her own pursuits. Ascertaining the *matter* of The Common Good in its concrete specificity is a task for persons clothed with political authority, who (ideally) have the knowledge and the power needed to establish that just public order in which communal flourishing consists.[41]

What does this imply for the business firm? First, that authoritative political action may legitimately limit or shape the social form of firms—for example, by prohibiting racial discrimination or making certain financial investments tax-free. But, second, the firm should normally assume that the just achievement of its own common ends as an intrinsically valuable form of solidarity is its main contribution to The Common Good in the broad political sense. The "adverbial" influence of public authority does not nullify the common ends of the firm or subsume them into a larger political project, any more than private-law contract rules deny the dignity of the merchant. On an Aristotelian pluralist account, formally intending The Common Good does not mean redefining the firm's flourishing around overt political obligations (much less the claims of other stakeholders), but it does entail standing ready to limit or alter the course of private action in light of the legitimate claims of politics. As explored in chapter 1, the corporate firm relies on an unusual blend of private action and delegated public authority, so it ought to face a heightened responsibility to public goals. But the absence of effective accountability in today's corporate charters suggests that incorporated firms are no better positioned than others to discern and carry out their outward-facing responsibilities.

Discharging duties toward any broader Common Good presupposes wider forms of common action. Without broader social forms, there could not *be* any broader common ends in the first place. Furthermore, as Simon suggests, wider institutions are essential for determining what a business's wider duties are, in concrete terms. The business executive as a private actor is not in a position reliably to ascertain this. Her position may give her knowledge and authority within her own firm, but it does not entail comparable insight into the situation and needs of larger communities, of which her organization is only a part. Asking her, as a private person, to ascertain and promote the ends of a flourishing political community, which she has neither the knowledge nor the coordinating authority to do, is like asking her to spin gold from straw. This helps to account for the unreal quality of many corporate claims to act in the public interest. Even a well-intentioned business could not unilaterally assess its own claims to corporate social responsibility, which can be properly adjudicated only from the perspective of the larger community.

The problem is that contemporary economies on the Anglo-American model typically lack institutions through which firms could discern and discharge broader responsibilities. The space between the firm and the regulatory state is dominated by the price-centered market, and markets are not such an institution. Price-centered exchange is not reliably sensitive to cases when aggregated private goods do not track common ends, which are just those cases when the appeal to common goods could make a real difference. Nor are general legal regulations a suitable vehicle, insofar as they change the rules for each individual actor, rather than coordinating any common action among firms. The most promising example in which broader common goods are effectively brought home to firms is found in coordinated market economies such as Germany or Scandinavia. In such systems, important decisions are taken via common action a level above the firm but below the state—for example, on the plane of a whole industry or region.[42] Where firms act in concert or with various communities, they are in a better position to take effective account of wider common goods. Comparative political economists delineate a menu of competing real-world options, which demand careful judgment.[43] But it is a worthy goal of any political economy to enact *some* such form of common action above the firm, so that businesses can grasp and live up to the just claims of external stakeholders, larger communities, and ultimately The Common Good.

GROWING TOGETHER

All these groups and unions have their effect, and limit and develop your life, make you do, or refrain from doing, what otherwise you would not, and in so far prevent you being a free and untrammeled citizen of the state. More than that, they penetrate your imagination and your thought, and alter not only what you do but what you want to do.

—John Neville Figgis

To work in a business is to participate in a moral project animated by an embodied conception of justice and shared excellence. The transformative reality of common action can be a selling point for fresh recruits to the business firm. "Think how much you'll grow in your first year here" ran one poster soliciting college graduates to a global consulting firm. As this recruiting pitch implies, a great deal more than money is in play, so the normative stakes are higher, and other, than a market imaginary will allow. This fact is as obvious to most management scholars as it is to plain persons in their workplace. On the other hand, if the predominant profit-centered mode of carrying on business is as problematic as I and other critics suggest, the higher normative stakes of a business should be as much a warning as an attraction for potential workers. "Think how much you'll be deformed here" is the unstated dark side of the same reality. Either way, the actual moral architecture of firms as common projects is an invitation to understand business organizations and the market economies they dominate in the richer terms of common goods. No one can remain a "free and untrammeled" merchant in a market system that is driven primarily by business firms, or rightfully ignore the questions of just and unjust solidarity that each of them raises. In this sense, a "pluralist" political economy is not something over the horizon; it is right in front of us. The first challenge of achieving our common goods is whether we can own the common ends that we are already pursuing and come to pursue them with fuller justice.

As a form of solidarity in its own right, the business firm is defined by the questions of *who* is party to its common action and *what* their just ends are. Since the firm is an order of shared work, the answer to the first seems to me clear-cut: the primary members are workers. The question of how workers can flourish together in justice is much more complex. It involves first specifying the shared ends that define the internal flourishing of the firm, which certainly include its material goals as well as intrinsically social goods. But a business firm is also oriented beyond itself, to the sale of goods on the market and to the goals its shares as a member of broader communities. The categories of "corporate social responsibility" have long been pilloried as squishy and vague. If the grammar of common action on its own cannot rescue these categories (no one else can either), it can at least diagnose the problem. A firm's wider duties, whatever they may be, are determined by the character of broader common action, and so they are a matter for political theory and political institutions, not business ethics alone.

Increasingly, however, the broader responsibilities of the firm cannot extend only to, or be specified by, political communities. In this chapter, I have applied the logic of common action to the hierarchical model of business that has been dominant over the last century or more. Integrated firms such as GM, ExxonMobil, or Microsoft have a moral density because they are built around a complex social form of production. In these firms we find collaboration and command, honor and status, shared culture and habits, loyalty and legends, rootedness and history and all the other features of a durable human community. These features cannot be reduced to prices or merely private action, and neither can the proper goals of such companies. But the firm in its present form is passing away, or at least losing its dominance. Nike, for example, is a footwear and apparel company that makes no shoes or clothes, having long ago outsourced production and distribution to other firms in the global supply chain. Likewise, the staff of a typical Hilton or McDonald's no longer works directly for those brands, but for hired contractors or subcontractors sometimes many layers deep. The digital revolution and the gig economy have only accelerated the decades-long shift between two rival ways to work together: away from cooperation under authority, toward price-centered market relations.

Ethical categories tailored to the monolithic, managerial firm cannot come to grips with the market contracts that increasingly appear at the heart of cooperative work. Workers and citizens must now tackle what I call "the Uber problem," which arises when leading companies convert their core activity from in-house production to market-based coordination. In such cases, should we return to the Chicago school with its theory of the firm as a nexus of contracts? Perhaps so, but there is still something beyond price in the new moral architecture of work. The frontier between the firm and the market is increasingly blurry, so the grammar of common action is an essential normative tool for mapping the new economy, no less than the old.

CHAPTER FOUR

THE UBER PROBLEM

In September 2019, the California state assembly passed AB 5, a law requiring most workers to be treated as employees, unless proven otherwise by those who hire them. Unlike independent contractors, employees are entitled to various labor law protections such as minimum wages, sick leave, unemployment coverage, and health insurance. The law was widely seen as an attack on ride-hailing giant Uber, which treats its drivers as independent contractors. The company's response was not slow in coming. Even before the measure was formally enacted, Uber joined forces with two competitors, Lyft and DoorDash, to oppose the measure politically. They each pledged $30 million dollars to fund a public ballot initiative (a form of direct democracy in California) that would override AB 5 and reclassify "app-based drivers" as independent contractors, but with a somewhat elevated level of benefits and protections. Their ensuing campaign for Proposition 22 was the most lavishly funded constitutional initiative in California history, soaking up more than $200 million from these three firms and smaller allies, who jointly outspent their opponents ten to one. The proposal was handily enacted by California voters in November 2020.

The idea of drivers as independent contractors is essential to both the self-presentation and the business model of such gig-economy firms, which is why they were willing to pay so much to defend it politically. Uber portrays itself as a neutral platform for "turnkey entrepreneurship," a way for drivers to "be their own boss" and gain the advantages of a self-sufficient life. Uber's app promises to connect drivers with riders, for a modest fee, so they can better contract with one another as part of the "sharing economy." Because Uber does not directly employ its drivers or own their vehicles, it reduces its risk and overhead, maintaining more of the flexibility and global scalability that go with digital products, even as it facilitates a very physical service. For their part, drivers gain real flexibility from their fleeting commitments to Uber, along with a large measure of precarity. Yet it is essential to Uber's success to exercise a significant measure of supervision and control over drivers, so that customers enjoy a service of a uniform high quality, which they credit to Uber (not the individual driver). There is a level of coordination in play that clearly differs from hands-off market contracting, so many drivers feel that they are engaged in a shared project with one another and with Uber. This sense of collaboration underpins drivers' recurrent, often fruitless, attempts to increase their clout with Uber, either through unionization (as was done in Seattle) or by legal reclassification as full members of the firm (as in California's AB 5).

App-based drivers are less enmeshed than employees, but more entangled than outside contractors. Their hybrid status is the paradigm of a political and intellectual puzzle that I call the "Uber problem." Are such hybrid workers inside or outside the common action of the company? Uber spent nearly $60 million on Proposition 22 to legislate its preferred solution, "contractors-plus," in California, a bellwether jurisdiction for tech regulation. Courts elsewhere in the USA, in Europe, and elsewhere have gone the other way, ruling that drivers are employees and should be treated as such.[1] But it is unclear that political brute force on either side can stretch the available legal categories to fit the realities of app-based driving as we find it today. Uber's drivers are neither employees nor independent contractors, but some third category in between. Similarly, ethical theories keyed to the managerial firm will miss key aspects of drivers' experience, no less than will the ethics of the open market. We cannot get a handle on the unfamiliar moral architecture of their work without using the grammar of common action to ask more basic questions.

Thus far in the book, I have been describing firms and markets as rivals, insofar as they embody two opposing modes of interaction: common action versus private exchange. All common action should be evaluated in terms of the just achievement of its built-in common ends. The primary reason to evaluate businesses under the rubric of common goods is their dense sociality. Traditional firms rely on authority and status, and on cultures of "norm-based productivity" rather than prices, not to mention the constitutive dependence of the corporate form on state power. But a prototypical price-centered market contract is not a form of common action. It aims not for intrinsically common ends, but for a "sum of private goods that happen to be interdependent," as Yves Simon puts it. Generally, the legal/social boundary between price-centered market exchange and collaboration in a firm also marks the frontier between private and common goods. What, then, should we make of cooperative work that is coordinated in detail through market contracts? Is it an intricate kind of market exchange, or a form of cooperation for shared ends that extends outside the firm?

This chapter will focus on Uber as an illustrative case, but gig drivers are not the only workers who have one foot in the market and one in the common action of the firm. Put another way, other industries face Uber problems of their own. For decades, large organizations have been deploying a whole arsenal of techniques to contract out parts of their work that were previously done in-house: franchising, subcontracting, offshoring, and so on. All this partial outsourcing creates what David Weil has termed "fissured workplaces," in which persons with various membership statuses—vested employees, temps, contractors—labor side by side. At a larger scale, lead firms such as Apple and Nike stand atop global supply chains constituted by a bewildering array of relationships of contract and control. In at least some of these market-based constellations, I will argue, a form of real common action lies athwart social or legal boundaries, uniting firms with outsiders in a single common project, albeit one that may lack a name or an institutional form. My brief excursus will not pretend to formulate the specific problems adequately, much less to solve them. Still, the basic logic that is needed to address Uber's problem could be extended to illuminate the normative puzzles raised by these complex social forms, in which some contractual relations outside the firm constitute forms of common action, while others do not.

UBER AND ITS EMPIRE

Uber provides the smartphone-era, gig-economy version of a taxi service. In order to get a ride in the "10,000+ cities worldwide" where Uber operates, all you need to do is download its smartphone app, enter some payment information, and tap in your destination. An offer is made to an available driver nearby; she accepts, arrives, and you are on your way. It's easy, quick, and cheap. Of course, the driver who picks you up will not be an employee of Uber, or at least that is the legal arrangement that Uber and its allies have secured in California. Uber does have over 22,000 conventional employees, who build and service its "technology booking platform." But on the company's official view, rather than working *for* Uber, your driver works *through* Uber's app but ultimately works for you, the passenger. Uber serves as a middleman, for a 20 to 30 percent cut, contracting temporarily with a driver only for the duration of the ride she provides. The number of drivers and riders on the road is controlled by market forces of supply and demand, with a little help from Uber's algorithms, which dangle incentives in front of passengers or drivers when one side is lacking.

In many ways, the scheme has worked enviably well as a business proposition. Though Uber did not turn its first profit until 2023, fourteen years into its life, its market valuation a year after its 2019 IPO was more than $50 billion. It has become the paradigm of digital disruption, inspiring a legion of gig-economy imitators that seek to become the "Uber for X" in their own industry.[2] For that matter, what *is* Uber's own industry? The company insists that it is only a technology firm, not a transportation business, in keeping with the notion that its 3.9 million "driver-partners" are contractors (or even clients—i.e., end users of its software). The image of a humble dispatching tool is essential to Uber's public narrative. Behind the scenes, matters look rather different, since Uber sets the terms of when, how, and for what pay drivers shall work. The massive asymmetries between driver and dispatcher create a potent form of power that is hardly consistent with free and equal bargaining on the market. The complexities of market-mediated power give rise to the distinctive moral and theoretical puzzle that I have dubbed the "Uber problem."

The realities of app-based driving suggest that drivers are not really within the structure of authority that is the firm as we usually understand it, but neither do they have full-fledged market relations to Uber. In the USA, Uber's drivers are generally solo operators who furnish their own vehicles, fuel, and maintenance.[3] They can log into the Uber app, provide as many rides as they like, and log out whenever they want. Flexibility and responsibility are the heart of Uber's recruiting pitch to potential drivers:

"Be your own boss." Yet the "turnkey entrepreneurship" offered by a ride-hailing app is not quite as independent as Uber's marketing arm makes it out to be. Fares are set unilaterally by Uber's ever-changing algorithms, and then offered to drivers on a take-it-or-leave-it basis. A driver has only fifteen seconds to decide, and neither the destination nor the total price is specified until after the driver accepts. Furthermore, drivers who accept less than a threshold level of the rides proposed to them, generally 85 or 90 percent, are liable to be suspended or barred from driving for Uber.[4] A GPS mapping program prescribes a route, and drivers can have their pay docked if a rider complains about any deviation onto a path deemed "inefficient."[5] And the app attempts to dissuade drivers from logging off, using perky encouragement ("Your next rider is going to be awesome") or monetary incentives ("Demand is very high in your area. Make more money, don't stop now!").[6] All of these features bespeak ongoing involvement rather than arm's-length contracts, which would leave drivers free to carry on business in their own way. By deploying a combination of autonomy and oversight, Uber keeps drivers close enough to control, but far enough to avoid responsibility.

As a creature of the smartphone era, Uber seems like something new under the sun, but its basic business model was established among conventional taxi companies decades before Uber was born. For much of the twentieth century, US taxi drivers were unionized and so enjoyed the labor protections of employees, such as wage floors, hour limits, and benefits. A major shift occurred in the 1970s, when taxi companies around the country first began to reclassify their drivers as "independent contractors" rather than employees. The taxi companies were trying to exploit a loophole established by the Taft-Hartley Act, an anti–New Deal measure of 1947, which exempted independent contractors from the right to bargain collectively. The core of the revised taxi arrangement was that the company, which owned permits issued by the local government, would lease medallion cabs to drivers at a flat rate for a fixed time period (ranging from several months to a single day). By reframing drivers as "entrepreneurs" in business for themselves, the cab companies could avoid many of the liabilities that employers usually bear, such as paying for idle workers or sick leave.[7] Uber relies on digital technology to push the same logic further, controlling an even larger workforce while owning even fewer assets. Dispersed local taxi dispatchers are replaced by a centralized app under a powerful global brand, while transportation "entrepreneurship" is made available to nearly anyone with a car, often in defiance of local laws,[8] thus removing the need for Uber to own and maintain a fleet of vehicles.

Uber and its forebears in the taxi world are pursuing a strategy of hyperspecialization that has become ubiquitous: do only that part of the work that you do best, and let others do the rest. This approach leads to strangely hollow brands: Apple is a computer company that makes no computers; Nike is a shoe company that makes no shoes. Both firms focus on design and marketing, leaving production and distribution—which are less profitable and easier to standardize—to others. Similarly, Uber and its yellow cab rivals are transport companies that do not transport anyone. What they do best is not rides but reputation; they offer the promise of a quick ride at a fair price, symbolized by a global tech brand or by local taxi medallions. Once the promise is made, the actual delivery of passengers is done by temporary contractors who are not integral members of the firm. Of course, in all these cases—from Apple to Nike to Uber—the lead firm exercises a degree of oversight to ensure the integrity of its all-important brand.

David Weil has given a name to this process of intense specialization: "fissuring." It is the opposite of the diversification pursued by conglomerates such as Warren Buffett's Berkshire Hathaway, which brings multiple unrelated operations under the same corporate roof. Fissuring involves first splitting apart unrelated businesses, and then trimming down the remaining operation until it is tightly focused on profitable core competencies. Extraneous processes that might otherwise be done in-house, by members of the firm, are farmed out on the market. In the 1980s, as Weil recounts, large firms began by contracting out administrative tasks such as HR, IT, and accounting, and then moved on to maintenance, cleaning, and security, all of which were once done by employees.[9] A more extreme degree of fissuring sets in when the core activity of the firm is itself split up, and portions are given over to franchisees, suppliers, or independent contractors.

Uber has taken this extreme division of labor very much to heart, relying on billions of short-term, tech-mediated contracts as a mode of coordinating transport. Yet as we have seen, Uber insists that it is not a transportation company, because it does no driving in-house. But many app-based drivers, who see the system from the inside, are not convinced by the putative distinction between Uber's main business and the market for rides. Their doubts are shared by the concerned citizens in California who backed AB 5 and by high courts in Germany, France, and elsewhere. All of them see drivers as essential players in Uber's core business. Still, given the realities of driving for Uber, it does not seem entirely right to lump its drivers, who pass so easily in and out of Uber's orbit, with employees of traditional hierarchical firms. The moral/legal binary of employee within the firm versus contractor out in the market are too crude to solve the puzzles raised by Uber, or by fissured work more generally.

THE UBER PROBLEM, TRANSLATED

We can draw on the grammar of common action to get a broader perspective on the Uber problem and suggest how it might be solved. In chapter 3, I outlined the four dimensions on which one can analyze the common action of a firm (or any other community): property, power, practice, and product. The members can achieve a true common good only when these four shared goals are rightly ordered to one another. I suggested that the normative core of well-structured common action is found in the goods of "practice," the intrinsically common goods of excellence that are especially distinctive of a given community: a university's pursuit of knowledge, a bakery's baking. The other three dimensions of common action should be ordered to, or flow from, this core shared activity. Interestingly, the priority of practice, which I presented as a moral demand, is echoed in the brass-tacks financial imperative of pursuing a core competency. The point of the extreme fissuring that we find in Uber is to strip the firm down to its core practice and let the market do the rest. At one level, then, fissuring seems praiseworthy, in that it organizationally prioritizes the dimension of common work that is normatively crucial, though for pecuniary rather than ethical reasons. On the other hand, the core practice (and its constituency) is not the only thing that matters when people together enact an answer to the question *Who are we to become?* The core practice depends on the other three dimensions of common action (and the persons connected to them), ignoring or maligning them only at the price of injustice. Whether these dimensions are pursued inside or outside the legal boundaries of a firm is quite irrelevant.

Yet the 4-P analysis of common ends does not straightforwardly apply to the Uber problem in the way that it applies to the hierarchical firm. Only when persons in various coordinated lines of work are engaged in a unified common project do they have some claim in distributive justice to share in the communal burdens and benefits. This is precisely what disaggregated firms are attempting to avoid, by separating the various dimensions of work through a market-based division of labor. To start by pressing the moral grammar of common goods would be to beg the crucial question: *Does Uber involve any common action at all?*

To be clear, the question is not whether the C-suite executives of Uber Technologies Inc. in San Francisco are working in common with its software developers and sales team. Obviously they are; the immediate common goal of their firm is to support and extend the use of the Uber app. The question at the heart of the Uber problem is whether the drivers who use the app are also members of that same community, or perhaps of some larger, more diffuse form of common action. Put another way, how many emergent social realities are in play when it comes to Uber and its drivers: one, two, or none at all? Once this fundamental question is settled affirmatively, we can move on to ask what the just goal of collaboration is, and who counts as a member. Yet in a doubtful case like Uber, it may be well to start by suspending judgment on this doubtful matter pending further evidence. One might first look to other, clearer social facts—such as the presence or absence of an intrinsically common goal or the use of mechanisms like authority, honor, or status—and then reason backward to answer the more fundamental questions about common action and its ends.

With Uber, there is indeed a single regulative goal in play—getting a ride; quick, safe, and reliable. As far as the passenger is concerned, the ride comes from Uber, which looks to her a good deal like a unified firm. Indeed it is crucial for Uber's global success that riders think "I got an Uber" rather than "I got a ride from Pradeep," in part because many drivers also drive for Lyft or other competing ride-hailing services. Behind the scenes, however, the picture is considerably more complicated, and this is where the rubber hits the road (pun intended). If we provisionally divide the single goal of getting a ride into the four key dimensions, who is performing each task, and how are they related? Uber Technologies Inc. stands firmly astride the two core aspects, the intrinsically common dimensions that I denoted as "practice" (attracting riders with a pleasant user experience and the promise of a reliable ride) and "power" (coordinating and overseeing drivers). But the other two dimensions of "property" and "product" remain largely outside the firm, since Uber Inc. neither owns the vehicles nor provides any actual transport. As I observed in the last chapter, these two dimensions are only extrinsically common, meaning that they are shared concerns only when they are made the focus of common action. They may easily appear instead as private goods to be bargained over, which is how Uber treats them. From the point of view of two key groups of workers—the software team and the drivers—the end product of providing a ride appears less the shared end of common action than the outcome of a nexus of contracts.

Normatively speaking, there may not be any problem with this. In chapter 1, I critiqued the Chicago theory of the firm as a nexus of contracts on the grounds that a nexus is not what a firm "actually is." The relations between boss and employee are not very like those between grocer and shopper, who have largely contractual relations. But the links between ride-hail driver and Uber's algorithmic dispatcher are a good step closer to the model that Chicago erroneously applied to the standard firm. A nexus of contracts model is normatively aboveboard, as far as the grammar of common ends is concerned, so long as it fits the social reality at hand. When the model fails to fit, two kinds of problem ensue, practical and moral. Practically, it is foolish to pursue through market contracts those goods that grow only from common action, because it just won't work. David Weil points out that some fissured firms compromise the quality and innovation of their own products by relying too much on temporary workers or outside suppliers.[10] More relevant to my concerns is the moral problem of misconstruing common action as if it were nothing but contractual exchange. A reductive normative vision cannot justly share out the common goods that it does not notice. For the case at hand, the key question remains: Are Uber and its drivers engaged in a form of common action?

Driving for Uber obviously lacks some key features of common action. Many of Uber's 3.9 million drivers have never met an employee of the company, so friendship and honor between drivers and employees are largely out of the question. Solidarity among drivers, on the other hand, is widespread. Alex Rosenblat reports that online driver forums, which jointly had around three hundred thousand members in 2017, are actively used for collective action as well as venting and advice.[11] Drivers in some localities have attempted, usually without success, to organize a union to bargain for better pay. More frequently, drivers team up informally to game Uber's system with a maneuver known as "surge pumping." If a sufficient number of drivers log off just as demand spikes (e.g., when a plane touches down at an airport), Uber's algorithm initiates rush hour–like "surge pricing," increasing each driver's take.[12] But even if drivers may engage in common action with each other, this does not yet imply that they share a common project with Uber itself.

Two key features of common action do characterize the relations between Uber and its drivers: oversight and control. Uber has faced numerous lawsuits alleging that it misclassifies drivers as contractors when they are in fact employees. In assessing these claims, courts have often found against Uber on the basis of doctrinal tests for employment, which focus on the hiring party's degree of control. The "common law of agency" test asks whether the principal "controls or has the right to control the manner and means of the agent's performance of work."[13] Uber tracks much more than drivers' ride acceptance rates and passenger feedback. It also subjects their cars to approval and monitors driving details such as hard braking and shaky phones (which indicates a phone on a driver's lap, hence likely inattention).[14] A second judicial tool, the "economic realities test," asks whether the agent's "opportunity for profit and loss" is determined by the hiring party. Uber's key argument is that it does not control when anyone drives or for how long, and in that sense it does not determine how much a driver can make.[15] This is true, but Uber does unilaterally set the fares, which vary by time and by driver. Uber dangles special promotions in front of new or prospective drivers, which expire once the drivers are firmly part of its network. Uber uses fleeting, machine-generated price "surges" to meet high demand, but sometimes drivers in the right place at the right time may not be offered the higher fares. Likewise, drivers who qualify for Uber's premium tier are sometimes given no choice but to accept fares at a lower level, despite their sometimes-large investments in premium vehicles. Contrast all these forms of control with a clear case of an online marketplace: Ebay, which does not control what is sold, how it is marketed, or the price.

If Uber and its drivers are not engaged in arm's-length market contracting, we must conclude that they are engaged in a form of common action. But what kind of common action is it? Courts in multiple jurisdictions have ruled that app-based drivers are employees, suggesting that Uber and its drivers form a single, diffuse association. In my judgment, this judicial conclusion speaks more to the paucity of available categories than to the social reality at hand. Uber wields authority over its corporate employees, and it also wields authority over its drivers. Authority bespeaks common ends. But how many common projects are there: one or two? There seems to be more than one social form at play, given the huge qualitative difference between the tasks of software-coding and driving, in terms of their goals, structure, and culture, a divide that is deepened by the algorithmic wall between them. We would be better advised, therefore, to see two social entities at play: Uber Inc. and a broader common project, which we might call Uber+. Uber Inc. would include the company's formal employees, while Uber+ extends to all its drivers as well. The two orders of common action are hierarchically linked but distinct. We might picture Uber Inc. and Uber+ as an inner citadel within a larger walled town or, in an image that highlights the power relations and normative problems of the current scheme, as an imperial power ruling over subjugated peoples. The larger, amorphous social entity of Uber+ lacks an organizational name or structure, but this is precisely why we need a capacious grammar of common action to serve where legal categories do not fit.

By infusing its driver contracts with features of common action, Uber Inc. takes on a heightened responsibility to the just flourishing of a larger common project that is generated, which I am calling Uber+. One way to recognize the moral reality would be to institutionalize Uber+ in some way, establishing relations of deliberation and accountability to answer the key questions of common action: *Who counts? How might they share their common ends in just fashion?* Seen very charitably, Uber's public campaign for Proposition 22 in California was an effort to answer just this need. As Uber CEO Dara Khosrowshahi opined, "What Prop. 22 is about is about starting to move into the best of two worlds: you've got flexibility, you're your own boss, you're your own CEO, but you do have protections."[16] It is conceivable, though unlikely, that the members of Uber+ might share justly in their common project without modifying the stark power differential between Uber Inc. and its drivers. Unionization would be a means to the same end and would give drivers considerably more clout with Uber than they generally enjoy.

Public scrutiny of the Uber problem has rightly focused on the hardship and injustice faced by drivers under the current scheme, but it is also worth asking what Uber Inc. loses by failing to recognize the common project of Uber+. The main loss is the injustice itself; when Uber Inc. needs data or concessions from its drivers, it simply takes them. Rather than asking drivers about their needs or experience, Uber's app simply extracts (often unethically, sometimes illegally) troves of data from their phones.[17] Price cuts are imposed from the top, occasionally accompanied by the specious justification that lower fares lead to larger driver income.[18] For drivers who demur, the exit door is always open. A firm that relies on lying and stealing is not flourishing, and Uber's reputation has suffered as a result. But Uber Inc. has also deprived itself of an important source of insight and innovation: its drivers. When it comes to understanding how Uber's app actually plays out on the ground, big data and AI are no substitute for the savvy and local knowledge of drivers. By treating them as consumers of software rather than collaborators in the provision of software-enabled transport, Uber Inc. contents itself with a worse product that it would otherwise have. The analogous exemplar would be Toyota, which famously values the skill and craftsmanship of its hands-on worker teams and has drawn many innovations from suggestions from the shop floor.[19] When workers move past prescribed tasks to engage actively in improving processes and products, both their individual work and the common project stand to benefit.

BROADER HORIZONS

Uber problems are by no means unique to Uber, since such puzzles are liable to crop up wherever common action and market exchange are combined. The key to solving these quandaries, in my view, is to think about common ends: what goals are shared, and by whom? Legal categories and the frontiers between firm and market are only a starting point, since the essence of an Uber problem is that common action can transgress such boundaries to link a firm with (ostensible) outsiders. There are numerous advantages to be gained by common action relative to exchange: greater coordination and control, deeper mutual learning, and potential for innovation. Yet the benefits of market exchange are perhaps even more palpable, especially in a world where the bottom line is so often taken as the last word: freedom of movement, fewer responsibilities, lower prices due to competition. At bottom, what underlies any Uber problem is that powerful lead firms want to have it both ways: both lower costs and greater control. The puzzle is not *that* this temptation is unjust, or *why*. As I argued in chapter 1, the benefits of common action can be justly enjoyed only through fidelity to common ends. The Uber problem is a problem of locating such common ends amid vast and shifting networks that rely heavily on market contracts.

Uber's own version of the problem turns on the algorithmic authority it exercises through its smartphone app. Though drivers may have little contact with Uber and its management, they are subject to invasive oversight and manipulation. Drivers have to submit their daily work, and in so doing conform their character, to shifting demands that they have little power to contest or modify. This degree of direction could only be legitimate if it conformed to the just flourishing of the common project. Uber's algorithmic management does not even attempt to meet this standard. Some drivers continue to regard their own contributions with dignity, but virtually all feel wounded by Uber's unjust combination of contempt and control.

Not all Uber problems resemble the plight of the app-based driver, so it is worth glancing briefly at the broader landscape that might be explored with a grammar of common action. Where else might we expect to see common action confusingly blended with market relations? Gereffi, Humphrey, and Sturgeon have developed a useful classification of five broad kinds of "global value chains," based on the complexity of tasks and the relative capacity of parties, ranked by increasing levels of explicit coordination and asymmetrical power:[20]

1. *Markets*: simple, standardized exchanges governed by price
2. *Modular chains*: highly capable suppliers perform complex but codifiable tasks
3. *Relational chains*: complex tasks that cannot be codified bring high-capacity firms into long-term contact

4. *Captive chains*: low-capacity suppliers are beholden to lead firms in carrying out complex tasks
5. *Hierarchy*: complex coordination under authority

At the extremes of this typology are the two institutions I focus on in this book, the market and the hierarchical firm, in which a specific form of common action is most clearly absent or present. Between them are three hybrid cases, which are all liable to Uber problems because they make extensive use of market contracts while relying on modes of power and coordination that are absent in the open market. Uber itself looks like a variant of the "captive" chain, since the drivers of Uber+ have little access to riders except through Uber Inc.'s technology. This classification of Uber suggests that the present chapter's analysis of app-based drivers might be extended by analogy to the common ends at stake in other paradigmatic captive chains, such as Nike and its global network of captive apparel makers. Conversely, the rich literature on sweatshops and offshoring might shed useful light on the normative situation of Uber drivers, as well as other gig-workers and franchisees. The obvious authority at the heart of captive chains, which Gereffi et al. rank just below the firm proper, marks off such relations as forms of common action uniting lead firms with their suppliers in the market.

The other two classes of hybrid governance point to rather different variants of the Uber problem from what we find in the gig economy. "Modular" and "relational" chains involve relative equality between cooperating firms, so they lack the note of "working under" a lead firm that we see in the captive drivers of Uber+. But if coercive authority is absent in these two types of global value chain, other modes of common action are actively present.

Relational manufacturing chains, which involve mutual formation and learning, are oriented to a product that no single firm can achieve on its own. As an example, in 1941 North American Aviation could not produce a sufficiently powerful fighter plane with locally available air-cooled motors, so it turned to the English firm Rolls-Royce, maker of the water-cooled Merlin engine. The resulting P-51 Mustang, uniting an American fuselage with a British motor, could only be described as an emergent common achievement—not "mine" or "yours" but "ours." The life of each firm was bound up with the cooperative project in a way that went beyond the balance sheet. If relational chains involve intricate collaboration around essentially common ends, it seems clear that they should be seen as forms of common action beyond the firm. I will return to such chains at the end of chapter 7, when discussing the notion of market exchange as common action.

A modular supply chain, by contrast, does not involve the active collaboration that distinguishes a relational chain, nor the authority central to captive chains. Hence the modular chain is not obviously a form of common action or a ground of solidarity in itself. Therefore, some modular chains likely fall into the same normative basket as typical price-centered market exchange. A bicycle maker, for instance, might order a truckload of custom-threaded bolts from a tool-and-die shop, without needing to refer to any goods or goals they share in common. Modular cooperation would be normatively distinct from the market mainly where "turn-key suppliers" and lead firms are both engaged in some larger form of common action. One way to understand this larger social form relies on Alasdair MacIntyre's idea of the goods of a practice. MacIntyre has argued that the goods of a complex, coherent human pursuit, such as bicycle racing, are necessarily common goods, though not goods specific to an organization. If this is so, then buyers and sellers engaged in the same practice are not total strangers to one another in the way that other merchants characteristically are. The Taiwanese firm Giant, the world's largest maker of quality bicycle frames, supplies top-tier bicycle brands such as Bianchi and Trek. But Giant's relations to these other brands are modular. Part of what allows their cooperation to be modular, as opposed to highly involved, is their shared commitment to the goods of the practice of cycling. Trek knows of Giant's commitment to international size and quality standards, while Giant knows of Trek's mission to embody and advance excellence in the sport. Their dealings are one moment in the larger common action of the "cycling community," allegiance to which affects how they should rightly approach their bargaining with one another.[21]

This brief sketch suggests that there are at least three distinct types of the Uber problem, which cannot all be modeled in the same way, because the social reality of each case differs significantly from the other two. Nor is there a one-size-fits-all solution for captive, relational, or modular market networks, least of all the simplistic strategy of more broadly applying the category of "employee." Even if it is the least-distorting available category for Uber drivers, it is not a silver bullet either as a means or as an end. In terms of practical efficacy, Veena Dubal has documented that the work lives of contract drivers who win employee rights via lawsuit does not necessarily improve.[22] Their labor situation may even get worse, as lead firms either evade or blatantly ignore legal stipulations intended to protect drivers. Here as elsewhere, political intervention that does not lead to a deeper moral imagination and better business culture can make little headway toward genuine common goods.

Furthermore, it is not unambiguously "better" to be an employee, and not all drivers want to be one. Which is to be preferred depends on the particular situation, as we can see illustrated in the parallel case of FedEx and its delivery drivers.[23] Much like Uber, FedEx classifies its drivers as independent contractors. They are required to lease branded trucks and given specific routes to drive, and their personal conduct is regulated down to the color of their socks. Many FedEx drivers have grown discontented with the arrangement, filing numerous lawsuits alleging misclassification. Unlike Uber drivers, however, FedEx drivers have not generally sought to be reclassified as employees. Instead, they have sought to be in fact what they already are in name—*independent* contractors who face less control from FedEx and are given greater latitude in the "manner and means" of their work. What is intolerable, for both FedEx and Uber drivers, is the unjust lack of fit between the social reality and the normative standards being applied.

The ambivalence of contract drivers illustrates a broader point about Uber problems, and about common goods more generally. The solution is not necessarily to increase the intensity of common action, and so to push all the different kinds of interfirm cooperation in the direction of the hierarchical firm. Firms are not "better" than markets, nor are common goods generally "better" than private goods, in some free-floating absolute sense. Common action does have a practical and moral depth that is lacking in impersonal market exchange. Market relations are characteristically more flexible and more competitive. Both are worthy and just when they match the goods being sought and the social reality of the cooperation at hand. Both are essential to human flourishing in a world like ours built around an extensive division of labor.

Uber problems arise because the limits of common action do not always track the legal/social frontiers between employees and independent contractors, or those between culturally scripted cooperation and ostensibly impersonal market exchange. The boundaries of a social entity have always been slightly fuzzy and could not be otherwise, since they depend on matters of judgment and moral evaluation. Who should count as a citizen, for instance, has been a contested political issue from the time of Aristotle to our own day. Who counts as a member of a firm may be equally contested. As technology enables ever more discrete and fine-grained contracts (just this task, just for today), the distinctions between cooperation under authority and market exchange grow fuzzier still. It may require considerable discernment to parse complex cases of potential common action to answer the question *Who justly counts?*, and it may require a notable degree of virtue not to take advantage of legal gray areas or loopholes.

On the other hand, at a sufficient distance from the firm's sphere of control and its core practice, the haze gives way to clarity and common action is definitely supplanted by arm's-length market contracting. To return to my imaginary bakery, it might be hard to say if the miller and the florist who often work with Pie in the Sky are engaged in a single order of common action with the bakery. But the vendor that annually supplies the bakery's chairs or napkins is plainly not.

The recipe for an Uber problem is active collaboration mediated by prices. Notice that the problem requires two social domains, operating on two different logics, to be present and in tension: common action in the firm and an open market oriented to individual gain. An important first step to improving the lot of app-based drivers, and others who suffer from fissured work, is to replace a private-good model of firms and production networks with a better imaginary that recognizes the common ends that are already present in businesses. This is what I have tried to do in part 1 of this book. But the problem cannot be fully addressed without considering the other half of the equation. Where overt cooperation fades, the concern for common goods in economic institutions shifts away from the firm and its analogues to a distinct mode of economic order: the price-centered market.

PART 2

ON THE MARKET

September 19, 1977, is still remembered as Black Monday. It was not only the day that Youngstown Sheet & Tube announced that it would close its largest foundry and lay off five thousand workers. In a larger sense, it was the day that the steel industry declared its divorce from Ohio's Mahoning Valley. Youngstown was once an icon of steel, but by the mid-1980s the market forces of recession, changing technology, and globalization had ground away fifty thousand steel jobs from the area. As of 2007 Youngstown was the poorest American city of over sixty-five thousand residents, by a wide margin. It was not for nothing that Bruce Springsteen titled his elegy for the Rust Belt "Youngstown." And just in case Black Monday didn't make the point clearly enough, the people of the Mahoning Valley have been treated to periodic reminders of the colossal indifference of global markets to their community. The latest object lesson came on November 26, 2018, when General Motors announced that its plant in nearby Lordstown, in operation for over half a century and still employing some eight thousand workers, would be "unallocated" along with four other US plants, in favor of cheaper labor in Mexico. Wages in Youngstown were already down 6 percent since the 2008 financial crisis. GM's stock rose 5 percent that day.

The numbers can also tell a different story about the market, a much larger story that, some think, puts the recent trials of cities like Youngstown in the shade. Since 1800, the average amount of goods and services produced and consumed per capita, worldwide, has increased by a factor of about eight and a half. The local increases are various, ranging from somewhat more than triple in parts of Africa to a factor of nineteen in places such as France, Hong Kong, and the USA. Lives are longer and healthier, with a larger portion of cultural goods available to more people than ever before. This great leap can be credited, in good part, to the spread of the market.[1] If Youngstown has declined, in this larger statistical narrative, it is only a partial descent from a summit that the market helped it to reach, and it is more than balanced by prosperity elsewhere.

It is no coincidence that the mythology of the market points in two familiar but opposing directions, epitomized in these two stories. The human experience of the market has been deeply ambivalent: riches and liberty for some, misery and effective enslavement for others, for many prosperity and alienation at the same time. Every durable modern democracy has made extensive use of markets, but so have many tyrannies. My goal in part 2 of this book is to rearticulate the moral architecture of markets in terms of common goods, but not to explain away either story as wrongheaded or unintelligible. I take the ambivalence of markets as a basic fact to be explained, and perhaps guided, the better to serve human flourishing. It is all too easy to polemically emphasize the good or bad dimensions of markets, as do the authors on whom I focus in the next three chapters. My method in part 2 will be more exegetical than my treatment of the firm, as I deploy the grammar of common goods to extract the key insights from several mutually opposed polemics as a way of getting at the complex market reality they are striving to understand.

This consideration of the market is a necessary sequel to my rearticulation of the business corporation in common-action terms. For good and ill, market prices sway much about the common action of firms—what ends they pursue, whom they engage as workers or customers, and how they fare. How we think about common goods in the market is certain to shift our sense of the business firm, and vice versa. Chicago's shareholder-value theory of the firm is compelling in large part because we usually see markets as spaces of private goods alone. Contrariwise, the real-world example of leading firms oriented to their own shared flourishing might highlight the common ends that are never entirely absent from markets. Ultimately, we need a grammar of common action if we want to understand the social reality of the market and its ambivalent relation to human concerns.

The received explanation is that markets promote prosperity and private gain (in the sense of the second story above) precisely because they are indifferent to any common ends (as shown by the first). If so, it stands to reason that they haphazardly help some communities and hinder others. In common-action terms, this received view boils down to three key claims: (A) politics is a form of communal action, but (B) markets are not, and therefore (C) the two domains can have no regular or necessary relation to one another. Put so bluntly, it should be obvious that this view is too simple, but what is wrong with it? The chapters of this section proceed dialectically through three sophisticated responses to this pervasive but inadequate account, moving from Friedrich Hayek's "spontaneous" solution through Karl Polanyi's "instituted" account of markets, and finally to the Italian "civil economy" school. At bottom, any three redactions of the market must answer two same fundamental questions:

(1) Are there communal actions and goals in market exchange?
(2) Is the politics that undergirds markets itself a form of common action?

I have chosen these three rival accounts because they crystallize the analytic options with special clarity, but they also represent important intellectual and political currents in the struggle to come to grips with the market economy (roughly: the libertarian, the social democratic, and the humanistic). All three views agree that politics and markets have a tighter relation than the received explanation lets on, and each view overturns one of claim A, B, or C as a way to critique or defend the market system (and, by implication, the other two views). Their positions are compactly summarized in table 5.1.

Chapter 5 begins with the best-known and most rigorous theory of markets: that of neoclassical economists who emphasize the benefits of impersonal price-based coordination. According to the economist's stylized individualism, there is no common action in markets, and therefore there are no common goods either, even if the "invisible hand" benefits many or all merchants in terms of private gain. In a sense, then, we value market coordination precisely because it does *not* promote common goods in the

Table 5.1. Three Rival Versions of Markets

—	Spontaneous	Instituted	Civil
Common Action in Markets?	No	No	Yes
Common Action in Politics?	No	Yes	Yes
Markets' Main Contribution	Private goods	Common and private goods	Common goods

strict sense. Friedrich Hayek aggressively extends the same logic to the legal and political framework of markets as well. His "spontaneous" theory holds that common action is as irrelevant to politics as it is to price-centered exchange, since both pursue private goods alone, and so he concludes that common goods are never relevant to the market as a public institution. Despite his real insights, I shall argue that his bid to establish continuity between liberal politics and impersonal markets fails, much as did the Chicago attempt to assimilate the firm to the market, and for much the same reason: common action (here, that of citizens) cannot be described and evaluated in terms of private, divisible ends. Yet some global markets do largely fit Hayek's spontaneous model, even if it fails to explain the many markets ensconced in domestic politics.

A less reductive view of politics features in the "instituted" model of Karl Polanyi, whose theory of market society as a moral economy is the subject of chapter 6. The analytic core of his position is that politics is a mode of common action, but price-centered exchange is not. Moral economists concur with the commonsense contrast between communalist politics and individualist markets, but Polanyi relies on economic history to show that they are systemically linked. The market has always been a publicly constructed space of private action, instituted in the service of some common project. Thus there is always a sense in which the common ends of some sponsoring community should take precedence over merchants' private goals. But the normative primacy of common ends is subverted where every economic factor is put up for sale, as in the ideal of the self-regulating market, which still influences public discourse today. I use the grammar of common action to clarify Polanyi's crucial but rough insight that certain supposed commodities central to a market system are actually (much like the flourishing of the business firm) intrinsically common concerns. If this is so, price-centered markets are politically ambivalent in large part because some forms of exchange should not, indeed cannot, be detached from the common ends of citizens, while other markets can. The instituted-market model helps us to grapple with all those politically managed markets where shared ends are never entirely out of sight, even if merchants do not have them in mind.

The primacy of common ends over impersonal markets, always indirect and sometimes direct, should raise some doubt that ordinary market exchange is as individualistic as the mainstream economist supposes. To explore this unfamiliar possibility, chapter 7 turns to the Italian tradition of civil economy that looks back not to Adam Smith, but to a luminary of the Neapolitan Enlightenment, Antonio Genovesi. This calling card of civil economy is the claim that that market exchange can be, should be, and often already is a form of common action. The civil economists thus posit a continuity in common goods that is the inverse of Hayek's individualism: markets and politics as nested domains of solidarity. In order to distinguish civil economy from both feudalism and authoritarianism, I propose the concept of "reciprocity pricing" as a possible way for merchants to honor the common goods that they share without losing the dynamism of decentralization. Despite their sensitivity to common goods, civil markets are no silver bullet, inasmuch as they inherit the drawbacks as well as the upside of common action. They are susceptible to the pathologies of human cooperation, and their extent is limited to the range of effective solidarity.

Ultimately, the goods of common action do not bear on all markets in the same way, so I propose making room for all three of these rival versions. Price-centered markets have virtues as well as vices, and it would be neither feasible nor desirable to replace all impersonal exchange with a common-action mechanism. Private goods are genuine goods, and sometimes merchants best serve The Common Good by declining to seek common ends, as the spontaneous model recommends, especially in markets at global scale. But politically framed markets depend far more tightly on successful common action, as the instituted model highlights, and neither merchants nor citizens can afford to ignore the shared projects underpinning exchange. Finally, the civil market captures the relational exchanges within industries and regions that are often essential to innovation and stability, where common action empowers merchants to do together what impersonal exchange alone could never do. Markets are pluralistic, so what we need is not a grand unified theory but an enhanced capacity to grasp and judge the various human relations and goals at stake in particular markets.

CHAPTER FIVE

THE END OF THE INVISIBLE HAND

Any inquiry into markets and common goods is well advised to begin among the economists. We all have some intuitive grasp of what markets are like, but the insights of economists are indispensable in order to think clearly about markets in their broader, politically salient aspect. My aim in this chapter is to explore the relevance of common goods for the canonical model of markets that (neo-)classical economists have relied on since Adam Smith. In brief, the model of "Strangers Selling Stuff" (SSS) construes markets as a site of free exchange of goods, coordinated by prices, among mutually disinterested merchants, set against a minimal legal background. The SSS conception, taught to countless millions of undergraduates, lucidly explains how price-centered markets reliably promote wealth and private gain. What is less clear in the textbook version of SSS markets is the role, or perhaps nonrole, for common action and its goods.

This chapter will focus on the work of Friedrich Hayek as an outstanding exponent and defender of the economists' canonical model. The large conclusion of his "spontaneous" approach, baldly put, is that common goods are relevant neither to market exchange nor to the law and politics that underwrite commerce. Some may therefore think that Hayek, godfather of libertarianism, is simply too far from political concerns about The Common Good to be a fruitful interlocutor. I disagree. Quite to the contrary, Hayek is obsessed with the problem of private versus common goods, a distinction that is absolutely central to his thought. His polemics about the dangers of pursuing shared ends do not diminish the power and elegance of his model of the market, which is well worth engaging. One of Hayek's great virtues as a theorist is that he patiently asks questions of social ontology—that is, he asks what a market *is*. He answers that a market is a form of rule-based social order that has no ends of its own, and so no place for social (in)justice nor for common goods. This is not per se a criticism of markets—at least for Hayek it is not—it is only an assertion that market exchange is oriented to aggregate private goods rather than common ends. The nonalignment of SSS markets with communal goods, witnessed a few pages ago in Youngstown, is rooted firstly in the social facts of impersonal exchange, not in merchants' moral or intellectual shortcomings.

Markets may be indifferent to The Common Good in the grand political sense, but *it* is not indifferent to *them*. Elections and even entire regimes hang on the outcomes of market exchange. Hardly anyone, including Hayek, would deny the political importance of markets, but the crucial questions concern the nature of the connection. Are there systematic links, direct or indirect, between the apparently indifferent market and the flourishing of various communities? Do merchants serve some common end even as they pursue disinterested exchange? Hayek's answer to both questions is, No. His "spontaneous" model of the market envisions no common action or common goals at any level of the market nor in its minimalist legal-political infrastructure. If Hayek were right about the total absence of common action and goals, he would be perfectly justified in deeming The Common Good to be vacuous and harmful as a moral standard for market order. He is not right, but that does not diminish the welcome rigor and lucidity of his theory.

In conversation with Hayek and the broader perspective of economists, this chapter will argue three main theses about common goods and the market. First, to the extent that the canonical model of Strangers Selling Stuff holds good, market relations are not sites of common action, so any common goods (or evils) relevant to the market must be the goods (or evils) of a community that is not itself a market. It is unfortunate but not incoherent that Youngstown languished even as the stock market marched on. Second, markets *do* have a necessary relation to politics and law. A clean separation between markets and other domains of human life is provisional, if not mistaken. We must look beyond merchants and prices, to see what makes their bargains possible. In these first two theses, I stand in broad agreement with Hayek and many other economists.

Third, Hayek is wrong to hold that markets under law are *not* oriented to common ends. To restate the double negative, the market seen in its political context is in fact oriented to the ends of the political regime in some positive, if often indirect way. Despite his insightful and elegant theorizing, Hayek's minimal account of the politics of the market is too minimal. He focuses on the private law, but this turns out to be an important vehicle for transmitting the larger common ends of a regime. And the legal system is insufficient in any event for the construction and maintenance of markets. Both ordinary experience and Aristotelian theory demand a richer account of politics and common goods in markets, which will lead us to the school of "moral economy" in the following chapter. The citizen qua citizen has reason to be proud of the market's material advances both local and global and ashamed of the failures represented in a place like Youngstown, since these are the fortunes of a shared political project, not only a growing or shrinking pile of aggregated goods.

THE NATURE OF MARKET RELATIONS

What is a market? Although my arguments about the business firm in part 1 made endless reference to the market as a rival form of economic order, it is worth re-laying the groundwork before embarking on an extended consideration of markets in their own right. The various meanings of the everyday word "market"—supermarket, stock market, black market, and so forth—derive from the distinctive relation that individual merchants (buyers and sellers) take up in those settings. How we characterize this foundational, one-to-one market relation will have enormous ramifications for thinking about the political role of markets writ large. An insightful place to begin, if not necessarily to end, is the economist's canonical account of market relations. This model can be usefully boiled down to a three-word slogan: Strangers Selling Stuff. I will refer to this as the "Smithian" model of exchange, in honor of Adam Smith, who is often (rightly or wrongly) credited with coining this account of trade.[1] On the SSS conception, what is distinctive about merchants is that they bracket all interpersonal considerations or social relations while bargaining, so that their transactions depend solely (or overwhelmingly) on the quality and price of the items being sold. Friedrich Hayek summarizes the main norms at play: "that they compete honestly according to the rules of the game, guided only by the abstract signals of prices and giving no preferences because of their sympathies or views on the merits or needs of those with whom they deal."[2] The ideal-typical merchant is totally indifferent to *who* is selling or buying—be it prince or pauper, friend or foe; only the stuff matters. As economist Samuel Bowles puts it, "Strangers make markets, and markets make strangers."[3] Or in the words of Frank Knight, founder of the Chicago school, merchants are "free from social wants, prejudice, preferences, or repulsions, or any other values not completely manifested in market dealing."[4] In order to ward off the creeping influence of social status, power, or authority, market relations presuppose legal freedoms as well as competition, so any merchant can "exit" a particular bargain at little or no cost. The upshot of this canonical take on market exchange is that merchants meet as strangers and equals who are guided solely by their private interest in the goods for sale. In this respect SSS markets are radically different from most social settings.

Admittedly, the economist's stylized model depends on bright lines that may be fuzzy in real-world situations: Is this a hard-nosed bargain or the start of a beautiful friendship, or both? Anonymous exchanges like online shopping or investing in mutual funds are obvious cases of the former. I may not even know if a person or an algorithm stands at the other end of the deal. Similarly, real estate transactions are normally rather impersonal, but a friend of mine eventually married the man (previously a stranger) to whom she sold her house. Furthermore, the case of Uber and its drivers in chapter 4 illustrated how market-based networks may rely on factors of authority and cooperation that defy the tidy distinctions of the Smithian view. Things are not always clear-cut. To take account of this variety, chapter 7 will relax the SSS premise that merchants meet as strangers and equals. But this chapter and the next will follow the lead of two main interlocutors, Friedrich Hayek and Karl Polanyi, who rely on the precision of the canonical model as a way to think clearly about the nature and political role of markets. The best reason to follow them, in my view, is that the model does helpfully capture important features of most market exchanges. It illuminates, for instance, why market transactions among friends are so awkward: charging the "going rate" is tantamount to treating a friend as if he were a stranger, while charging anything else seems unfair. And the parsimony of the economist's model also makes it easier to see that typical market relations are not a form of common action in their own right.

Adam Smith famously observed that "it is not from the benevolence of the butcher, or the brewer, or the baker, that we expect our dinner, but from their regard to their own interest."[5] That merchants' primary motive is self-interest, in the sense of each one getting a good deal for themselves, follows from the absence of shared purposes at the bargaining table. But this self-interest is less pernicious than is sometimes alleged. First, free exchange will take place only if it appears beneficial to all parties. Market exchange is not war by other means, so we may say that its overall point or goal is the joint benefit of all the exchangers. In addition, simply by stepping onto the market and seeking a good deal in the ordinary way, we do not become *Homo oeconomicus*, the egoistic calculator who has no ultimate regard for any other human being. Some early neoclassical economists authors did posit such an unreal figure,[6] but the canonical model does not require heroic assumptions about human selfishness.

To describe the self-interest we see in markets, we need only the weaker doctrine of "non-tuism" (not-you-ism), which holds that merchants are typically not concerned with one another's purposes—that is, that "I" am not primarily interested in "Thou."[7] The label is awkward, but this sensible axiom captures the mutual disinterest that is characteristic of buyers and sellers seeking a good deal on the market, without excluding generous or public-spirited motivations in other domains of life. As economics Nobel Prize–winner James Buchanan puts it, "The theory of markets postulates only that the relationship be *economic*, that the interest of his opposite number in the exchange be excluded from consideration."[8] To borrow an example from P. H. Wicksteed, who coined the term "non-tuism," St. Paul of Tarsus did not need to suspend his sanctity in order to make and sell tents as a way of funding his missionary efforts. But even though his market dealings were means to noble or generous ends, he would have regarded his relations with Corinthian tent-buyers as just that: means to an end. Not, therefore, as forms of solidarity sought for themselves.

The notion that buyers and sellers on the market are interested in good deals rather than in forming new communities is almost too familiar to need restating. But one key implication of non-tuism is often left unexplored: buyers and sellers are not engaged in genuine common action around a common end. This follows from the merchant's characteristic focus on prices, not persons. It is telling that among all the modern words for social realities—school, club, league, alliance, tribe, and so on—there is no generic word for a social bond between buyers and sellers. For the Aristotelian pluralist, the explanation is straightforward: they have no such bond. An irreducible "we" is required to generate any common end, but a price-focused exchange of goods does not create any solidarity of this kind. True, merchants bargaining over the price of a car or a plumbing repair could say with perfect grammatical correctness, "*We* are doing business," or, "*We* are negotiating." But such a "we" is purely instrumental and contingent. It is instrumental in that they negotiate in order to secure private benefits, whether goods, services, or money, not to forge solidarity among themselves or to do something *together*, as friends or teammates do. It is contingent because the same private good might, in principle, be obtained more cheaply from a vending machine or a robot or by one's own effort. Whatever can be obtained in a nonsocial way is not an essentially social goal, as common ends are. Unlike virtually all other familiar social roles—parent, soldier, judge, colleague, employee, and so on—the interactions of merchants are understood to aim at what Yves Simon terms "a sum of private interests that happen to be interdependent" rather than any essentially common end. At bottom, then, even when price-centered exchange is mutually beneficial, what merchants have in view is at most a convergence of private goods rather than solidarity in some properly common end.

THINGS UNSEEN: MARKET ORDER AND COMMON ENDS

One can hardly glance at the news without reading a headline such as "the market reacted to the trade deal." What so greatly interests investors, regulators, and citizens is not the solidarity among merchants, or lack thereof, but the aggregate results of their exchanges. The overall trends of market exchange may enrich a firm, leave a region desolate, or ideally promote what Adam Smith called "universal opulence." It is tempting, therefore, to think of a broad system of price-centered market exchange as a shared project oriented to common ends, despite the mutual disinterest of particular SSS merchants. This, I shall now argue, is a mistake. Despite its undeniable political consequences, the merchant's world writ large is as indifferent to common goals as individual merchants are to one another. This indifference is no accident. To the contrary, the market's orientation to individual goods is central to the possibility of precise, dynamic, and large-scale coordination—what is often called the invisible hand of price-centered competition. Friedrich Hayek's account of market coordination-without-a-coordinator helps us to see that any common ends relevant to the Smithian market must belong to a community beyond the realm of merchants.

Hayek draws out the ontological and normative dimensions of the canonical market model with a clarity that few other economists have attained. His argument, briefly put, is that the price system is a form of spontaneous order governed by abstract rules, so it cannot be conformed to some overall plan or concrete shared goal while still performing its coordinating function. Though Hayek is no proponent of The Common Good, Aristotelian or otherwise, his overall vision can be usefully translated into the grammar of common ends: a system of market exchange enhances the private goals of merchants precisely by avoiding common action among them. But no translation is perfect, and it is worth flagging the main flaw in Hayek's argument right at the outset. He claims too much—holding implausibly that market order is individualistic not because it is impersonal, as I argued just above, but because *no* rule-governed order of any kind can track common ends. The next section of the chapter will show that this cracked foundation undermines Hayek's larger vision of continuity between the worlds of the merchant and the citizen. Politics cannot plausibly be modeled on the lines of atomistic market exchange. His arguments about the beneficial absence of common goals among merchants qua bargain seekers are far more persuasive when kept in their place.

Hayek's main explanation of market prosperity develops the classic doctrine of the invisible hand. According to Adam Smith's famous metaphor, merchants who attend only to price-signals and private gain effectively promote general affluence, without knowing *how* they do so. As Hayek summarizes, "Each [merchant] is made by the visible gain to himself to serve needs which to him are invisible,"[9] the needs of all others involved in the market. His distinctive explanation of this unintended coordination focuses on the informational benefits of market prices. Hayek conceives prices as a kind of shorthand language, which is able to capture and express far more information than any human tongue. "We must look at the price system as such a mechanism for communicating information if we want to understand its real function."[10] The semantics of prices are very simple, in that they only go up or down, and for Hayek this is the key point. Even though the factors that go into price formation are unfathomably complex, the resulting price is clear and easy to read. This simplicity allows indefinitely many merchants to respond appropriately to situations far beyond their conscious awareness.

For example, very few persons need to know whether a rise in the market price of cobalt is due to war, or tariffs, or new uses of cobalt, or something else. For the vast majority, the price signal is enough to induce them to respond properly, by economizing on cobalt. Some of the marginal uses of cobalt will be swapped for other metals, until supply and demand equilibrate around a market-clearing price for cobalt. By focusing on prices, which are easy to adjust and easy to read, a system of market exchange allows "fuller use [to be] made of the existing knowledge" of the best uses of things,[11] even though individual actors cannot see beyond their own situation. The market price concatenates their fragmentary knowledge into an accessible public symbol with just enough content to guide and coordinate action.

By responding primarily to prices, individuals are able to dovetail their own plans, in a precise and flexible way, with the innumerably many others connected to the tin trade. This process will tend dynamically to put goods to their most beneficial uses, and thus it is a "wealth-creating game." Even if the process never actually reaches the theoretical Pareto-optimum point in which no more mutually beneficial exchanges could be made, it allows each merchant to avail himself of more knowledge than he could get otherwise. By comparison, a merchant guiding his bargains by his own severely limited grasp of society's needs would be shooting in the dark. As Adam Smith acidly notes, "I have never known much good done by those who affected to trade for the public good."[12] Thus a system of price-centered exchange enables a more efficient and productive coordination.

Very few thinkers have thought as deeply as Hayek about the kinds of order that could produce unintended social benefits of this kind. His social ontology is centered on a great binary between two ideal-types of social order: deliberate and spontaneous. A deliberate or "made" order is any kind of social arrangement that is set on foot to achieve concrete purposes. The great majority of familiar social forms fall under this category, including "the family, the farm, the plant, the firm, the corporation and the various associations, and all the public institutions including government."[13] Despite their variety, such organizations each reflect "a deliberate arrangement of the use of the means which are known to some single agency."[14] They tend to be "relatively simple" and "usually concrete," the better to be effectively surveyed and coordinated by the commands of a manager.[15] Of course, some organizations are quite complex, in which cases the central authority may stipulate only "the assignment of particular functions and the general aim," with abstract rules filling in the gaps.[16] Nonetheless, on Hayek's view, any organization is fundamentally controlled from the top down, or from the outside in, by means of "command and obedience" oriented to some "single scale or hierarchy of ends."[17] (I note in passing that Hayek here agrees, in his own way, with the claim in part 1 of this book that corporate firms are oriented toward a complex shared goal, not to aggregated individual ends.)

A spontaneous or "grown" social order, by contrast, is self-generating in that it emerges from its participants responding to general rules of conduct rather than to commands imposed from "outside."[18] Individuals' actions may be carefully planned, but the overall pattern is not a product of anyone's intention. To repeat Hayek's favorite citation from the Scottish Enlightenment thinker Adam Ferguson, a spontaneous order is "the result of human action but not the execution of any of human design."[19] Hayek writes as though most spontaneous orders arise by historical accretion or accident—that is, spontaneously—but this need not be the case. He admits, "It is possible that an order which would still have to be described as spontaneous rests on rules which are entirely the result of deliberate design."[20] Present function is more decisive than the origin of the rules. An order can be called spontaneous so long as persons and goods are moved concretely by the rule-governed pursuit of private goals rather than authoritative arranging.[21]

A spontaneous order resembles a game—say, basketball or backgammon—in that the rules set the terms of play but do not fix the outcome. Hayek therefore argues that a spontaneous order, unlike an organization, has no concrete ends of its own. "Since such an order has not been created by an outside agency, the order as such also can have no purpose, although its existence may be very serviceable to the individuals which move within such order."[22] The point of a rule-based order is mainly to facilitate the pursuit and evolution of participants' own ends. For Hayek, the market is a paradigm case of such a spontaneous, instrumental order.

Up to No (Common) Good

How should we think about the relevance of common goods in large-scale market contexts that are "invisibly" but effectively coordinated by price signals? Hayek's views on the matter come out most strongly in his criticism of the discourse of social justice. What his polemics aim to show is that the market and its outcomes cannot coherently be regarded as socially just or unjust. Claims of (in)justice require a perpetrator, a responsible party. But neither the rules of the game nor particular merchants playing the game determine what goes on in a market. Therefore, they are not responsible for its outcomes; in a sense, no one is. For Hayek, talk of just or unjust markets is "nonsense, like the term 'moral stone.'"[23] Common good and social justice are cognate concepts, which always travel together. So if Hayek's polemics hit home, they also show that SSS exchange "for the common good" is another bit of pious claptrap.

Hayek makes his own case difficult, in that he frankly acknowledges that not all market distributions are pleasant, or optimal, or even rational. He does insist that, as a general matter, market orders "will enhance for all the prospects of achieving their respective purposes,"[24] but he is equally adamant that merchants will often fail on the market due to no fault of their own. The outcomes may be ugly: "The manner in which the benefits and burdens are apportioned by the market mechanism would in many instances have to be regarded as very unjust if it were the result of a deliberate allocation to particular people."[25] As an example, suppose that restaurants in Canada started by Honduran-born women fail at twice the rate of similar restaurants started by native-born Canadian women. Could one not say that any such regrettable state of affairs offends social justice or The Common Good, just because it is humanly regrettable? Of course, if The Common Good somehow included every bit of human flourishing and excluded every bit of human failure, then the Hondurans' misfortune would be repugnant to the ideal. But this kind of lazy moralizing is far too quick. Strictly speaking, appeals to common goods and related claims of social justice apply only in specific social forms. We cannot judge without first asking which shared ideals are relevant to the case at hand.

Hayek adopts a juridical perspective limiting the domain of justice to the imputable actions of persons or groups, not mere states of affairs. "Strictly speaking, only human conduct can be called just or unjust."[26] A phenomenon like bad weather, undesirable though it may be, cannot be unjust, because no one is responsible for it. Similarly, concrete outcomes in the market (such as restaurants' patterns of success or failure) do not result from the intentional action of any identifiable person or group. Therefore a market allocation "can be neither just nor unjust, because the results are not intended or foreseen, and depend on a multitude of circumstances not known in their totality to anybody."[27] Thanks to the dispersion of responsibility, the outcomes of a stylized market are normatively more akin to natural facts than to intentional human action. This analogy may seem false to Hayek's own boundaries of justice, since markets are a mode of human conduct and weather is not. The key point for Hayek is that neither one has a human author who could rightly be praised or blamed, so the two domains are equally impervious to claims of justice.[28] If no one is responsible for the Hondurans' misfortune, what they suffer is not injustice.

Yet we still want to assign blame for market misfortunes, and the other likely target for blame is the rules themselves. In practice it is always possible, and often accurate, to claim that the whole game is "rigged" in favor of someone or other. Perhaps there are language-based regulations tailored to impede immigrant restaurateurs, under the guise of impartial guidelines. Hayek would respond that a market cannot be manipulated in this way while remaining a true spontaneous order. What underlies any market are "just rules of individual conduct" that "tell each what he can count upon, what material objects or services he can use for his purposes, and what is the range of actions open to him."[29] These rules are typically negative in character and (relatively) universal in that they do not apply to specific individuals. The paradigmatic example is the law of property, tort, and contract. Rules of this kind do not determine market outcomes any more than the rules of basketball specify who wins a given game. They only set up what counts as fair play. To the extent that ad hoc rules are in fact targeting specific persons or groups, Hayek would classify such rules as commands in disguise, which are in conflict with the basic mechanism of a market order. In other words, a rigged market is not a real market. If the Canadian restaurant market is rigged, Hayek would advocate not a better realization of social justice among restaurants, but a genuine return to some set of market rules under which claims of social (in)justice cannot validly arise.

For the SSS merchant in the midst of other merchants, "there is no individual and no co-operating group of people against which the sufferer would have a just complaint, and there are no conceivable rules of just individual conduct which would at the same time secure a functioning order and prevent such disappointments."[30] Hayek emphasizes the problem of verification. He thinks no human agency wise enough adequately to evaluate the concrete deliverances of a complex market in terms of efficiency, justice, or any similar standard. We cannot know enough apart from the price system to verify, say, the viability of the Honduran- and Canadian-owned restaurants. If we did, we wouldn't need the competitive market in the first place. "It would be patently absurd to sponsor a contest if we knew in advance who the winner would be."[31] It would be more than impolitic to press claims of social justice against law-abiding merchants, or claims of distributive justice against the rules of the market. To hold someone to account for what they did not, indeed could not, do—this would itself be a form of injustice. No merchant qua merchant is responsible for the apparent wrongs suffered by the immigrant restaurateurs. The inapplicability of all community-facing forms of justice implies that no common good is at stake among SSS merchants.

There are two further reasons, drawn from the general grammar of common action, why market outcomes are not a properly common good (or evil). First, considered from the perspective of the merchant, the market itself is not a project that can flourish or fail to flourish. Any community flourishes when its members achieve their common ends, but merchants do not share a distinctive set of ends with one another. At most, competitive markets that are free of manipulation and monopoly power will be more serviceable as a common utility, much as roads will serve drivers better if they are free of bumps and potholes. But any good that is achieved will be the private flourishing of merchants, not the flourishing of the market itself.

Second and more fundamentally, markets writ large do not involve common action any more than microtransactions do. There is a quasi-categorical difference between particular one-to-one exchanges and large-bore outcomes: the gap between intended gain and unintended benefits. Could we say that the common ends of various communities count among the unintended but real beneficiaries of the price system? For the sake of argument, let us grant that mutually beneficial exchanges proliferate wonderfully in a market system, as the invisible hand doctrine predicts. Suppose even, contra Hayek, that every single merchant measurably benefits. This tells us that private stocks of good increase. What Stefano Zamagni has called the "total good," defined as the aggregate of all private goods, grows.[32] Even if literally everyone is richer, however, this tells us nothing about any common end, which is not reducible to an aggregate. A common good is the flourishing of an order of common action that is intended (at least in part) for its own sake, for the irreducibly social goods it generates. There is no more common action in the SSS market writ large, a vast network of interlocking exchange relations, than there was in its component parts. Where there is no common action among persons, there is no common good. Without common action among merchants, the evaluative standard of common good is not directly relevant to the market constituted by their exchanges.

For Hayek, the absence of common action and goods in a market is not a problem; quite the contrary, it is the source of the market's greatest virtues. It frees merchants to pay attention to prices, which allows the "full use of social knowledge" that Hayek considers the key to prosperity. And in a pluralistic world it makes "peaceful reconciliation of . . . divergent interests possible," since it allows for societal collaboration without joint pursuit of common ends. But it also means that in order to apply the metric of common goods to market exchange, citizens would need to look to some teleological common project that is not itself a market. As we will see, Hayek mistakenly claims that no such community is essential to the price system, and thus wrongly concludes that purely private, negative market freedom is possible and even desirable. From a wider point of view, his failure to recognize a frame of common action around private exchange renders his account of impersonal markets far less persuasive than it might have been.

An Amendment

Before we leave Hayek's version of market theory, I pause to register a criticism. Though he correctly identifies a gap between impersonal, price-centered markets and the ends of common action, the underlying argument is unsound. Hayek gives the right answer for the wrong reasons. It is a serious error to hold, and his conclusion about markets does not require him to hold, that any abstract, rule-governed order is free of common ends.

Recall that Hayek's broad social ontology turns on a distinction between a "made order" serving the concrete purposes of particular persons and a "spontaneous order" that follows abstract rules and supposedly lacks goals of its own. The latter, he avers, "not having been made, . . . *cannot* legitimately be said to *have a particular purpose.*"[33] There are two problems to flag here. The first is Hayek's conflation of social ends and particular conscious purposes. The priority of ends over purposes, for which I argued in chapter 2, implies that the two categories must be distinct. The normative ends of a school, for instance, are not determined by the personal goals of a particular principal or set of teachers, as Hayek's argument seems to imply. An elementary school, as a social form, has the end of educating the young even if its teachers happen to be uninterested in kids or in learning. Failing to achieve its built-in end is what makes this a bad *school*, and not just an unpleasant daycare. Emergent common ends, which are the substrate of any common good, are built into a social entity and so are quite different from the conscious purposes of identifiable individual persons.

The larger mistake flowing from this first error is Hayek's denial that any abstract, rule-governed order can have ends of its own. This second mistake is more damaging to his overall project, because the abstract-concrete divide defines both his social ontology and his advocacy for liberal freedoms. He proclaims, for instance, that "when we obey laws, in the sense of general abstract rules laid down irrespective of their application to us, we are not subject to another man's will and are therefore free."[34] Hayek is quite right to argue that a social order defined by abstract rules cannot be fundamentally oriented to "known particular results." But it does not follow that a rule-governed order cannot be oriented to common ends, since common ends are not confined to "known particular results." Our basketball team's common goal may be centered on winning *this particular tournament*, but the flourishing of a relationship between parent and child does not depend on any such discrete achievement.

For the Aristotelian pluralist, it is the presence of common action, not the pursuit of known concrete goals, that is the most reliable marker of common goods as against coordinated self-interest. Yves Simon writes that "a good is common if, and only if, it is of such nature as to call for common pursuit and common enjoyment."[35] Such goods may, indeed must, involve patterns as well as particular objects, so Hayek's abstract-versus-concrete distinction is beside the point. Every common good includes justice, solidarity, and friendship as essential elements, and they are patterns rather than particulars. For Aristotle himself, the paradigmatic common end is that of the political regime, and a regime is not oriented to some specific goal (e.g., victory over the Persians or a certain distribution of wealth), but rather to a "way of life" that the citizens share in common. The laws of a regime shape the citizen's way of life precisely by honoring certain abstract principles. Aristotle claims, for instance, that an abstract rule allowing the free poor to vote valorizes equality, while denying them suffrage honors wealth. Goods in common are always more than concrete outcomes.

In order to reach his illuminating conclusion about the lack of common goods in market relations, Hayek ought to have focused not on the rule-governed or spontaneous character of the market as we know it, but on its impersonality. The "rules of the game" direct buyers and sellers to focus not on their social relations, but rather only on the price and quality of the benefit at hand. This mutual indifference is what makes common goods so little applicable to conventional market exchanges. On the other hand, the market's rules enjoining impersonality could be relaxed, as we will explore in chapter 7. If there were a standing custom of giving one's neighbors a 10 percent discount, such a market would be quite as spontaneous and resistant to individual purposes as the "impersonal process" that we are familiar with, even if it lacked some of the flexibility and universality that Hayek celebrates in the price system. But it would *not* be indifferent to common goods, in this case the goods of neighborhoods.

Thanks to the deep flaw in Hayek's otherwise impressive social ontology, he fails to imagine not only how repersonalized markets *could* serve common ends, but indeed how anonymous markets as we know them already *do*. As I will explore in the next chapter, Karl Polanyi and the school of moral economy show that modern markets have always served as key parts of a substantive political vision precisely in their anonymity. Hayek found such a vision of markets embedded in a teleological community unappealing, and likely incoherent, since he thought common ends were incompatible with spontaneous order. He sought instead to set the price system within an implausibly individualistic legal and political frame, which was itself modeled on market order.

FROM PRICES TO POLITICS

The present chapter has been considering the market in isolation, as a distinct domain of human affairs with its own set of rules, motivations, and reasoning. This sequestering approach follows the path laid down by economists, who begin with a version of the state of nature: Robinson Crusoe, alone on his island. As Hayek's mentor Ludwig von Mises puts it, "In order to conceive the market fully one is forced to study the action of hypothetical isolated individuals."[36] Many of the seminal insights of the tradition that descends from Adam Smith, to which Hayek is a notable contributor, begin with such a stripped-down account of markets apart from any social or political context. By focusing only on buyers and sellers in their market roles, this parsimonious account also helps to bring out the role, or rather the nonrole, of common ends in prototypical market exchange. At this level of analysis, it is only a hair too blunt to say, with Hayek: common goods have nothing directly to do with markets one way or the other. Whatever common ends may be affected by particular exchanges or by a competitive price system, they must belong to some community that is not itself a market. Morally formative common goals and other distinctive features of cooperative action do not, indeed cannot, appear in accounts of market efficiency that focus only on prices and divisible private goods.

Yet even Hayek recognizes that the analytic separation of markets from politics and other domains of life can only be provisional. Any broad vision of political economy must eventually explain three things: (1) market exchange, (2) political affairs, and (3) the link between the two. Viewing market exchange in isolation gives us only part of the story, for it does not tell us either the end or the beginning. We never see the denouement, morally speaking, since for buyers and sellers alike a market exchange is just a means, not an end. The real human worth of markets will depend partly on how the price system affects adjacent forms of solidarity; many critics have alleged that pecuniary incentives tend to "crowd out" higher human motives.[37] The final tally will also depend on what merchants choose to do with the goods they have exchanged. As Edmund Burke wryly comments, "The effect of liberty on individuals is, that they may do what they please: We ought to see what it will please them to do, before we risk congratulations."[38]

More important for our purposes is the absent beginning of the story: the fact that market exchange cannot get off the ground without the authority of law. At minimum, market relations depend on the enforcement of basic rules of ownership and exchange. Even Robinson Crusoe and Friday on their island would need some tacit understanding of property and promise keeping, in order to render their exchanges sustainable or even intelligible. In any real-world market scenario these rules include genuine rules of law enforceable by a judge. Because these constitutive rules are in the hand of one who is not himself playing the market game, even the staunch market partisan (and Hayek is among the staunchest) recognizes that one cannot fully do away with law, and thus with politics, at least as a background condition for the market. In this way, questions about common ends and the market lead beyond the restricted perspective of the merchant to query the market's place in a larger political landscape.

The link between markets and politics is where the rubber hits the road for Hayek, since the practical point of his theory of spontaneous market order is to protect it from the encroachment of government or other authorities. More broadly, the primary goal of his postwar writings is to articulate a law-focused conception of politics that is compatible with market order and thus with liberty as he understands it. The core of Hayek's broader political economy, which I will sketch all too briefly, is the claim that all three dimensions focus on individual action and private ends alone. I have already discussed the most plausible dimension of his model: the exclusion of common ends from market exchange as such. It remains to expound and critique the other two elements: Hayek's model of liberal politics as an individualistic, spontaneous order and his claim that markets depend primarily on private-law rules that draw no one into common action. These flawed ideas amount to a blanket denial that political economy needs a grammar of common action, a denial that Hayek himself cannot consistently maintain.

Supporting Private Ends: A Divided Vision

For Hayek, the most essential role that government plays in the market is the maintenance of "an appropriate legal system, a legal system designed both to preserve competition and to make it operate as beneficially as possible."[39] As we saw, a spontaneous order can arise only when individuals act according to a set of abstract rules, and not just any set of rules will do. Hayek emphasizes that the bedrock rules of a competitive market order are categories of private law: property, contract, and torts. He quotes David Hume approvingly on "the three fundamental laws of nature, that of stability of possession, of its transference by consent, and of the performance of promises."[40] Laws of this kind are generally abstract and negative: abstract in that they apply to classes of people or situations rather than particulars; negative in that they mainly aim to prevent injustice rather than to orient action to ends.

The main function of the law in a spontaneous order is not to achieve some particular state of affairs, but to allow persons to coordinate expectations in constantly changing circumstances. And the best way to do this, for Hayek, is through the "delimitation of protected domains"—that is, through the definition of property and other rights that mark off what I may or may not do and what others may or may not do to me, in a given situation. If the private law has a goal or purpose, it is to realize an order of actions in which these just expectations (or expectations of justice) are met—that is, the rules are followed, the game is played fairly. "Only when it is clearly recognized that the order of actions is a factual state of affairs distinct from the rules which contribute to its formulation can it be understood that such an *abstract order can be the aim of the rules of conduct.*"[41]

Hayek also acknowledges a more positive role for government in supporting real-world markets. He views government as society's "maintenance squad," which is tasked not with producing any particular goods, but rather with keeping social mechanisms "in working order." The key mechanism is the legal system itself, which exercises the government's "coercive function."[42] But government as an organization also plays an indispensable "service function" by deploying its large resources. Following a classic insight noted already by Adam Smith, Hayek observes that the competitive price mechanism will fail to provide enough of certain necessary public goods, such as roads and other infrastructure. It therefore falls to nonmarket actors, often government, to provide them. Hayek is surprisingly broadminded about the admissible range of public goods that the government might provide, and he has chagrined many partisans of small-government by his warmth toward a strong social safety net, or even, in principle, a universal basic income.[43]

The reason for Hayek's openness to such ideas is that he is concerned less with the *volume* of government involvement in the market than with the *kind* of involvement. As he remarks, "Planning and competition can be combined only by planning for competition but not by planning against competition."[44] Some kinds of government "services" exist alongside the price mechanism and even facilitate its operation, while others supplant it through authoritative command. Entitlement schemes, for instance, operate according to general rules and so do not greatly interfere with the free workings of the market. At least *some* measures of this kind are "required to make competition as effective and beneficial as possible." Hayek reserves his principled opposition for methods of direct command that replace the market mechanism, putting coercion in place of free, price-guided individual decisions.

Even as he makes space for law and politics, Hayek tries to maintain the blunt conclusion that common ends sought for their own sake have no place in markets. Stated positively, he tries to hold on to the idea that market relations have merely instrumental value to merchants seeking private goals. He will not be able to maintain this stance consistently, however, since he sees that the market does demand a degree of real moral commitment. Demands of this kind cannot be squared with a merely instrumental valuation of market relations. If the market must be described and justified in terms of morally consequential membership, one cannot finally dispense with reasoning about common ends, as Hayek would prefer to do. He is unwilling to admit that he has implicitly reopened the door to morally formative common goods, so his account vacillates between an instrumental and a moralized account of markets under law, and of politics itself.

Hayek's exclusion of common goods is at its strongest when one considers only private law. There are no more common purposes in markets seen in a private-law context than there are when one considers buyers and sellers alone. Indeed, assuming merchants are law-abiding, there is no significant difference between these two perspectives. The private law simply articulates the (largely) negative norms that the individuals are already following. As Hayek puts it, "The aim of jurisdiction is the maintenance of an ongoing order of actions."[45] Merely invoking or following the laws of property and contract, which are indeed backed by political authority, does not seem to involve buyers and sellers in a shared hierarchy of ends. Private law alone cannot coordinate any common projects or transmit any common ends, much as wood cannot conduct electricity.

Yet Hayek recognizes that markets also need public legitimacy, and, like many other economists, he tries to secure it by demonstrating the instrumental value of the market as a convergent good, which serves the private ends of many individuals. Citizens should support the market just because "any person picked out at random" is likely to regard it as a desirable mode of social coordination. On occasion, Hayek even avails himself of the Aristotelian vocabulary of The Common Good, only to reinterpret it in a utilitarian direction: "The common good in this sense is not a particular state of affairs but consists in an abstract order . . . which will increase everybody's chances as much as possible, not at every moment but only on the whole and in the long run."[46] At first glance, the market economy and its legal order can be conceived as public utilities much like the power grid, mere instruments for the sake of the private ends or purposes that they serve.

Once we move past the surface rhetoric of Hayek's account, however, the market and its demands appear in a quite different light. Unlike some neoclassical theorists, Hayek makes clear that not all merchants will win and that many will fail from sheer bad luck, sometimes with devastating personal consequences. The unavoidable risk of "severe hardship and privation" is the price of maintaining the market system.[47] What is to motivate the individual merchant to support an "impersonal process" that only promises to boost prospects "on the whole and in the long run"? As John Maynard Keynes famously commented, in the long run we are all dead.[48]

If I am going to suffer catastrophic losses over the short run during which I have to remain solvent, then I have no *instrumental* reason to support the rules of the market game (e.g., by following the private law or by opposing government intervention). The political foundation for a system this capricious must be principled, even disinterested.

Sustaining a market demands a certain degree of self-discipline and even self-sacrifice. For Hayek, markets are not gotten for free: "Freedom can only be had a price and . . . as individuals we must be prepared to make severe material sacrifices to preserve our liberty."[49] Instrumental rationality, by which one constantly consults one's own bottom line, could not justify such sacrifices, so the market must rest on something deeper. Hayek holds that market order demands a certain "moral attitude" from merchants, which is to "compete honestly according to the rules of the game, guided only by the abstract signals of prices and giving no preferences because of their sympathies or views on the merits or needs of those with whom they deal."[50]

We can glimpse here that for Hayek the "rules of the game" concern both the negative and positive pillars of market relations, both the typical normative boundaries and the characteristic motivations that markets require. On the negative side, one is to deal "honestly," which means not lying, cheating, stealing, or otherwise breaking the law. But mere law-abidingness is not enough to achieve the efficient coordination that is the jewel in the crown of a market order. For the law does not, and indeed could not, enforce the price-centered motivations that fuel the market engine. Abstemious monks, for instance, might not break the law, but their concern for God and neighbor would orient them to concerns other than prices and so would impede the full use of social knowledge that Hayek sees in the ideal price system. Prices have a moral weight; for Hayek they are a matter of principle as well as prudence. "It would mean not merely a personal loss, but a failure in their duty to the public, to employ a less efficient instead of a more efficient person, to spare an incompetent competitor, or to favor particular users of their products."[51] Adopting a market attitude is, on this view, a civic duty. Considerations other than price *ought* to be disregarded (among them the direct pursuit of common ends by political means) for the good of "the public."

The Inevitability of Common-Good Reasoning

Hayek puts forward two different models for relating the market and the common good that are not obviously compatible. It would seem that markets are either a piece of "utilitarian machinery" that facilitates the pursuit of individual ends,[52] or they are a transformative moral order that imposes positive duties, justifies personal sacrifice, and forms individuals in light of some common vision. Hayek faces a dilemma: both models cannot be unqualifiedly true, yet each has at least a grain of truth.

Hayek seems to think he can retain both models at face value because of the peculiar character of the market order that he advocates. A merchant's price-centered attitude may seem to refuse all moral considerations. Yet if we follow Hayek's argument closely, moral judgment is not suppressed but only displaced from the ignorant agent to market institutions, which are supposed to concatenate all the relevant information and purposes into a definitive signal, something that individual insight usually cannot do. Given my own severely limited knowledge, if I want to do right by my fellows, I can do no better than to dance to the market tune.[53] Using the price system is not callous or amoral; it is only humble. Moreover, merchants in a market system should not focus on the instrumental value of the rules. "Though these [abstract] rules ultimately serve particular (though mostly unknown) ends, they will do so only if they are treated not as means but as ultimate values, indeed as the only values common to all and distinct from the particular ends of the individuals."[54] Because no one knows all the particular purposes the rules will serve, merchants should, and often do, take the rules themselves *as if* they were ends.

Hayek tries to have his cake and eat it too, by positing the rules of market order as if they were a morally weighty common end that is valued for itself, which is at the same time a mere instrument. This kind of paradox is meant to persuade the losers at the market game to keep faith with a system that was supposed to facilitate their ends. Providing solace of this kind is a traditional role for the concept of The Common Good, which citizens can share and promote even in the very act of self-sacrifice. Soldiers, police officers, and occasionally normal citizens are called upon to lay down life or health in defense of the community. Their sacrifices are typically repaid with honor. The losers at the market game, by contrast, will never be congratulated for having honestly followed the rules. It is hard to imagine the people of economically devastated Youngstown drawing much comfort from Hayek's teaching that the rules of the market are ultimately instrumental to the very private ends that they are *not* realizing.

Hayek puts too much weight on the power of ignorance to transform the character of market order. If I have no appreciation for art but I keep a Cézanne in the front hall as a way of impressing whoever may walk through my door, the instrumental worth of the painting does not become intrinsic value for me simply by being indefinite. Neither should a public utility earn my respect as an end in itself, simply because I may not know all the uses to which it is put.[55] There is nothing amiss, of course, about some form of social order being instrumentally and intrinsically valued in different respects. I may value my participation in a professional choir both for the salary it pays me and for the shared experience of creating beautiful music. But the intrinsic value of the choir's common action does not derive from its value as a tool for my purposes, and indeed it is apt to shape what my purposes are. Likewise, markets require and encourage a certain kind of person, who will act on a certain set of motives in market contexts. The fact that a market is also instrumentally useful does not draw it back down to the level of a public utility, indifferent to the moral quality of its users or their relations.

The lack of fit between Hayek's two foundations of market order unsettles the earlier conclusion about the irrelevance of common goods. Insofar as market order draws on a certain "moral attitude," it calls merchants out of themselves to participate in a common stamp of character, and thus is more than a mere instrument. If this attitude is very nearly that of the indifferent *Homo oeconomicus* who leaves all considerations beyond self-interest in the (invisible) hands of the price system, this is an expression of a typical liberal political paradox: the common project of . . . not having a common project.[56] And while a real-life liberal regime may be a paradox, it is not a market. Despite his qualms and cavils, then, Hayek's account does evoke a view of market order as an aspect of a soul-forming political regime, a feature of politics that his account of the Great Society explicitly denies.

Great Society versus Political Regime

On Hayek's view, the wider reason why markets under law do not serve any common good is that a legitimate state has no common ends of its own. Even apart from the fact that private law cannot unify action around shared goals, Hayek's liberal society has no such goals in the first place. This helps to explain why he thinks the "moral attitude" of merchants leaves them innocent of any common projects. Here I will only gesture at the larger political vision that Hayek erects atop his theory of spontaneous order. He argues that an idealized liberal polity, which he calls the "Great Society," is itself a spontaneous order because it is ultimately governed by the rule of law, rather than by command or authoritative direction. As we have already seen, Hayek thinks (mistakenly) that a social order coordinated by abstract, negative rules cannot reflect any shared ends. Its "purpose" is merely to maintain relations of justice among its constituent members as they pursue whatever their own purposes happen to be. If this notion of spontaneous, purposeless order was nourished historically by reflection upon markets, Hayek bends the concept back onto politics, with unfortunate results.

His account depends on a sharp separation between government and political society. Government he calls "one organization among many,"[57] a bureaucratic hierarchy serving concrete purposes, especially the provision of public goods. The citizens of a liberal political society, by contrast, are related not by shared goals but only by their observance of the abstract rules of law as they go about their own purposes. "A Great Society has nothing to do with, and is in fact irreconcilable with 'solidarity' in the true sense of unitedness in the pursuit of known common goals."[58] On Hayek's conception, therefore, to set markets in legal and political context is to situate one spontaneous order within another. There is no fundamental tension between the basically instrumental character of market and polity, both of which are conceived as means for serving individual ends.

"The Great Society and its market order" are connected by more than an analogy, since for Hayek the market is the primary ordering device within political society.[59] The civil organizations that make up a polity are not themselves markets, but "the interdependence or coherence of the parts of the Great Society is purely economic. . . . It is the market order which makes peaceful reconciliation of the divergent purposes possible."[60] On this picture, to promote the "general welfare" in politics is primarily a matter of maintaining the spontaneous order of the market. This overriding goal implies that, for Hayek, citizens share no distinct common good or end that could be sharply distinguished from their interest in the market. Public order is only a matter of coordinating private goals; it adds nothing to them. Hayek's liberal citizens can and should make a full-throated defense of competitive market order as that end—or rather, that ends-free, means-oriented order—to which the polity is itself oriented.

This exclusively "nomocratic" construal of political society parts ways with the Aristotelian tradition and also, in my view, with common sense. For Aristotelian pluralism, any political society, and indeed any emergent social form whatever, is inescapably "teleocratic," in that it aims at some common good or end, and could not do otherwise. Aristotle himself takes it as obvious that "the city is some sort of community and that every community gets established with some good in view."[61] On his account, every political community aims at some positive overall vision of human life, which determines its particular regime. But this vision is primarily a feature of the laws of the city, rather than a directly commanded project of the rulers. As Aristotle writes, "Where the laws do not rule there is no regime."[62] Above all, it is public law establishing who shall rule and why (either in explicit black-letter fashion or, more typically, by custom and tacit assumption) that orients the city and its citizens toward a common end. "For whatever the authoritative element conceives to be honorable will necessarily be followed by the opinion of the other citizens."[63] So even an association defined by laws and rules entails a shared end.

Hayek's focus on conscious purposes and commands, forged in his death-struggle against authoritarianism, renders him blind to the subtler teleological drift that inevitably characterizes any scheme of public and private law, which orients citizens in the direction of a common goal. To imagine the rule of law without noticing the corresponding form of common life and its ends, as Hayek fails to do, is to miss the most distinctive feature of actual polities, their regime. Or, perhaps better, it is already to advocate a particular regime, namely democracy. As Aristotle and Tocqueville observe, it is typical of democrats both ancient and modern to downplay elements of the city besides exchange and agreements about injustice, the better to emphasize equality and freedom.[64] But even democratic laws create a regime oriented to a common way of life as its end, in pursuit of which democratic citizenship can be seen as a form of solidarity, or even civic friendship.

The Aristotelian claim about teleocratic politics is largely a descriptive, empirical one about the tendencies of regimes, whether conscious or unnoticed. Whatever the proponents of democracy or oligarchy may *say* about their limited aims, it is clear from what they *do* that their regimes cannot avoid promoting a rather full-orbed political vision of a life lived according to what Hayek calls a "hierarchy of ends."[65] Of course, such an abstract project is quite different than the "known common goals" of Hayek's hated central planners; there is a "spontaneous" aspect to the solidarity of a political regime in Aristotle's sense. Nonetheless, no actual political regime could be described as a fully ends-free system, as Hayek insists that a spontaneous order necessarily is. The Aristotelian view has all the weight of experience on its side of the dispute. On this point, Hayek's model is not incoherent; it is simply wrong. His vision of aimless politics has never been realized, nor could it be. The model of spontaneous order is insightful in many ways, but it cannot be extended from markets to all of political life, and is therefore incomplete.

Its incompleteness throws a further obstacle in the way of Hayek's previous large claim, namely that the private-law connection between politics and the market allows the price system to proceed independent of any shared ends. This is somewhat plausible as an idealized theory of of how to maintain an ongoing market, even if it does miss key features of how modern markets actually work.[66] But as an explanation for the origins of our market system, it fails completely. The role of private law, as Hayek depicts it, is the largely conservative one of "maintaining an ongoing order of actions." But the market revolution in the West, as we will see in the next chapter, was more of a tsunami hitting social practices from without than a slow shift of the tide. Indeed, right at the core of the postwar neoliberal project, which Hayek so deeply influenced, is the constructivist thesis that markets have to be promoted and propped up by political means. This act of market construction, whether ancient or modern, is a public project carried out in service of a political vision. In certain key respects, markets are "made," not "grown."

There is a remarkably robust connection between modern liberal democracy and the market. As Peter Berger observes, "One can say on empirical grounds—not because of some philosophical principle—that you can't have democracy unless you have a market economy . . . [but] the relationship is asymmetrical. . . . You can have a market economy without democracy."[67] For all the acuity of his analysis of markets, Hayek's purely "spontaneous" approach fails to explain this connection fully. Both liberal polity itself and the moral infrastructure of the market are morally thicker, messier, and more ends-oriented than Hayek will allow. It is something of a compliment to say that Hayek's theory is *too* elegant, *too* rigorous, but of course elegance is not preferable to truth. According to his contemporary Raymond Aron, Hayek attempted to reduce moral problems to merely technical ones because he "succumbed to the temptation to do away with political rule and political prudence."[68] To put the same point in terms from Charles Taylor, Hayek's overreliance on the concept of spontaneous order tries to settle questions at the level of ontology that are properly matters of advocacy. The fact that Hayek's reductive arguments fail does not prove any kind of positive case, Aristotelian or otherwise. But it does illustrate that approaching political affairs with a set of market concepts is a fraught and probably futile project.

CAN WE AVOID COMMON GOODS?

Here, again, is the big question that I have enlisted Hayek to help answer: Is a market system a way of pursuing common ends together that must be evaluated with a moral grammar of common goods? More concretely, do we see common goods at the level of exchange, or in its political underpinnings? By aggressively generalizing the economist's market model into a broader vision of political economy, Hayek's own response is a blanket "No" at both levels. He argues that the invisible hand of price-centered competition is only one type of abstract, spontaneous order, while the liberal Great Society is another. On the premise that no social order can be oriented to shared goals if it is governed by rules rather than commands, Hayek sees no place for common ends either among merchants or among citizens, nor in their private-law connections. Politics and markets are alike in their focus on private goods. But the premise is false, and Hayek's overly narrow view of common ends leaves him vacillating incoherently between instrumental and moralized justifications for market relations. Nonetheless, I hope this chapter will add something to Hayek's reputation as a clear-eyed theorist of common goods (notwithstanding that he staunchly denies they are public concerns). His polemics show how much it would take to exclude common action from political economy in a comprehensive way: the political setting of the market would itself have to be a mode of individualistic transaction.

No political order can be plausibly described in these terms, so Hayek cannot successfully exclude common goods from politically framed markets. Nonetheless, there are some important markets that strongly resemble Hayek's spontaneous model: treaty-governed international markets. A multilateral treaty like NAFTA would seem to be oriented to the aggregate goods of the nations that are party to it, not to any irreducibly communal goal. As I will explore in chapter 7, a model free of all common goods may gain important real-world traction when it comes to vast global markets, but it cannot well explain the domestic political economies where Hayek erroneously applies it.

Even so, Hayek's private-goods account yields an invaluable formulation of the core dilemma of markets: SSS exchange can have no direct relation to common goods—and yet anonymous markets are essential for functioning modern societies! The canonical model of "Strangers Selling Stuff" implies that neither particular bargains nor the aggregate effects of anonymous trading constitute common ends in their own right. If this is so, SSS markets can have no common goods of their own. And yet in one sense, it is good that they do not. Many of the chief benefits of markets stem directly from the absence of common action among merchants. The moralist cannot simply declare that merchants should promote common goods, and end the discussion. The beneficial absence of common action in SSS exchange must be prudentially weighed against the shared goals of some adjacent community that is not itself a market. Hayek acknowledges no such community, so he sees no relevance for common goods. The upcoming chapter will consider the patchwork approach of "moral economy," which embeds impersonal SSS markets within a frame of morally formative common action. Ultimately, this alternative vision will furnish additional reasons to reconsider the canonical SSS model, so chapter 7 will finally turn to the lesser-known tradition of Italian civil economy, which highlights the common action and sociality that is never fully absent from market exchange.

We can concretely grasp the need for these further steps by speculating about what Hayek might say about a community such as Youngstown, which has seen its livelihood yanked from beneath its collective feet by the whims of the market. He makes such admirably clear and coherent use of the economist's canonical model that one can have a pretty good guess. Hayek would certainly not blame General Motors or US Steel for pulling out of the Rust Belt, since keeping their factories in place for reasons of sentiment or loyalty would have been a "failure in their duty to the public." Nor would Hayek necessarily blame Youngstown and its civic or business leaders for failing to avoid the disaster of Black Monday. Unforeseen and unmerited hardship is a risk to be run by anyone playing the market game, including whatever regions are currently booming. The "severe hardship and privation" that the shifting market sometimes leaves in its wake is no more a matter of praise and blame than the devastation of a tornado.

For that very reason, Hayek might call the plight of Ohio's Mahoning Valley a sign of health, a sign that the twin spontaneous orders of the price-system and liberal politics are still functioning more or less freely. This disaster is what is supposed to happen, insofar as Black Monday is the flip side, regrettable but inevitable, of a system of free coordination that promises to boost the chances of all. You couldn't avoid such misfortunes without deserting spontaneous markets entirely. On a Hayekian view, citizens need not ignore the trials of a Youngstown and might even offer public assistance as a way of buying off discontent. But they should not seek to avoid future failures of the same kind. If one asks where The Common Good comes into this judgment, Hayek's answer would be, in a word, it doesn't. The decline of the Rust Belt is neither the realization nor the frustration of some common purpose, because he cannot discern any common ends in a system governed by abstract rules.

If Hayek's economistic view is a good place to begin, thanks to its clarity about markets, it is not a good place to end, on account of its partial view of politics. The problems of the Mahoning Valley were not intended by anyone in particular, and no one was in a position to prevent them (except perhaps for General Motors, though its degrees of freedom may have been severely constrained by its competitors). But Hayek's political analysis of such situations depends implicitly on the common ends that it explicitly rules out. Only a citizenry of tremendous fortitude could look on the tempests of the market and not be shaken, or moved to shelter themselves from future storms. Forging the degree of shared commitment needed for the citizens of Youngstown to accept their fate without grumbling would be a political achievement of the first order. The maintenance of markets and the collective habits of graciously winning or losing at the market game can only be a substantive part of this common vision, never simply a logical consequence of liberal politics as a form of order. In this light, Youngstown would make a claim in justice on some broader common project. And the role of politics in constituting exchange is far broader and deeper than serving as an impartial umpire. Since they do not arise spontaneously, free markets have always been as much a political project as a political premise, as the moral economy of Karl Polanyi will help us to see.

CHAPTER SIX

FORUM AND EMPORIUM

When it was constructed in 1885, and again when rebuilt in 1935, the Chicago Board of Trade Building was the tallest edifice in the city: a fitting testament to the importance of its stock exchange for a metropolis that was doubling in size every decade or two. It is also fitting, though less obviously so, that the CBT took the title of tallest building from Holy Name Cathedral, for the two were alike in surprisingly many ways. Both were topped with statuary and adorned with stone engravings, yet it is the similarity between the goings-on in their vast central halls that should interest us more. The action began with the ringing of a bell. Men (in the fin-de-siècle era it was only men) in traditional habiliment assembled in a ritually-designated spot at the end of a flight of steps: in one building up, in the other down. Both conducted their affairs in a liturgical language that was as rigidly traditional as it was unintelligible to the outsider. In the one, it was Latin ("Dominus vobiscum." "Et cum spiritu tuo."); in the other a brusque shorthand ("I am limited, I'm ½p out in 250." "I could deal one way." "Very well, you may open me." "Give you ½p." "Sorry, I'm a buyer at 127½."). In both, boys or younger men flitted about the periphery of the action, serving the older protagonists who they aspired one day to become. The two halls, just a mile and a half apart, were rather different in volume and tone, with frenzied shouting as against singing and silence. But the language and rhythms of the body were in both cases as essential as speech: palms in to buy, palms out to sell, palms together to pray, palms down to bless. Most importantly for us, both rituals epitomized the concerns of a great number of absent persons and powers, concerns that could touch matters material, political, or transcendent, or all three together.[1]

There is more going on in market transactions, of which commodity exchange is a paradigm case, than the coordination of individual plans. Under the hood, so to speak, one finds shared norms of right conduct that suffice on their own to refute the cartoonish view of the market as a morality-free zone. But the rules of the game do not explain themselves. How did commodity traders come to speak their own private language? Why do we accept markets in stocks but not in slaves, markets for surrogate wombs and fashion advice but not for votes or admission to elite colleges? These are not mere concatenations of individual choices, any more than a religious ritual is. Market patterns can be fully explained and justified only by referring to the transformative moral projects that all communities entail.

To make my own agenda clear, the grammar of common goods cannot be kept perpetually at arm's length from the market if we want to understand its moral architecture. How and where should we apply the logic of common action? We might test it on either of the two key levels of markets: merchants and their bargains, or the social frame of exchange. Chapter 7 will investigate the radical proposal that ordinary buying and selling is itself a form of fraternity with common goods of its own. But the civil economists' claim that merchants *are* generally striving for solidarity will seem just as hard to swallow as Hayek's notion that citizens are *not.* The present chapter, by contrast, respects the widespread sense that politics aims at shared goals, and markets at private gain. On the "instituted" model, it is the market's social frame that involves common action, not price-centered exchange. This model differs from the commonsense view, however, by its keen sense of the entanglement between the two domains. Large-scale market formation has always been a political project,[2] so self-interested merchants are drawn indirectly, and often unwittingly, into the shared goals of the communities that endorse and uphold SSS exchange relations. Yet the influence runs both ways: any community that institutes widespread market exchange will find its own common ends profoundly shaped, and not infrequently hindered, by the very lack of common action among merchants.

The tradition of mainstream economics is poorly equipped to deal with the "moral ecology" of the market.[3] The protagonist of most economic theory is a "rational fool" who cannot fathom modes of human action other than the disinterested exchange of private goods.[4] He is all too apt to construe the cultural and political background of the market as if it were itself an aimless instrumental order, much as Hayek's spontaneous model does. The more sensible point of departure, going back to Plato and Aristotle, is to imagine the polity as a great household, or a ship of state, or a body politic—in any case as a species of common action around common ends. As Hayek implicitly recognizes, politics tends to transform everything it touches in its own image, so a morally thick, communalist conception of the political regime would threaten the idea of a fully instrumentalist, ends-free market.

Threatening though such a notion may be to standard economic theory, it is foundational for an alternative twentieth-century approach to the market: the tradition of moral economy.[5] The canonical figures of this broad movement include historians such as R. H. Tawney and E. P. Thompson, anthropologists such as Marcel Mauss and Margaret Mead, classicists such as Moses Finley, and the hard-to-categorize figure on whom I shall concentrate in this chapter: Karl Polanyi. At the heart of the moral economy school is the claim that the competitive mechanism of the emporium is not a form of common action and is therefore discontinuous (in one sense, as I will explain) with the dense civic action of the forum that upholds it. Therefore, the modern market breaks with age-old patterns of securing human livelihood, by adopting "a rationalized economic system [in place of] a system in which exchange of goods was not a mechanical but a moral transaction, bringing about and maintaining human, personal relationships between individuals and groups."[6]

Yet discontinuity is not the whole story for the moral economist. To stand in this alternative intellectual universe is to bring into focus also the forms of solidarity and collective goals that give the market system its stability, much as they did in any premodern arrangement. A wide comparative perspective shows that a primary concern of any economic system is to align the forces of production and exchange with political goals of stability and shared flourishing within a moral order. In other words, with some conception of The Common Good. Against this background, the individualist market ceases to look like the uniquely efficient rational solution to the "economic problem" and begins to look more like a paradoxical and parochial answer that reflects a prevailing liberal regime.

The project of this chapter is to develop a constructive account of markets and common action, drawing critically on Karl Polanyi's patchwork model of atomistic SSS exchange within communalist politics. I will first lay out his method and findings—which are less well known and less elegantly theorized than the economist's invisible hand—and then integrate and clarify them with the grammar of Aristotelian pluralism. The overall trajectory of ancient and modern political economy reveals market formation to be a political project, instituted in service of some shared vision. However little Strangers Selling Stuff may appreciate the fact, their trading belongs to a transformative moral order that must ultimately be assessed in terms of common goods. What worried Polanyi, and should worry us still, is that the aspirations of modern liberalism have obscured this civic foundation and allowed the beneficial logic of the invisible hand to metastasize into an all-consuming ideology of the self-regulating market. The insightful core of his critique is that the "fictitious commodities" of land, labor, and money are common ends that cannot be coordinated well and justly by anonymous private exchange. It is no part of my project, however, to support Polanyi's strangely simplistic conclusion that market societies should be rejected *in toto*. His own patchwork perspective suggests that market exchange can be variously instituted so as to serve flourishing communities, whether by firm political guidance or (in an option that Polanyi, again strangely, never contemplates) by relaxing the norm of merchant impersonality. In any event, common goods can never be justly left out of account, for a market economy *is* a moral economy.

ON MORAL ECONOMY

The first task of this chapter is to conjure, all too briefly, the imaginary of the moral economist. The intellectual tools of moral economy become, in the hands of a master such as Karl Polanyi, a deep source of insight into the modern market world. But these insights are approached more easily by first considering the nonmarket economies where they lie much closer to the surface. What we must first do, in a word, is to set aside the verities of the economics textbook so as to look with the eyes of the anthropologist. Once we have in hand some of the key ideas that anthropologists have gleaned from studying primitive economies, we will be in a better position to make use of Polanyi's analysis of the market world.

The theoretical heart of the moral economic perspective is the idea of the embedded economy.[7] It is almost a truism of anthropologists and classicists that "man's economy, as a rule, is submerged in his social relationships,"[8] as Polanyi often repeats. Across the premarket world, from ancient Athens to the Pacific Islands and even some peasant villages in the developed countries of today, nearly all goods and services are produced and exchanged within the context of relations of status and authority.[9] In a traditional embedded economy, it is not the coordination of anything like a price-centered market but instead the norms and needs of many other institutions—for example, family, religion, politics—that determine what is made and how it is allocated. Polanyi argues that this social integration of economic life is accomplished in three main modes, which can also be combined: reciprocity (gift and countergift), redistribution (movement to and away from a political center), and householding (production for one's own use).[10] In each mode, thick social norms encroach so closely onto the task of provisioning human life that there arises no specifically "economic" domain of life with its own distinct purposes and modes of conduct. What we would now call "the economy" is theoretically and culturally invisible, camouflaged by the institutions and social relations in which human livelihood is sought.

To put some flesh on the idea of an embedded economy, consider Margaret Mead's description of the situation of a tribesman from Papua New Guinea, whom she observed in the 1930s:

> A typical Arapesh man, therefore, is living for at least part of the time . . . on land that does not belong to him. Around the house are pigs which his wife is feeding, but which belong either to one of her relatives or one of his. Beside the house are coconut and betel palms which belong to still other people, and the fruit of which he will never touch without the permission of the owner. He hunts on the bushland belonging to a brother-in-law or a cousin at least part of his hunting time, and the rest of the time he is joined by others on his bush, if he has some. He works his sago in others' sago clumps as well as in his own. Of the personal property in his house that which

> is of any permanent value, like large pots, well carved plates, good spears, has already been assigned to his sons, even though they are only toddling children. His own pig or pigs are far away in other hamlets: his palm trees are scattered three miles in one direction, two in another: his sago palms are still further scattered, and his garden patches lie here and there, mostly on the lands of others. If there is meat on his smoking rack over the fire, it is either meat which was killed by another, a brother, a brother-in-law, a sister's son, etc.—and has been given to him, in which case he and his family may eat it, or it is meat which he himself killed and which he is smoking to give away to someone else, for to eat one's own kill, even though it be only a small bird, is a crime to which only the morally, which usually means with the Arapesh mentally, deficient would stoop. If the house in which he is, is nominally his, it will have been constructed in part at least from the posts and planks of other people's houses, which have been dismantled or temporarily deserted, and from which he has borrowed timber. He will not cut his rafters to fit his house, if they are too long, because they may be needed later for someone else's house, which is of a different shape or size. . . . This then is the picture of a man's ordinary economic affiliations.[11]

In this embedded economy, everyday essentials such as food, clothing, and shelter, which in a market would be allocated through prices, appear as ingredients of various cross-cutting social relations. The use and movement of those items can be thus seen and regulated, in a fairly straightforward way, as a dimension of the common action of family, neighborhood, clan, and so forth. Polanyi comments that "such a situation must exert a continuous pressure on the individual to eliminate economic self-interest from his consciousness to the point of making him unable, in many cases (but by no means all), even to comprehend the implications of his own actions in terms of such an interest."[12] To act in a market-like, disinterested way, by ignoring the position and concerns of one's counterparties, would be viewed as "morally deficient" and would be so socially costly that, all things considered, it would very seldom pay.

The Arapesh example should not mislead us into thinking that moral economies of this kind were necessarily small or simple. The famous *kula* trade of the Trobriand Islands, first described by Bronisław Malinowski, comprised a complex exchange system conducted over hundreds of miles, in open boats and over many years, without the assistance of money or prices.[13] The participants in this aristocratic trade had a partner in both the clockwise and counterclockwise directions along the rim of a roughly circular archipelago, whom they met annually or with even less frequency. White-shell armbands of great prestige traveled in one direction around the ring, and equally prized red-shell necklaces moved the other way in a slow dance that could bring the very same object back to a previous "owner" after ten years or more. Though engaging in the *kula* was a privilege and an obligation for persons of a certain standing, the gift exchanges themselves occurred with a great show of modesty and generosity on the part of all concerned. The perilous *kula* voyages were important social and political events that also gave occasion for more prosaic barter involving less ceremonial objects, but even the sharp bargains of this *gimwali* exchange must be disguised as something other than straight haggling, perhaps by "accidentally" dropping an item to be exchanged, to be discretely picked up later. Though the *kula* trade was notable for its spectacle, it is by no means the only long-distance or large-scale exchange system of its kind. Marcel Mauss described an earthier but equally obligatory custom of *wasi*, in which mountain villagers left a part of their produce at the house of a partner in a maritime settlement, to be reciprocated in due time with a catch of fish.[14]

The study of such embedded economies forms the imagination of the moral economist, who is especially sensitive to the ways in which an economy reflects and is governed by larger social goals. In primitive economies, there is no distinct intellectual puzzle about how to organize an economy around common ends, just because there is no separate standard of "market efficiency" that could pull against the overall flourishing of family, sect, or clan. The roles and norms that govern economic life just *are* the roles and norms of various communities oriented to various common goods. There may be tensions and perplexities, of course, wars and rumors of war, but economic problems are not separable from the general challenge of flourishing together.

As far as the anthropological data go, economies thus bound up with common action are so widespread that they can be considered a "natural" or baseline state. Contrast this with the "state of nature" myth favored by economics textbooks, the story of Robinson Crusoe alone on his island.[15] There are no common ends for Robinson Crusoe, since there is no one to share anything with, and the market models that are built on his solitary rationality have no room for common ends either. To the extent that economistic models are correct and comprehensive in describing the world of the market, as Hayek suggested, the study of primitive embedded economies has little to contribute to our understanding of ourselves, except as a nostalgic or utopian alternative. Yet we have seen that Hayek's model of an aimless spontaneous order fails to explain the political and legal framework of the price system, so it falls silent about any larger common ends that may be at work. I contend that the historical work of Karl Polanyi, steeped in the logic of the moral economy, can go a long way toward completing the picture of common action and the market.

THE MARKET IN HISTORY, AND IN POLITICS

Laissez-faire *was planned; planning was not.*

—Karl Polanyi, *The Great Transformation*

What is natural does not have a history, except in the slow eons of evolution. This may explain Hayek's relative lack of interest in the history of markets, which he paints as spontaneously evolving behind the back of human actors.[16] For Polanyi and the tradition of moral economy, the modern market is not so much natural as "naturalized." Over the past several centuries, market relations have become "second nature," a customary way of being together that is so deeply and widely pervasive that we can scarcely think our way past it.[17] But an acquired custom does have a past, and one of Polanyi's most influential contributions has been to draw theoretical insights from the inflection points in the history of market order, where aspects that are normally submerged rise to the surface. I rehearse Polanyi's historical survey here as a way of illustrating the on-the-ground social realities that the patchwork model of common action is meant to explain. That history, in a nutshell, recounts centuries of incremental change (sometimes "spontaneous" but often dictated from above), abruptly culminating in the cataclysmic imposition of the self-regulating market system during the period 1780–1830.[18] It is not wrong to describe this long metamorphosis—in the terms we just introduced—as a move from an embedded to a disembedded economy. But this black-and-white phrase describes only the ideology and the not the reality of the change, since no actual economy could be entirely lifted clear of its social frame in common action. For Polanyi, "the idea of a self-adjusting market implied a stark utopia"—in other words, the move toward a pure market system was a politically motivated and ultimately futile attempt to undo the nature of human society.

Told at full length, the story of the market would extend back into the haze of prehistoric times. Virtually all societies have made some place for barter or market exchange, which is thus a fourth well-attested mode of ordering human livelihood alongside reciprocity, redistribution, and householding. Until quite recently, however, market exchange played a small and confined role, usually dealing with long-distance trade.[19] Such markets as existed were, as a rule, severely hemmed in by "custom and law, religion and magic" in order to limit their potential for dissolving social bonds.[20] The rise of markets in Europe from a sideshow to the dominant principle of economic organization was not a smooth organic development, in Polanyi's telling; it was the result of conscious political intervention. "Internal trade in Western Europe was actually created by the intervention of the state" by forcing open "fiercely protectionist" municipalities and princedoms in the fifteenth and sixteenth centuries.[21] Despite the increasing size of the markets forged by nascent nation-states, it was "the traditional element of regulation, not the new element of competition" that prevailed in Europe's growing markets for some centuries.[22] No longer governed by custom or magic, mercantilist markets were still kept on a short political leash. "Markets and regulation, in effect, grew up together."[23] Down to the Industrial Revolution, political intervention both created and controlled Europe's markets.

The trend of tight political control, a vestige of the embedded economy, was quickly and decisively overturned in the key development that lends the title to Polanyi's best-known work, *The Great Transformation*. In the early nineteenth century, first England and then all of Europe relinquished close political oversight in favor of the free, price-centered, "self-regulating" market. Polanyi's account of this crucial period, which is also the setting for E. P. Thompson's landmark *The Making of the English Working Class*, centers on the political effort to create markets for everything that goes into economic life. The creation of a labor market was particularly destructive of traditional ways of life, since it involved valuing and moving human beings by means of an impersonal price system, on a scale that had never been attempted before. The suffering that ensued among workers was immense, but as Polanyi mildly comments, "Improvements . . . are, as a rule, bought at the price of social dislocation."[24]

What made this destructive project politically possible, on Polanyi's view, was the growing popular and scientific conviction that markets were natural, the same genre of conviction that lies (often unacknowledged) beneath the economist's canonical model. "For the self-regulating market was now [in the 1830s] believed to follow from the inexorable laws of Nature, and the unshackling of the market to be an ineluctable necessity. The creation of a labor market was an act of vivisection performed on the body of society by such as were steeled to their task by an assurance which only science can provide."[25] Several changes resulted from this great intervention, changes that would appear quite puzzling to those who thought free markets merely brought man back to his natural state. First, it actually increased the need for political oversight of the economy: "To make Adam Smith's 'simple and natural liberty' compatible with the needs of human society was a most complicated affair. . . . The introduction of free markets, far from doing away with the need for control, regulation, and intervention, enormously increased their range. Administrators had to be constantly on the watch to ensure the free working of the system."[26] Second, opposition to the changes from both ends of the political spectrum was more or less spontaneous, continuous, and long-lasting. As Polanyi wittily puts it, "*Laissez-faire* was planned; planning was not."[27] The political history of the later nineteenth century across Europe was in large part a history of various legal and revolutionary attempts to cope with the advance of markets. Polanyi famously calls this prolonged reaction, together with the free-market project that provoked it, the "double movement." If anything, the reaction was more "natural" than the market project, because the former aligned with the time-honored "principle of social protection aiming at the conservation of man and nature as well as productive organization,"[28] goals to which the SSS market per se is indifferent. The push and pull of markets and social protection is a dynamic that is still powerfully at work in politics today.[29]

In more theoretical terms, the transformation toward a market system could be called the "Great Disembedding," because it saw the economy break free from the norms of kinship, religion, and politics, so that it could be socially imagined as a distinct sphere of human life unfolding according to its own "natural" processes.[30] According to the ideal of the self-regulating market economy, as Polanyi describes it, "order in the production and distribution of goods is ensured by prices alone."[31] All problems of supply or demand are solved by the invisible hand, so to speak, by merchants raising and lowering their prices. As we have seen, one can order an economy by means other than prices, such as by political fiat or social custom. The ideal of the self-regulating market is defined in opposition to all so-called interference from nonmarket sources. It requires "markets for all elements of industry, not only for goods (always including services) but also for labor, land and money."[32] Any nonmarket limits on key inputs might, at some point, prevent a given market from finding its price, sparking a crisis of excess or deficiency requiring political intervention. Only when all these elements trade on "numberless" discrete markets, and link up to form "One Big Market,"[33] can the price mechanism operate autonomously over time.

Thus far, Polanyi's account seems to depict the historical unfolding of a system that in many ways resembles Hayek's vision of the "Great Society," with more emphasis on its "nonspontaneous" origins as an overt political project, a dimension that Hayek recognized but downplayed rhetorically.[34] If this were the extent of Polanyi's theory, it would shed only a feeble light on our efforts to understand the market's civic role through a grammar of common action. But Polanyi, as a moral economist, is also acutely aware that the ideal of the self-regulating market did not, and could not, accurately capture the full reality of market order.

THE FICTION OF AUTONOMOUS MARKETS

The crude merchant-versus-citizen imaginary envisions a price-guided economic domain operating alongside, and largely independent of, the world of politics and civil society, serving their purposes indirectly by increasing wealth and opportunity. Polanyi shows that the domains of politics and the economy, while distinct, are far more entangled. The SSS market system does not simply serve the pregiven projects of civil society, whatever these may be; it radically transforms them, because "a market economy can function only in a market society."[35] If a self-regulating market required only, say, that the market for grain be linked to the markets for hogs and straw, its political implications would be slight. But the market also demands the inclusion of the "fictitious commodities" of labor, land, and money, which are "none other than the human beings themselves of which every society consists and the natural surroundings in which it exists. To include them in the market mechanism means to subordinate the substance of society itself to the laws of the market."[36] The result of the "Great Disembedding," then, was not an autonomous market economy rendered independent of society, but an inversion of their traditional relations of priority: the world turned upside down. For Polanyi, the move toward the self-regulating market gave rise to "a whole society embedded in the mechanism of its own economy—*a market society*."[37]

Polanyi's central notion of "fictitious commodities" does not entail that humans cannot treat land, labor, and money *as if* they were commodities, for we clearly can. His claim is that they *are not* commodities. To consistently pretend that they are, not only rhetorically but institutionally, is to engage in a vast collective fiction—that is, a departure from reality, which will prove as unjust and destructive as treating a marriage as nothing but a source of income and free meals. Land, labor, and money refuse to behave "as though they are produced for the market—that is, to be stored, transported, and withheld from sale until their true price is revealed."[38] The nineteenth-century attempt to treat these three goods like any other commodity proved as damaging to the economy as it was to the overall prospects of human flourishing. Let us look more closely at these three fictions.

(1) "Labor" is just another name for human activity as it relates to the economy, and the market ideal demands that it should be measured solely (or primarily) by prices in the form of wages. But human activity cannot be intelligibly divorced from richer moral and social

considerations. Polanyi remarks that, "in actual fact, man was never as selfish as the theory demanded. . . . On closer investigation, he was found to be acting on remarkably 'mixed' motives, not excluding those of duty towards himself and others—and maybe, secretly, even enjoying work for its own sake."[39] Even in a market system the worker does not aim primarily "at safeguarding his *individual* interest in the acquisition of material possessions, but rather at ensuring social good will, social status, social assets. He values possessions primarily as a means to that end. . . . Under capitalism . . . his *standing with his fellows* will depend upon the level of his income."[40] In the "heroic period of laissez faire,"[41] British policy sought to reduce the human dimensions of work to material gain alone; for the rest of the nineteenth century it reaped what it had sown in the form of social turmoil and political backlash—the action and reaction of Polanyi's "double movement." When a century's worth of political dust had settled, "the labor market was allowed to retain its function only on condition that wages and conditions of work, standards and regulations should be such as would safeguard the human character of the alleged commodity, labor."[42] It is no accident that human work today is overseen by nonmarket institutions ranging from the Department of Labor to the practical moralists of the pulpit, the advice column, and the TV drama *The Office*. At bottom, they all sing variations on the same tune: labor is more than a commodity, even when it sports a price tag.

(2) "Land" is a catchall term for the aspects of the natural environment that underlie every human activity, even in today's knowledge economy. Traditionally, the social and moral restrictions on human interactions with nature were many and complex. Consider the elaborate laws of land inheritance that lie behind Jane Austen's novels: the drama of *Pride and Prejudice* arises because Mr. Bennett is not free to simply sell his land and give the proceeds to his daughters, rather than entailing it to a distant and disliked relative. The move to a self-regulating market, which (in Polanyi's account) took hold shortly after Austen's death in 1817, required that that land be considered primarily for its market value. In the words of Jeremy Bentham, who inspired profound land reforms in the 1830s, "The condition most favourable

to the prosperity of agriculture exists when there are no entails, no unalienable endowments, no common lands, no right of redemption, no tithes . . ."[43] In a vision like Bentham's, Polanyi writes, "labor and land are made into commodities, which, again, is only a short formula for the liquidation of every and any cultural institution in an organic society."[44] For "land" in the broad sense "invests man's life with stability; it is the site of his habitation; it is a condition of his physical safety; it is the landscape and the seasons. We might as well imagine his being born without hands and feet as carrying on his life without land."[45] Thinking of land in mere money terms leaves these human dimensions substantially out of account, along with political concerns such as food security or materiel for war. It is no surprise, then, that the nineteenth-century attempt to put a price on nature met with reactions as various as romantic agrarianism and territorial nationalism. Today, human interchange with the environment is a concern of practically every US government department from Energy to the EPA to the FDA, and of nearly any civic group one can name. Again, there is a market for land, but price is no more than half the story.

(3) "Money" would seem like the paradigmatic market institution, since exchange requires some medium of exchange. As Polanyi tells it, the high-water mark of a market-based approach to money was the gold standard, consolidated in England in the Bank Charter Act of 1844. By fixing the ratio of currency to gold reserves, the gold standard left the supply of money to the forces of supply and demand, supposedly safe from political meddling. Yet throughout the later nineteenth century "the market administration of purchasing power would periodically liquidate business enterprise,"[46] thanks to the deflationary roller coaster that the gold standard set in motion. It is only a slight exaggeration to say that by construing this central dimension of exchange as itself a commodity, rather than a social institution of reciprocity, the market economy was implicitly committed to destroying itself every decade or two.[47] The wild and destructive ride of commodity money was not brought under control until the advent of effective central banking after the turn of the twentieth century, when the supply of money was brought more firmly under the control of political

institutions such as the US Federal Reserve. Only when money was anchored outside the market could the market itself function smoothly over longer periods, and only then could merchants relate to one another on reasonably stable terms.[48]

THE SOCIAL FRAME OF ANONYMOUS EXCHANGE

On Polanyi's account, then, there are two main dimensions of market order that cannot be fully explained as a spontaneous coordination of individual projects: its origins and the ongoing integration of the "fictitious commodities." Both require a much fuller account of the politics of the market than we saw in Hayek's notion of the private law as a political referee. As to its origins, the history of the market is a story of political construction and maintenance, not of organic growth. It took concerted effort by the state to shift an economy off its historical modes of embeddedness, such as medieval feudalism and even early-modern mercantilism. "The road to the free market [in the 1800s] was opened and kept open by an enormous increase in continuous, centrally organized and controlled interventionism."[49] As to its ongoing function, a system of unimpeded laissez-faire slides quickly from competition toward monopoly, which is a kind of perverse analogue to the embedded economy in that it reintroduces power into the price system.

Even more crucially, the essential factor markets for land, labor, and money can be produced and maintained only as common political projects. On Polanyi's account, in order to present them as though they were self-standing commodities, a subsequent act of collective interpretation is needed. Since these key factors are dimensions of common action, they are common concerns and could not fail to be such, even when we agree to put them under the discipline of the market. It is more honest, in a sense, to approach them as "political footballs" rather than aspiring to scientific detachment, which can endanger the whole system by obscuring the fact that the market is a vast and morally consequential political project. For Polanyi, it is this "reality of society" that the fictions of the market are meant to cover up, as a way of earning for the market program the political respect due to "nature."

Though Polanyi's framework was derived from historical data, it has proven highly influential on leading empirical models of state and market within political science. In his 2018 study *Marketcraft*, Steven Vogel notes that there is a "virtual consensus" among scholars of many disciplines that markets are "complex institutions that must be created and sustained by the visible hand of the government."[50] Much like Polanyi, Vogel aims to shift the terms of public and scholarly debate away from a zero-sum tug-of war between "market" and "government" as fully contrasting forms of order, since they presuppose as much as they oppose one another. As Vogel puts it, the ongoing maturation of markets usually depends on "re-regulation" rather than deregulation, so more market and more government usually go hand in hand. Nor should one forget that "the government is the largest consumer, employer, lender, borrower, insurer, and property owner in modern market economies."[51] Vogel's comparative study of industrial economies in the postwar period confirms Polanyi's thesis that no durable market develops without the political action that is often mislabeled as government "intervention."

Polanyi's now-classic analysis, supplemented by contemporary findings, provides us a rich vein of historical and theoretical resources for understanding the links between market exchange and common action. On this picture, I will argue, the market system turns out to be as much a recapitulation of the historical rule of the economy embedded in society as an exception to that rule. To the extent that the modern market is indeed a historical anomaly, this can be credited to the liberalism of the encompassing order rather than the unique political location of today's economy. Before attempting a concrete interpretation of the liberal market regime, however, we need to develop a better abstract model of markets and common ends that can serve where Hayek's continuity account falls short. To elaborate such an account I will rely on another historical touchstone of the moral economy school— ancient Greece, to which the mature Polanyi increasingly turned as part of his (ultimately fruitless) quest to envision a decent, marketless society. The advantage of classical Greece, by comparison with the modern era, was that its newborn market stood in stark contrast to the communalist principles of the prevailing regime, and so could not hide its valence with respect to the common goods of politics.

MARKETS UNDER COMMON GOODS

"I have never yet been afraid of any men, who have a set place in the middle of their city, where they come together to cheat each other and perjure themselves." Cyrus [the Great, Emperor of Persia, d. 530 BC] intended these words as a reproach against all the Greeks, because of their having market-places where they buy and sell, which is a custom unknown to the Persians.

—Herodotus, *The Persian Wars* 1.153

We return to the theoretical puzzle left unsolved by Hayek's economistic approach: how to situate the market in relation to common action and shared ends. Hayek sidestepped this challenge by claiming that a liberal "Great Society" does not itself have any common ends and that, even if it did, the market depends on politics only for private law, not for common action. Our task, then, is to draw on Polanyi's insights to constructively theorize what the failure of Hayek's argument only implied: that the market is intimately related to the political regime, serving the common ends of citizens in some positive sense. A model built on Polanyi's account of the instituted market will, and probably should, have a certain paradox about it, because it will have to portray private action as publicly authorized and explain common projects that culminate in individual activity. This sort of twist seems to be constitutive of liberal orders, as I will discuss in the next section. Modeling the contemporary market in these terms is thus a backhanded way of confirming the moral economist's rule of thumb that broader political norms overshadow the economy.

Polanyi assumes a sharp conceptual distinction between market exchange and sociopolitical action as two contrasting forms of order, and he never admits that the reality may be less tidy. Concerning the market relation itself, Polanyi differs very little from the economics textbook's zone of price-centered, disinterested exchange, where merchants meet as strangers and equals. But he enormously enriches the account of where SSS exchanges come from and what makes them possible, replacing Adam Smith's idea of a natural "propensity to truck, barter, and exchange" with a historically grounded view of the market's political origin and presuppositions.[52] If the natural or baseline state of human affairs is an economy knotted up with norms of common life, then open market spaces are a sign of political intervention, not inactivity or restraint. "There was nothing natural about *laissez-faire*; free markets could never have come into being merely by allowing things to take their course."[53] To find a significant dimension of an economy lacking direct reference to any dimension of common flourishing is itself a sign of common action that changed this basic orientation and prevents it from springing back to its "natural" state. In other words, the disinterest of SSS market relations is a social product, not a natural fact or a mere aggregate of individual behaviors. In their day-to-day activity of trading for private gain, merchants can be said to be conforming to a role that was forged, and even prescribed, by the activity of politics. The pursuit of gain may thus be described both as individual end, which is how merchants are apt to see it, and also as a common end of a certain kind. This duality can be perceived most easily where shared political concerns sharply contrast with the methods of the market, as in ancient Greece.

Much like Rome, classical Athens grew too large to be supported by its hinterlands, so it became highly dependent upon imports for its food supply (*trophē*). Athens therefore took pains to ensure that the Piraeus, its harbor town, housed a bustling international market for grain. By treaty, all ships bound for Athens received special treatment in the grain ports of the Black Sea. Likewise, all merchants bearing grain were offered special legal status once they arrived in Athens, which other noncitizens did not enjoy. Xenophon in his *On Revenues* proposed honoring deserving merchants with seats in the theater.[54] These benefits were open to all, irrespective of status or origin. By focusing on the commodity, not the person, Athens opened up genuine market relations around grain.

We can see in this example that Athens's political interest in its *trophē* prompted the *polis* to expand and endorse the market for grain. "Foreign policy *was* food policy."[55] A reliable *trophē* trumped the interests of Athenian shipowners or merchants who might have benefited from a protectionist grain trade. To be sure, grain traded on an administered market, not a laissez-faire free-for-all. Athenians were prohibited from exporting grain even if prices were higher elsewhere, and a return cargo of grain or some other necessary commodity was a condition of every sea loan.[56] Merchants from other Greek cities could buy only limited quantities of the grain that arrived in Athens, even if they were willing to pay a premium for it.

The market was kept at arm's length from the city, both physically and socially. The grain emporium at the Piraeus was several miles distant from Athens, connected only by a fortified road called the "Long Walls." And because of the threat that sharp dealing was thought to pose to common life, citizens of any standing rarely stooped to trade on the emporium, or at least did not boast about it.[57] There was little chance for a market mentality to spread from the grain trade to, say, the control of land, since the noncitizens (metics and foreigners) who did the bulk of the trading on the emporium were generally prohibited from owning land in Attica. Retail merchants on the *agora*, a marketplace inside the city proper, might be low-status Athenians, but they too were closely overseen by "grain commissioners," who offered a standing bribe of public honors for selling grain at the conventionally recognized "just price" of five drachmas per medimn, no matter what the wholesale price was.[58] If the prevailing price rose too high, many Greek poleis would use a public fund (sponsored by the wealthy) to buy grain at the market rate and would resell it to their citizens at five drachmas. Athens's grain market, then, was moved by many forces beyond supply and demand, but this very impurity shows forth the basic point all the more clearly: it was for political common ends that Athens opened a market space wide enough to ensure a reliable *trophē*—but no wider. For the merchant, "whose only fatherland is profit,"[59] these boundaries appear as limitations. But from the perspective of the polis, the social relations and practices circumscribing the market were the very stuff of Athens's common life, which the grain market had been instituted in order to promote.

If this is the typical or even necessary civic backdrop of the market, as Polanyi maintains, then merchants must be seen as (perhaps unwitting) collaborators in a grand political project that has opened up a space for market relations to take place and that works continually to keep that space from expanding or contracting unduly. There are thus at least two fundamental roles in the instituted market, two perspectives that the individual can adopt. The originating role, if we follow Polanyi, is that of the statesman, the maestro whose political prudence orchestrates the extent and location of markets in light of the common ends of politics.[60] When the citizens or magistrates of Athens elected to enlarge or support the grain markets by political means, they acted as statesmen. But SSS markets also require merchants, whose calculating rationality does not acknowledge any common goods. Even while emphasizing the social ecology of markets, one must acknowledge the merchant's perspective as widespread and phenomenologically valid. The grain traders of Athens were basically concerned with turning a profit on their shipping runs, not with the *trophē* that the statesman had in view. The two perspectives are mutually exclusive but hierarchical. The statesman has to be aware of how merchants think without entering into their point of view, the better to govern it. The merchant qua merchant takes no account of the statesman's point of view and so can be no more than an unwitting participant in the larger project of an instituted market.[61]

With two opposing views available to the individual, there is necessarily a third option, not so much a perspective as a perplexity: the one who must decide between the two points of view. Suppose that if I sell my grain now, I will realize a large profit but hurt the war effort. Should I act as a statesman or a merchant? Conflicting goods of this kind are not unique to the instituted market. If I am a father and a basketball coach, my dual role may put the common ends of family and team into conflict. As Alasdair MacIntyre writes, "Each individual as a practical reasoner has to answer the question of what place it is best that each of those goods should have in her or his life."[62] The tension is yet more acute in the case of the instituted market, however, because the perspective of the merchant is (by stipulation) incompatible with the perspective of the citizen, rather than merely in tension with it, and yet the merchant's role is authorized by the common action of the polis. The merchant who hurts the war effort seems to act both in accord with the city's common end and against it. She furthers it in a formal sense by playing an authorized role but hinders it by her concrete act. It was perhaps to avoid such dilemmas that Athenian citizens customarily did not engage in the grain trade (or in any commerce at all, if they could avoid it).[63] The role of citizen is less fraught if it is not mixed with that of merchant.

The perceptive statesman will realize, as the Athenians apparently did, that there is a price to pay for market spaces, the "opportunity cost" of a good forgone. The decision to prosecute any particular exchange follows on a prior choice to engage in market relations at all, which incurs this cost. Since market exchange on the SSS model precludes common action, it is precisely common goods that are an opportunity cost of markets.[64] The choice to exchange grain (or clothing, or fuel, or iPhones, etc.) on a market is a choice *not* to exchange as part of common action, by means of reciprocity or redistribution, which would "make common" some benefit that shows up on the market as private. This "making common" generates or sustains a variety of properly common goods in addition to the item in question.

Market exchange has a civic cost, then, even when it is economically "efficient." Relational goods are not "priced into" a market transaction.[65] Tradable goods and performances may abound among the "strangers and equals" in a market, but common goods simply vanish (if merchants are not perfect strangers, then this will not be perfectly true, a possibility I explore in the next chapter). In the example of Athens, an adequate *trophē* was deemed more important, for good and obvious reasons, than the embodiment of the common life in the economy of grain. Any common goods in this domain were forgone for the sake of the overall flourishing of the polis, which would presumably encourage common goods in other realms such as culture, education, or sport. So the opportunity cost of markets may be well worth paying, but the statesman or citizen cannot overlook that it must be paid.

Our model has begun to reconnect the market exchange and common action that it began by distinguishing quite sharply. At this stage, the social map looks rather like Swiss cheese, with an array of empty market spaces defined by the thick texture of common life that surrounds and limits them. These bubbles of disinterest are not themselves forms of common action, but they are instituted for the sake of various communities, which allows the statesman to deliberate about market patterns roughly in cost-benefit terms: on the liability side the absence of common goods and the merchant's studied indifference to politics, and on the asset side the rich harvest (both of wealth and of negative freedom) that a well-crafted market can reap.

The statesman should ask, "If we foster markets *here* or *here*, thereby forgoing common action in those areas, what will be the effect upon the overall flourishing of the polity, and what will be the stamp of character it impresses upon its citizens?" Albert Hirschman's classic account of the rival historical views of market society elegantly categorizes the main historical responses to this question, some of which see the market as good and others as bad, some as strong and others as weak.[66] Montesquieu and many classic liberal thinkers thought that relying upon *le doux commerce* as much as possible would improve citizens by making them diligent and peaceable. Rousseau, like the ancient Greeks and most civic republicans, disagreed.[67] However one assesses the effects of markets on virtue and the polity overall, to see them as instituted in Polanyi's sense is to accord them a larger and more constructive public role than the mainstream economist grants.

THE LIBERAL MARKET REGIME

Not all market-oriented systems are democratic, but every democratic system is also a market-oriented system. Apparently, for reasons not wholly understood, political democracy has been unable to exist except when coupled with the market. An extraordinary proposition, it has so far held without exception.

—Charles Lindblom, *Politics and Markets*

When it comes to understanding the contemporary world, the foregoing model of markets as tools, community-free zones created by and for politics, is not fully satisfactory. It fails fully to capture the significance of the aspiration to organize liberal political economy by means of the market mechanism alone (or above all). Hayek thought such a goal both achievable and desirable; with Polanyi, I would say it is neither. For such a broad political project requires more than allocating particular domains or commodities as marketable, as the ancient Greeks did in order to enhance the common life of citizens. It requires in addition that central common ends be themselves treated in market terms. Because market exchange and common action are (on the normal SSS account) mutually exclusive forms of order, such a change demands a profound transformation of moral and political vision, one that culminates in something like Hayek's "Great Society," an imagined polity that is itself little more than a market. For those habituated to perceiving only coordinated private goods, it becomes difficult to fathom the very idea of a common good, whether in "the economy" proper or in other corners of public life.

A tool that transforms its users is more than a mere instrument, and such is the market within the liberal regime on Polanyi's account. As a way of grappling with the broad trends of liberalism, as outlined above, he critiques the "fictitious commodities" of a "market society." These are terms of his own coinage, never sufficiently spelled out, and his rough theoretical vocabulary ends up obscuring as much as it illuminates. Recasting some of his crucial insights in the grammar of common ends will yield a more rigorous model of the market that is supple enough to shed light on the normative tensions of our own world. Translated into the terms of common action, the gist of Polanyi's complaint runs as follows: as a way of maintaining the market, liberal political economy aspires to treat common goods as though they were private goods. Much like the assessment of firms by profit alone (which we can now see as a special case of a wider trend), this involves a kind of willful blindness, both in descriptive and normative terms. Markets are so central to modern democracy that Polanyi's critique amounts to a wholesale (though not entirely warranted) rejection of the liberal regime. In order to clarify and reframe Polanyi's thought, I must first sketch the broad contours of liberalism in terms that are, I hope, sufficiently familiar and commonplace that they will not arouse too much disagreement.

The paradoxical moral architecture of the modern market world cannot be limned by studying classical Greece, whose nascent market did conform to Hayek's notion of the price system as a *mere instrument* of more substantive projects, a kind of vast public utility. The goal of the Athenians was indeed a morally minimal market, one that would do no more than provide necessary resources for the densely textured moral project of their common life. This explains why they worked so hard to keep the emporium in its place; granting the market political priority would let the tail wag the dog. The early market system of the Greeks was a tool to enhance what Benjamin Constant called the "liberty of the ancients," their capacity for political efficacy and a flourishing common life.[68] The republican instinct for collective self-rule was effaced in the classical liberal authors and the institutions they inspired, in favor of the freedom of the individual, Constant's "liberty of the moderns." This species of freedom consists of the right to "do all that the law permits," in Montesquieu's famous phrase, or as Hayek would have it, "to use one's own knowledge for one's own purposes" by any legal means. Calling up a recurring theme of this chapter, one can envision liberal freedom as "a perfected state of nature: the citizens enjoy the advantages of the state of nature (they 'act as they please') without suffering from its inconveniences (they are freed from war and fear)."[69]

Despite the modern emphasis on the individual, a liberal state can still be called a political regime in a broadly classical sense, in that it provides an authoritative order or hierarchy for the heterogenous goods that clamor for dominance in human life.[70] Ronald Beiner articulates its paradoxical core in these terms: "Liberalism itself instantiates one particular vision of the good, namely, that choice in itself is the highest good. . . . Liberal society does have an ethos. Under the liberal dispensation, the ethos is—lack of ethos."[71] Liberal polity commits itself publicly to private freedom, or (heightening the tension) to the common project of not having a common project. The political instrumentalities employed in this project make clear, however, that liberal freedom is not simply private, as is the unconstraint of the prepolitical "state of nature" famously envisioned by Locke and Hobbes in the 1600s. On the other hand, the fact that liberal freedom is exercised largely by the individual qua individual makes the liberal citizen apt to overlook its roots as a common achievement.

Market-focused economic liberalism in the line of Bentham and Ricardo is a kissing cousin of the liberal political tradition of Hobbes and Locke, younger by about a century and developed in good part as a way of consolidating and extending the elder's achievements.[72] "[A] modern oeconomy . . . is the most effectual bridle [that] ever was invented against the folly of despotism," as Sir James Steuart wrote in 1767.[73] Guided by the invisible hand of prices, the SSS market mechanism mirrors the shared political ideal of facilitating the freely chosen projects of individuals. As a system embodying negative freedom, the price mechanism is, or is supposed to be, in the driver's seat of the economy, with politics serving as its "maintenance squad."

This prioritization of private goods marks a momentous shift, which turns the Swiss-cheese model of ancient markets inside out. One can now envision a "liberal archipelago" in which the market is not a bubble of anonymity within a thick common life, but is rather the encompassing sea of private-goods coordination that forms the context for islands of community pursuing common ends.[74] This indifferent market sea surrounds whole countries (think of the IMF or the "electronic herd" of international finance[75]) just as much as it encompasses individuals, families, or the associations of civil society. Sailing free on this sea, the law-abiding merchant is answerable to no one, only to abstract rules of impersonal exchange. Still, because the practical absence of felt authority is itself the goal of the liberal political project, we can regard the individual liberty of the market as politically embedded, in that it reflects and reinforces the norms and goals of the prevailing regime and must be maintained by it.

I now turn to Polanyi's critique of this pervasive liberal vision, a vision that I have tried (but probably failed) to describe in a nontendentious way. There are many real-world dimensions of inequality or oppression on which one could critique actual liberal states, but Polanyi takes issue with the central ideals as ideals. On his account, the dream of liberalism that no one will be under the thumb of any particular others is built on a foundation of sand: the shared fiction that everything is or can be a market commodity. The self-regulating market requires such a fiction because every key input needs to be up for sale for the system to be stable and free. But some key inputs are not commodities, according to Polanyi's "empirical" definition of a commodity as anything "produced for sale." So, he wants to say, the alleged freedoms of the market are unjust or impossible.

Where does Polanyi's critique actually lead? It is clear that he wants to marshal the idea of the "commodity fiction" as the fulcrum of a critique of market society. As stated, however, Polanyi's argument is inconclusive, or perhaps it fails outright. There is not anything wrongheaded or unjust about selling things that are not produced for sale, or about treating things under conventional fictions. On the auction block at Christie's, a Picasso or some other great work of art is treated much like commodity flip-flops produced and sold in their billions, and the culture of art appreciation has not collapsed. Moreover, the notion that a gold medal is to be prized more than a silver or a bronze is an unobjectionable social fiction. Other fictions are even praiseworthy: the liberal premise (inherited from Christianity) that all persons are fundamentally of equal worth has been decried down the centuries as a fiction that obscures real differences in talent, wisdom, or virtue. Simply styling land, labor, and money as fictitious commodities will not do the normative work that Polanyi wants, as part of his critique of self-regulating market ideal.

Polanyi's critique of economic liberalism is more perspicuous if we treat it as an implicit argument about common goods and the market. Many things—most "goods" and many "services"—may be ordered either through common action or by price-centered SSS markets. What is crucial for justice is that the mode of order at hand be recognized and respected. So, where red-shell necklaces are a badge of honor, as in the *kula* trade, it would be a socially corrosive insult to put them up for sale. But there would be nothing wrong with my putting a piece of jewelry up for auction on eBay, assuming it has no such connection to any common project (which rules out selling my wedding ring). There is nothing in jewelry itself that encourages or resists commodification, normatively speaking. In this sense, it was open to the statesman of ancient Greece to treat grain as a commodity or not, to fix or float its price, in view of the larger concerns of the *trophē*.

On the other hand, there are some goods that cannot be justly marketed—essentially common goods such as friendship, honor, shared practice, and so on. By operating on the non-tuistic SSS market, merchants treat their wares as private goods, which is clearly incompatible with treating them (in this particular context) as common goods. To put a price on common goods may bend them in the direction of the market ideal, but, unlike jewelry, in no social context can they cease to be the ends of common action, because otherwise they would not exist at all. In all such cases, the commodity fiction is necessarily an unjust (and not just an ill-advised) approach to the goods in question. Treating common goods as commodities is damagingly reductive because it ignores their irreducibly social dimensions, and thus harms the persons whose shared ends they are, who have a vital interest in their fulsome and just common achievement. And many such reductions just don't work, as we saw exemplified in the failure of the gold standard.

It seems clear that Polanyi means to describe land, labor, and money as something like essentially common goods, though he lacks the theoretical grammar to do so. He writes, "As the organization of labor is only another word for the forms of life of the common people, this means that the development of the market system would be accompanied by a change in the organization of society itself."[76] Of Polanyi's three objectionable factors, only money is inescapably social in all cases. Land and labor would be relevant to Robinson Crusoe, but in a large-scale social context they will almost always be tied in with forms of common action. Very seldom could their social and moral dimensions be justly left out of account, which helps to explain why the commodity fiction has failed to cover them entirely, such that they remain the object of intense political scrutiny and regulation. Members of a market society are torn between the prevailing ideology, which bids them to treat land, labor, and money (and by implication, for Polanyi, our entire common life) as unproblematically marketable commodities, and the ubiquitous personal experience that this way of treating them proves impolitic and unjust.

Aristotle wrote that defective political regimes do not correspond to "what the city actually is," so they cannot truly serve the common good of all their citizens. In essence, Polanyi wants to make the same point about a liberal market society. For those who care to look, it is clear that labor, land, and money continue to be produced as aspects of common action in its many forms, but they are misconstrued as though they were morally unencumbered, the better to be moved by price alone. This authoritative misinterpretation is encouraged, though perhaps not mandated, by the liberal politics that continually underwrites the "juggernaut market." What is behind the commodity fiction, or generally the façade of liberal neutralism, obvious to political contenders but concealed from the average citizen, is a set of power struggles that help to determine the fate of labor, land, and money. Michael Ignatieff, writing about the apparently neutral state, trenchantly observed that "for all the apparent relativism of liberal society—our interminable debate about what the good in politics consists in—in practice a shared good is administered in our name by the welfare bureaucracies of the modern state."[77] The same insight might be applied, mutatis mutandis, to the institutions of the supposedly neutral and autonomous economy.

Market patterns in land, labor, and money (and to a lesser extent, in other commodities as well) do embody a shared vision of the common good, since they force merchants into a certain way of interpreting the common action underlying these goods—namely, as if it were only private exchange. Recognizing the market's foundations in common action would add a decidedly personal and political dimension to what otherwise seems to be an impersonal process. But explaining the competitive market in such terms would seriously harm its liberal credentials, in that it would no longer epitomize the individual negative freedom that is often seen as the glory and the ultimate justification of the liberal political regime. Now, it is true that the broader liberal regime could (and, in my view, should) be articulated and evaluated in the richer language of common goods, as a way of fully acknowledging "what the city actually is," what it aims to be, and the gap between the two. The same goes for the market. But this deeper vocabulary would require citizens to put aside the morally desiccated language of the balance sheet and clothe themselves, theoretically and institutionally, in the garb of the moral economist. And that would amount to another great transformation.

Though Polanyi did not turn to studying Aristotle until well after writing *The Great Transformation*, his landmark analysis of market society is evidently trying to recapture a view of politics as world-shaping or "architectonic." It is not easy to represent the resulting conception visually. Drawing on earlier metaphors, one could imagine the liberal archipelago floating on a market sea, where the sea itself has political boundaries that influence the weather of individualistic supply-and-demand, rather like a vast wave pool. But this image is unsatisfactory, in that the market is (and for Polanyi, should remain) "outside" politics. Today, the dominant nation-states and international institutions create and sustain the sea of the global market, even as it surrounds them and in many ways escapes their control. Drawing on an image of Pierre Bourdieu's,[78] one might envision the field of force surrounding a magnet, by which iron filings external to the magnet are moved by its action. The point that I am struggling aptly to illustrate is how the pervasiveness of the market both is and is not a dimension of liberal common action. If this fails to be finally coherent, well, that may be Polanyi's point.

STRONG CONCLUSIONS

We are not here concerned with actual, but with assumed motives, not with the psychology, but with the ideology of business. Not on the former, but on the latter, are views of man's nature based. *For once society expects a definite behavior on the part of its members, and prevailing institutions become roughly capable of enforcing that behavior, opinions on human nature will tend to mirror the ideal whether it resembles actuality or not.*

—Karl Polanyi, "Our Obsolete Market Mentality"

The central ideas of Karl Polanyi, like the broader tradition of moral economy, are sparklingly insightful but often enigmatic and inconsistent. By connecting many disciplines in which he is not fully trained—economics, history, politics, anthropology, classics—he crafts what we might call theoretical aphorisms, but little that is systematic. This is not an accusation that Polanyi is not a rigorous thinker; on the contrary, in some regards he may be too rigorous. Like the economists he relentlessly attacks, he ascribes more explanatory value to a parsimonious theory of markets than shifting human affairs will bear out. Even as Polanyi tirelessly argues that market exchange is never the whole story, his polemics come to rely on the SSS view that price-centered self-interest is what actual markets are all about.[79] In his critical register he seems to forget, somehow, that the stylized model is only a model. Furthermore, he persistently speaks as though a pure vision of a comprehensive, self-regulating market was the goal, and even temporarily the result, of all the liberal movements that shaped nineteenth-century political economy.

Polanyi defends his reliance on an economistic ideology of the market on the grounds of its outsized influence, as we see in the epigraph. The normative upshot of his argument is as stark as the categories on which it is built: a liberal market society is basically corrupt, because its central economic mechanism turns on a set of unjust fictions. This blanket rejection drove Polanyi, in the years following the publication of *The Great Transformation*, to seek "good, non-market" alternatives to capitalism and socialism in societies such as ancient Athens and Mesopotamia and early-modern Dahomey in west Africa. What he found, according to his friend, the management guru Peter Drucker, was that market exchange was more prevalent and the societies were less good than he hoped, in that they usually relied on internal slavery and domination to maintain their stability. The failure of Polanyi's quest for a third way, and his evidently mistaken prophecies that the end of the market was near, made him a "deeply disappointed man" by the end of his life, or so Drucker unsympathetically saw it.[80] But there was little else Polanyi could do, so long as he held on to his rigorously consequent analysis of the injustice of the market system and its centrality to the liberal regime.

Polanyi's shortcomings become painfully clear when compared to a less precipitate critic: Aristotle, who argues that defective political regimes are defective because they are partial. Such regimes fix on a part of the truth about their constitution as if it were the whole truth. The dogmatic supporters of oligarchy or the rule of the free poor, Aristotle observes, "suppose that, because they are both speaking up to a point about justice in a sense, they are speaking about justice simply."[81] Aristotle's practical response is a moderate "mixed regime" that combines a number of partial positions into a system of institutions embodying a fuller perspective on who and what counts politically. The higher goal of removing all errors and arranging matters in light of the full truth of human affairs would issue in a "regime of virtue," but this goal Aristotle does not regard as a practical possibility.

Starting in a similar place, Polanyi admits that properly limited international markets for "nonfiction" commodities can be a real political boon, such that the liberal market ideal is also built on the absolutization of a partial truth. But his solution for realizing the goods of common life, in contrast to Aristotle's, is to reject rather than to counterbalance the prevailing market regime. Although Polanyi admits that there is no "inherent tendency of markets towards excrescence,"[82] he regards the market ideology as so potent, so alluring for the liberal temper, that a liberal society will always gravitate toward the market in its leading ideas and institutions. In other words, he thinks that liberal political economy cannot be moderated.[83] It is curious to see a thinker so attentive to the moral dimensions of an economy write off all practical accommodations to and adaptations of the market mechanism as finally unavailing. It seems that Polanyi's long polemic against the ideology of the self-regulating market, like Hayek's crusade against socialism, finally drew him into the categories, even if not the conclusions, of his opponent.

Despite the inadequacies of Polanyi's overall evaluation, the "instituted" model is indispensable for understanding SSS exchange within a framework of common action. Polanyi brilliantly weaves together classical economics with the thicker social inquiry of moral economy to show that SSS markets have always been a publicly constructed space of private action. The resulting patchwork greatly improves upon the pure individualism of Hayek's spontaneous account, pointing up the causal primacy of common action without denying the potential benefits of the invisible hand. And there is no reason why the instituted model of thin markets within thick politics cannot respect the moral priority of common ends over private purposes (in cooperative contexts), which I defended in part 1. In a well-instituted market, the coordinated self-interest of SSS merchants can materially promote common ends to which they remain formally indifferent. This happy outcome demands a hierarchical relation between the two parts of the patchwork, of the kind we saw exemplified in ancient Athens. Citizens' concern for their common goods ought to predominate, both morally and institutionally, over the aggregate private goods of the markets that they establish and maintain by common action. Of course, assigning markets to a subordinate role is no guarantee that a healthy configuration will be found in practice, but it is a start.

This normative structure is impossible to maintain when common ends are conflated with private goods, as they usually will be if the political language of common goods is lost. Polanyi's exhibit A: the "fictitious commodities" that are so central to modern markets. In reality, even when land, labor, and money are presented as ownable property, they are ultimately no more a matter of aggregate private goods than is the flourishing of the business firm. I see an instructive parallel between the ideal of the self-regulating market and Chicago's shareholder-value corporation. In both cases, a morally reductive vision that is blind to the difference between private and common ends ultimately inverts their proper priority. Simply ignoring common goods does not eliminate them; it only gives illicit priority to those who gain a private advantage from the "efficient" movement of divisible goods at the expense of broader common ends. Land, labor, and money should be (and in a sense always are) the object of the political struggle to maintain a just common order among the citizens who share the multiform goods of human life.

Engaging with Polanyi shows, if nothing else, how essential is a grammar of common action for articulating the social reality of the market system. His moral economy is more useful as critique than as a guide, but it does provide one crucial ingredient of a constructive vision: the world of market exchange is itself a kind of patchwork. The frontier between common and private action does not only demarcate politics from the market; it also divides some types of exchange from one another. In Polanyi's somewhat unhelpful vocabulary, there are "genuine" and "fictitious" commodities, and they cannot be evaluated on the same terms. When it comes to ballpoint pens, SUVs, and other merchandise produced for sale, the political project of maintaining markets is crucial in setting the stage for private exchange. Common ends are only indirectly relevant to "genuine" commodities, but no less powerful for all that. What is good for GM is good for America, as the saying went, so everyone who buys or sells a Chevrolet is doing a favor for Uncle Sam. If the merchant is furthering the (dominant vision of The) Common Good, then she is not acting only for her own private ends. Even where merchants remain personally indifferent to the common projects of citizens, the market system resembles a traditional moral economy, embedded in larger common action, far more strongly than it initially seems.

The fictitious commodities are a different story. If Polanyi is right, they are the substance of society in disguise, and their corner of the market patchwork is never a domain of purely private action. Merchants who traffic in land, labor, and money are dealing directly with irreducibly social goods, with aspects of a common project. Unlike pens or cars, these goods are not normatively open to purely private barter, but must remain, in view of the common ends at stake, a matter of common action and attention. Chapter 3's four-dimensional approach to common goods—analyzable as Property, Power, Practice and Product—can always be applied to the fictitious commodities. Polanyi's hasty conclusion that they must necessarily be yanked from the market is mistaken, but not incoherent. He argues on rigorously Smithian lines: anonymous SSS market exchange is indifferent to common ends, but land, labor, and money cannot be rightly ordered without reference to common goods, and therefore they ought to be removed from the SSS market. On the other hand, Polanyi clearly sees that neither traditional hierarchy nor the authoritarian state offers a viable, decent alternative to market coordination under modern conditions.

Polanyi's patchwork analysis of market society founders on this dilemma, stuck between injustice and unviability, because of his strangely uncompromising adherence to the SSS model of exchange. Bafflingly, he does not even notice a seemingly obvious solution to the puzzle of the fictitious commodities: drop the ironclad assumption of impersonality. Where economic relations are not anonymous, they need not be indifferent to common goods. Polanyi himself points out that modern land, labor, and money are already partially under the sway of institutions beyond the market, thanks to the historical double movement by which "the extension of the market organization in respect to genuine commodities is accompanied by its restriction in respect to fictitious ones."[84] There is no need to despair, as Polanyi ultimately did. One might conclude instead that the need to re-embed the fictitious commodities (and the unfeasibility of nonmarket options) presents the most pressing reason to imagine a more richly socialized version of exchange.

Intellectually messy such compromises may be, no less than the tangled social reality of boardrooms and stock exchanges, which we glimpsed at the Chicago Board of Trade.[85] Still, this human complexity would offer a beachhead for reembedding and so circumscribing the market, if one could only think of it in less theoretically pure terms. In the next chapter, I will take the step that Polanyi declined to take. The dilemma of the fictitious commodities points to a heretical possibility that lurks behind the moral economist's whole nested approach to markets: Why not change the rules of the game? If exchange could be instituted as a kind of merchant solidarity, it might bend toward common goods of its own and of the political communities that always underwrite markets.

CHAPTER SEVEN

ON SOCIAL CONTRACTS

The world's largest pickle factory is in Holland, Michigan, a town of thirty-five thousand on the shores of the Great Lakes. The plant is owned by H. J. Heinz Co., the ketchup giant, which is itself controlled by Kraft Foods and Warren Buffett. Despite these tight links to global markets in food and finance, the pickleworks has been notably loyal to the town, in contrast to messy Rust Belt divorces like GM's split from Youngstown. It was 1898 when local farmers committed to providing sufficient cucumbers for the Pittsburgh-based Heinz, and the plant still processes over a million pounds of pickles per day in high season. But the prosperity of Holland, which is immediately apparent to any visitor, does not depend primarily on the fickle allegiance of huge market players such as H. J. Heinz. The economy of western Michigan is anchored in companies that were founded in the area and never left. Some of these, such as Amway cosmetics or Steelcase furniture, are titans in their own right. A thriving ecosystem of lesser-known firms makes wind turbines, auto parts, and batteries for the global supply chain.

Family control and deep local roots have helped to foster a regional business culture that is not determined exclusively by labor costs or competitive pressures. One industrialist, Edgar Prince, donated a sidewalk snowmelt system to extend Holland's shopping season, as well as operating a one-man real estate trust to ensure that downtown landlords would be committed long-term. Beyond philanthropy, firms such as Padnos Scrap Iron and Cascade Industries proactively hire ex-convicts in addition to creating programs to train and mentor local graduates. The roster of civic-minded businesses is long. But one notable dissenter, according to locals, is the Heinz pickleworks. Despite its longevity in Holland, it is controlled from afar and has never departed from a market-centric stance to the point of explicitly supporting the town as part of its operational mission.[1]

The Heinz pickleworks and its peers in Holland reflect two rival answers to a vital question: Is the market a political sphere for citizens' public action or a merely "economic" sphere of private trading? Heinz enacts the long-dominant view of the market as Strangers Selling Stuff: a sphere of contract and self-interest, which (depending on one's political leanings) may or may not need public regulation in order to align with the common good. Inspired by Adam Smith, this view underlies the main arguments of the previous two chapters on Hayek and Polanyi, who agree that market exchanges do not count as a kind of common action, though they disagree about the nature and relevance of the political context. Firms like Padnos Scrap and Steelcase embody a rather different vision, one that does not restrict the point of markets to private goods alone. They seem to regard thriving civic society as one proper goal of exchange rather than a mere by-product. As Fallows and Fallows recount in their recent travelogue *Our Towns*, viable firms and localities operating on such a hopeful view are not hard to find in America today. But this alternative approach to the market has long lacked a convincing theoretical expression in English-language discourse, so the phenomenon has been easy to overlook or to reinterpret in the terms of coordinated self-interest.

The theoretical lacuna has been better addressed abroad, notably by the Italian school of "civil economy," which draws on Adam Smith's Enlightenment contemporary Antonio Genovesi. This tradition reenvisions the market as a fully social piece of an integrated civic system in which the economy aims directly at public ends. According to civil economists, markets should be seen as a sphere of mutual assistance and even fraternity, therefore as a potentially binding and civilizing force. Merchants in a civil market aim to benefit both themselves and their counterparty in much the same way that good citizens or team members aim at some common good shared by all. For Genovesi and his disciples, markets and states alike are bound together not by interdependent self-interest, but rather by public trust (*fede pubblica*) in the reciprocated goodwill of others.

The project of this chapter is to engage with the tradition of civil economy as a resource for understanding how market relations could bear directly on the common good. For the civil economists, all markets are potentially forms of common action, and many, as we see in Holland, already are so in fact. I will argue that what distinguishes civil exchange from standard markets is that concern for common goods is (aspirationally) built into the norms on which merchants trade, without detracting from their primary focus on prices. The mechanisms by which this integration might be accomplished are, to this point, rather underspecified in the leading authors of the civil economy tradition. Building on a hint from Marshall Sahlins, I propose that the doctrine of a "social coefficient" could distinguish civil markets from a fully impersonal price system on the one hand and a nonmarket status economy on the other. According to such a doctrine, the background market price should be adjusted based on the common concerns shared by particular exchanging parties—local community, ethnic identity, participation in a threatened industry, and so on. One key advantage of this approach: less need for government regulation to steer an efficient "civil" market away from specifically social pathologies such as inequality or cultural depletion, since such concerns could be built into the structure of the market itself.

Overall, the socially and morally thick markets of civil economy do provide an attractive ideal of how some key market relations *could* work, notably those problematic markets flagged by Polanyi, which cannot help but deal in common goods. But the account's reformist potential is limited in two ways. A civil market is limited in scope by the range of effective common action, and is also beset by the typical downsides of social cooperation among flawed human beings—subjection to power, potential for marginalization, high transaction costs. Some markets are simply too big or diffuse to be meaningfully "civilized," and any potential benefits must be weighed against moral and material risks. Despite its appeal, then, civil economy is no universal solution. But if none of the three models considered in chapters 5, 6, and 7 can gain a decisive advantage, are we simply at an impasse? To conclude this three-chapter section, I will use a brief case study of the automobile industry to suggest that we adopt a pluralist approach to markets, holding ourselves ready to apply now this and now that model of the market, as the social facts dictate.

INVISIBLE HANDS

It is a truth *almost* universally acknowledged—in stump speeches, op-eds, and Econ 101 textbooks—that markets are a domain of coordinated self-interest among Strangers Selling Stuff. I have called this the Smithian view, since its intellectual pedigree is usually established by means of choice quotations from Adam Smith's *The Wealth of Nations*. Few would disagree that "it is not from the benevolence of the butcher, the brewer, or the baker, that we expect our dinner, but from their regard to their own self-interest."[2] The implied egoism is usually redeemed by a still more famous proof text: "[Every individual] intends only his own gain, and is in this, as in many other cases, led by an invisible hand to promote an end which was no part of his intention."[3] The SSS merchant may be largely indifferent to moral or political concerns, but all the more attentive to the price signals that coordinate individuals' diverging plans and projects so effectively.[4] The market seems to work a kind of moral alchemy, using competition to transform the base metal of self-regard into civic gold. But this synthesized version of civic virtue is not quite the equal of the pure (and possibly mythical) Aristotelian or republican forms in one signal regard: it remains indifferent to any common good. Market prices may give the merchant good reason to refrain from trafficking weapons to her nation's enemies, or to invest in local communities rather than offshoring, but they may well not.[5]

Now, neoliberals of the strict observance could grant that such temptations are possible and yet advocate for a lightly regulated SSS market as the most reliable way to realize the common good. In some cases, no doubt, they are right. But the simple account of the Invisible Hand is helpless when market incentives begin seriously to undermine the political bases of the market itself. To take today's most prominent example, the worldwide rise in authoritarian populism and opposition to free trade is fueled by market inequalities, or so most commentators think.[6] Doubling down on unfettered markets is not a plausible response, from any point of view. Even if a market solution could be forced through, it would only intensify the political turmoil and undermine its own long-term viability.

For a more complex theory of the workings and ends of markets, we should return to Adam Smith himself, who was no crusader for laissez-faire. The idea that Smith envisioned individual satisfactions as the whole point of markets (or of human action in general) is a founding myth cooked up by twentieth-century economists.[7] Smith's humanistic defenders often point out that he wrote two books, and the one he esteemed more, *Theory of Moral Sentiments*, is focused on human connection and sympathy, not self-interest. Indeed, for Smith the "most important" achievement of commercial society is not wealth at all, but "order and good government, and with them, the liberty and security of individuals."[8] Like other classical economists, Smith was also much concerned with the market's distribution of resources among the contending classes of political society. Just two sentences after his oft-cited line about the self-interest of butcher and brewer, Smith observes that "nobody but a beggar chuses to depend chiefly upon the benevolence of his fellow-citizens."[9] The interest that markets promote, then, is not only prosperity but also public freedom from a degrading state of feudal dependence or beggary. The success or failure of a market, on Smith's fuller view, is to be judged not only by an aggregate metric like GDP, but equally, and perhaps primarily, by political ends such as liberty, equality, citizen character, and class concord.[10]

Despite these richer political metrics, there is an important truth in the idea that Smith sees markets in SSS terms as an impersonal realm of coordinated self-interest. He writes, "I have never known much good done by those who affected to trade for the publick good."[11] The job of merchants qua merchants is to make the best deals they can make, not to set limits around the market or to ensure that price incentives pull in the direction of the common good. Such tasks fall to the regulator, legislator, or citizen, looking upon markets from without. In the Econ 101 version of Smith (who bears a suspicious resemblance to Hayek), almost the whole of the job is to furnish public goods and to prevent corruption in the legal system, so that the price system can blow where it wills. A deeper reading of Smith reveals something much closer to the "instituted" model explored in the previous chapter, which involves deep and consequential tensions between two very different sorts of social coordination. His "system of natural liberty" requires active political engagement with the limits and tradeoffs of markets in matters such as education. Technocratic or legalistic approaches alone will not do.[12]

It is far from obvious, to put it mildly, that modern democratic politics can handle the civic challenge that markets pose. We have largely offloaded the task of overseeing markets to bureaucratic regulators. The financial crisis of 2008 showed that these "experts" are apt to be overconfident in market forces, hoodwinked by complex financial schemes, or just bought off. One can only hope that the common good would be safer with a democratic citizenry that has taken market oversight into its own hands.[13] But it is really only a hope, nothing more, for it has never been tried under the conditions of a modern nation-state.

The long-term historical evidence is not encouraging either. Historian Bas van Bavel has suggested, from studies of premodern societies from Iraq to Holland, that markets have a life-cycle of about five centuries in which an initial wave of prosperity yields to decline as markets erode their own civic foundations.[14] Widespread markets for essential goods and services arise in the context of relative political equality and freedom. Expanded market competition on these terms initially yields prosperity, but also growing inequality. Eventually, the winners at the new market game (who may be a different group than previous elites) are able to exploit their increasingly strong position to seize political power and change the rules in their own favor. Because effective price-based allocation depends on a degree of material and legal equality, market mechanisms eventually give way to other forms of economic order. For example, the relatively free and equal city-states of medieval Tuscany parlayed a market system into several centuries of flourishing. But over time, as Machiavelli later lamented, urban market elites dispossessed the lower classes of both freedom and property, and the region declined in power and wealth. Van Bavel's historical analysis finds a surprising ally in the conjectures of Adam Smith himself, who implies that the moral and material downsides of commercial societies will land them back in misery after a few centuries of broad opulence.[15] Some would say that our wave has already peaked.

However things may turn out for us, Smithian views (whether in their more nuanced, original form or in a cruder, neoliberal version) still set the broad terms of public debate today: Do we need more private market action or public government regulation? Trench warfare across these battle lines rages on, even as populists paint both approaches as illegitimate tools of elite power. On the populist view, the same forces that reap the benefits of the market have accumulated so much regulatory power that legal oversight can no longer effectively oppose them.

The market can be bent to serve common ends, then, but mainly in institutional conditions that it tends to undermine. What a market society needs, to paraphrase James Madison, is an enlightened statesman at the helm, or at least an empowered citizenry. As Smith admits, what it produces is often something else, a fittingly gloomy conclusion from the father of the "dismal science." Yet the conclusion is hard to avoid, given the SSS premise that markets are indeed a domain of self-interest and could not be otherwise, if they are to do their job. But what if this foundational premise is not true? In order to set the debate on a new footing, we should look away from misty Scotland to a sunnier center of the Enlightenment: Italy.[16]

CAPITALISM WITH ITALIAN CHARACTERISTICS

All our [Italian] economists, from whatever regional background, are dealing not so much, like Adam Smith, with the wealth of nations, but with Public Happiness.

—Achille Loria, 1904

The Italian school of civil economy proposes a solution more radical than better regulation: abandon the public/private, state/market binaries entirely, not by looking beyond the market but by theorizing more closely about it. The fountainhead of this humanistic alternative to self-interest is Antonio Genovesi (1713–69). He was a Catholic priest who did early work in Latin on metaphysics, but was also an Enlightenment humanist and the holder of the world's first chair in economics, at the University of Naples. A student of Giambattista Vico, Genovesi made Newtonian physics a central reference for his great work in economics, *Lezioni di Economia Civile* (1765), which exerted a broad influence across the Atlantic world, especially in Latin America. The only major language into which the *Lezioni* were never translated is English, but a growing literature has reintroduced Genovesi to English speakers, headlined by Stefano Zamagni and Luigino Bruni along with Robert Sugden and Adrian Pabst.[17] They all reject the SSS model of the market as an individualistic domain that can be induced to track common goods (not without tension, and perhaps hopelessly) only by external political power. Drawing on Genovesi's thought, they see markets as a fully social domain of life that is continuous with politics and civil society. On this view, the market is a domain of cooperation as well as competition, a sphere of solidarity as well as contract. Its "efficiency" is to be judged on social criteria alongside atomistic metrics such as wealth or GDP. Markets on this model are more than a prop to shared political flourishing; they are partially constitutive of it. There is an obvious aspirational element here, but the claim of the civil economists is that their vision of civilized markets oriented directly (i.e., intentionally) at common goods is rooted in the social realities that we already know, not just in utopian dreams. But to see this one must dig all the way to the cracked foundations of the Smithian view, to shore up the account of markets with a better vision of human nature.

The dominant SSS view is a preeminently modern vision, rooted in the Scottish Enlightenment and building upon what Machiavelli called the "effectual truth" about human beings as they are—to wit, vicious and selfish. As Smith's friend David Hume put it, "Political writers have established it as a maxim, that, in contriving any system of government, and fixing the several checks and controuls of the constitution, every man ought to be supposed a knave, and to have no other end, in all his actions, than private interest."[18] A crucial part of the appeal of SSS markets is that the Invisible Hand is fueled by just such self-interest, rather than demanding any more exalted motives. If the deepest "effectual truth" about human nature is *homo homini lupus* (man is a wolf to man), as Hobbes supposes, the unintended mutual adjustment of the market may be the best approach to building institutions.

But Hume acknowledges just a few sentences later that his politically useful maxim is "false in fact." The postulate of knavish self-interest is false in the familiar sense that humans are often self-forgetful and altruistic—for example, as parents. But it also misses the mark where persons act for *shared* interests, and this is preeminently the case with friends and concerned citizens, who act for goods that are held in common. It is on this classically political dimension of human nature that civil economy focuses its anthropology. In place of Hobbes's wolfish humanity, Genovesi asserts a more balanced principle: *homo homini natura amicus* (man is by nature a friend to man).[19] For the civil economist, the durable and effective truth about human nature is not unreconstructed self-interest, nor yet heroic self-sacrifice, but interests shared with others.

Through this anthropological lens, the market exchanges that are commonly seen as coordinated self-interest may be described in richer human terms. In the SSS view of the market, the good of one's counterparty is a mere instrument to one's own benefit, and no one has in view the joint good of both parties on an equal footing, still less their relation as a shared good in itself. According to the doctrine of the Invisible Hand, mutual benefit is indeed supposed to occur and to be widespread. Crucially, however, it is unintended. On Smith's picture, even if you benefit from my actions, I am not acting *so as to benefit you.* Our market relation gives me no reason not to deceive or defraud, or otherwise take advantage of you, if I can get away with it. Such behavior is ruled out where merchants enact exchange as a form of mutual assistance, or what Bruni and Sugden have termed "fraternity."[20] For Genovesi and his followers, the fundamental intention of merchants is, or should be, "to be useful to one another."[21] If so, merchants are not oriented solely to private goods, but also to a common end that delimits their just interests as members—firstly of their own tiny community of exchange, and perhaps of something larger. In other words, civil exchanges are not simply a matter of "you benefiting me" (self-interest), or even of "me benefiting you" (altruism), but rather "we benefit one another" (reciprocity).

A fraternal market stance runs with the grain of human nature, if Genovesi's anthropological proposals are correct. What does such an intention look like in practice? In many cases, in its outward appearances—what is exchanged and at what price—the civil market may not be easily distinguishable from SSS exchanges. But the inner moral picture—how the merchants themselves view what they are doing—is very different. Because the agents have a different disposition toward the market, they will not attempt, for instance, to squeeze every last penny out of every bargain, each one trying to capture all the gains from trade for herself.[22] And one of the goods of every "civil exchange" conceived in this way will be an affiliation, even a friendship, the good of a relation willed for its own sake.[23]

As we have seen in previous chapters, the SSS market stands in a fundamental tension with political common action and its goals, because they operate on two entirely different principles of social order. Common goods are in question only when one is dealing with shared ends (which are accessed through common action). On the SSS view, markets are not a domain of shared ends, so they are indifferent to the common goods of politics and its shared actions. For the civil economy tradition, on the other hand, there is no such categorical divide between markets and other forms of social order, because markets too are a form of fraternity or common action.

By positing a continuity in common goods between markets and politics, civil economists boldly reverse the "economics imperialism" afoot in recent years, epitomized in Gary Becker's proclamation that everything in human affairs, including marriage, childrearing, and crime, is an SSS market, explicable by private goods.[24] For Genovesi and the civil economists, reciprocity is the principle of all human affairs, markets included. There is no outcrop in the geography of the human soul, on which a purely self-interested market could be built. On this view, it would be deeply wrong-headed to assess civil markets by reductive mathematical techniques rather than the rich but rough ways of ordinary political deliberation.[25] Markets are just one more instance of the reciprocal relations that go into civil society, all of which express human sociability and the striving for happiness in common.

Since the civil market is continuous with society and politics in this sense, no moral gymnastics are required to show how it could be that merchants act for common ends. Acting directly and intentionally for common ends is the governing norm of the civil market just as it would be in any other social domain, on a civic republican view. But if we take our cue from Aristotelian pluralism, The Common Good is always a tiered or multilayered goal, reflecting social flourishing at various levels. In the case of civil transactions, beyond the "market friendship" embodied in each particular exchange lie a range of other communities—familial, professional, local, and ultimately political. The civil merchant's basic receptivity to common ends opens the door to the full range of communal goals that factor into the ultimate goal of the market economy on the Italians' view: public happiness (*pubblica felicità*).

VIRTUOUS EXCHANGE AND FLOURISHING COMMUNITIES

For the civic humanist, happiness is a common good—it can only be achieved in solidarity by observing what Genovesi calls "the true and useful maxims of justice and happiness of life in common."[26] Moreover, shrewd institutional design is never sufficient on its own.[27] The sustainable flourishing of any of particular community also requires (and in a sense just *is*) virtuous character, however this may be defined. Because markets are themselves an integral part of civil society, they too require both personal and public virtues if they are to achieve this loftier end.[28]

Chief among the civic virtues that Genovesi highlights is "public trust" (*fede pubblica*). Now, even die-hard market partisans would concur that trust among merchants is an essential lubricant for a contract-based price system. As Genovesi notes, "Where there is no trust, there is not security of contract nor any force of laws."[29] But the public trust of civil economy goes much farther. He argues that truly civil markets, which are focused on reciprocity rather than legal enforcement, require a three-tiered structure of trust: ethical, economic, and political. The three layers combine to underwrite a shared sense that one's fellow merchants are precisely *not* calculating egoists who will do whatever they can legally get away with.

For Genovesi, trust at the ethical level is a wide-ranging matter of "mutual confidence among persons, among families, among orders, founded on the opinion of the honesty, the religion (that is, the fear of God), the probity and the honor of contracting parties."[30] The economic tier of trust concerns the feeling of "security born of the certainty of funds on which debts are grounded." As Polanyi emphasized, a reliable monetary system is essential for ensuring stable terms of reciprocity on which merchants can relate to one another. The level of political trust is "born of conventions and promises backed by civil laws, the laws of religion, public customs and habits, and overall by the wisdom and strength of the state [*imperio*]."

Together, these three layers of trust serve to assure the civil merchant not only that the wheels of the market are going to turn but that the market as a whole is duly ensconced in a larger unifying framework of common action. As Genovesi writes, "Public trust is therefore a bond that ties together and binds persons and families of one State to one another, with the sovereign or other nations with which they trade . . . without which there can be so solid and lasting mass, and all is but fine sand and dust."[31] Markets conducted in the spirit of such trust are a binding force not merely because they interweave the self-interest of merchants but because they bring merchants together in a morally formative solidarity.

These interlocking layers of trust imply that a fully realized civil market would have to respond in some way to multiple common goods. The civil merchant's goal of "mutual benefit," all by itself, need not involve anyone beyond the immediate parties to the transaction. This already counts as a significant corrective to any SSS model, and this is the level at which contemporary civil economists such as Zamagni and Bruni have focused. But the ultimate vision must be more capacious, to be truly humanistic: the key role of larger common projects in "market friendship" is amenable to wider considerations: once I care about you, the door is open to considering all your various common goods and how our little exchange may bear upon them.

At each stage of their approach to markets, then, Genovesi's disciples of our day offer a slight but significant corrective to Adam Smith and the impersonality of the SSS market. At the level of fundamental anthropology, the proponents of civil economy see human flourishing as a matter of public and private friendships, social relations that are valued in-themselves and not merely as a way of obtaining necessary goods through Smith's "natural propensity to truck, barter, and exchange." The civil market is an expression of this basic orientation to common flourishing rather than a mere support or preamble to it. Exchange can be a site of fraternity where the dominant intention aims at mutual assistance for the sake of a common good rather than interdependent private benefits. This implies, further, that market exchanges must be set in a larger political context where these common goods can be grasped and acted on. Civil markets are continuous with civil society in the infrastructural, material sense, but also in their basic fraternal orientation to common goods. And so, as Achille Loria writes in the epigraph to the previous section, market exchanges are not basically to be evaluated in terms of the "wealth of nations" but in terms of a broader category of "public happiness." They develop not only private virtues of the merchant but also the virtues of the citizen and "public faith," which is an excellence of the community itself.

With all these cards on the table, we can assess the cash value of the civil economy proposal. What does it add to the human project? What could a civil market do that "strangers selling stuff" cannot? Because civil merchants are seeking common goods, in principle they have the necessary norms and motivations to take account of the social costs and benefits of exchange without being forced to do so from without. A product or process that contributed to, say, community cohesion or reducing inequality would have higher civil market value than one that did not, while generating pollution would be a disvalue. I postpone for a moment the question of how civil merchants and prices could effectively "learn" about these social costs and factor them in. Assuming they could, an idealized civil market might "internalize externalities," in economics jargon, because prices would better reflect the total cost and benefits, not just those that fall on the individual merchants. Taxes and regulation are the economics textbook's remedy for the problem of externalities, but they are blunt and often ineffective instruments. If civil markets could do more of this job themselves, using the individual initiative and knowledge that are the key to market efficiency, the price mechanism might reduce its civic costs and better promote communal flourishing. But how, even in theory, could this be done?

RECIPROCITY, THE MARKET, AND THE GIFT

The notion of promoting multiple common goods through exchange seems to place an impossibly heavy burden on the fellow feeling of civil merchants. Even if they are decent and open to mutual benefit, they have neither the ability nor the duty to promote The Common Good in some full sense, which is the concern of political actors. A fraternal stance does not erase the difference between markets and politics, nor convert merchants into saints or statesmen, but it does amplify the goals that exchange might promote. As we saw with Hayek in chapter 5, a decentralized price-system allows merchants to promote a range of goals that exceed their conscious awareness, relying indirectly on the knowledge of others. He thought that such unintended benefits were limited to private goods. I will argue that civil exchange among ordinary, limited humans could use a similar mechanism to promote a range of common goods as well, provided that the prices themselves reflect the shared concerns in question.

Let us first ask how any system so freighted with moral and social desiderata could even count as a market economy in the first place. Genovesi adds in many ideals absent from typical SSS exchange: fraternity, shared happiness, and so on. Now, a Porsche with a kitchenette and a retractable bed in the back wouldn't really be a sports car; it would be a Winnebago in disguise. Similarly, the civil market looks a good deal like a disguised version of premodern "moral economies," in which economic exchange is so embedded in other social institutions that it is all but indistinguishable from them. This is part of the charm of the civil economy vision, but the question is whether it retains the characteristic mechanisms of a market system, and so some of the liberty and dynamism that mainstream economists emphasize. Let us suppose with Hayek that the distinguishing feature of any market is the price system, more precisely the free exchange of private property coordinated by prices. All the major writers on civil economy claim this mechanism as centrally important to their own ideals.

A civil market must be focused on prices, then, if it is to be recognizable as a market rather than a system of centralized control. But to be a *civil* market, it must aim at common ends. Why doesn't the priority of prices entail the priority of private goods? As we saw in chapter 5, Hayek notes the absence of authoritative command in standard market relations and concludes that there can be no common goods among merchants. But we also noticed that Hayek's reasoning was erroneous; the absence of felt authority does not necessarily entail the absence of common goods. In a putative nation-state such as Somalia, the absence of centralized authority is indeed a good clue that there is no longer common action uniting the various corners of the country, and thus no common goals either. But personal friends or ballroom dancers do not erect a governing authority to coordinate their relations. Still, we know that there is a common good among dancers because of a much more obvious feature of such relations, namely reciprocity. Reciprocity involves an open-ended expectation of giving and receiving, which can take place only within an ongoing relation of solidarity, not a one-off transaction. If I lend today without counting the cost, it is only because I expect that at some unspecified future point you (or, e.g., some other teammate) will reciprocate, because I expect our friendship (team) to continue, and that is what friends (teammates) do. Reciprocity does require common action, then, so it has a necessary orientation to a common good. But reciprocity need not be commanded or ordered from on high, so it is perfectly compatible with individual free choice or with the market conceived as a rule-governed, price-centered order.

The civil economy vision needs a decentralized social principle such as reciprocity in order to orient price-centered exchange toward shared ends without lapsing into authoritarianism. This raises a serious challenge. Can all these moral addenda be funneled through the fairly blunt instrument that is market price? If we ask whether prices alone can fully and precisely reflect all the concerns that the civil economists want to build into their markets, the answer seems to be, No. Because price levels potentially reflect all the factors affecting supply and demand, no particular price necessarily reflects true reciprocity or concern for public happiness, and so on. The high cost of regionally made shoes may reflect aspirations of solidarity, or it may indicate no more than a dearth of fine leather. Moreover, relational goods don't have a strict market price, in that they cannot be reliably exchanged for nonrelational commodities. So achieving common goods cannot only be a matter of hitting pregiven price targets. The key is, rather, in expanding the mechanisms by which prices are formed. The initial objection gets the matter backward. We should not ask whether prices necessarily reflect the pursuit of common ends, but how the pursuit of common ends should affect prices. A given price structure in a civil economy might really, though contingently, reflect merchants' concerns for one another and their common goods. One could not conclude as much simply by reading off the numbers; it would be necessary also to consult the inner world of the agents and their intentions.

Merchants themselves might come to regard prices as sensitive to concerns of shared flourishing if they practice what I call "reciprocity pricing." If the present chapter makes an original contribution to the theory of civil economy, it is this notion. To trade goods everywhere at a single market price (adjusted only for costs of transport and the like) is to enact the idea of merchants as strangers and equals. In order to embody the pursuit of common ends, the price of goods would have to deviate from the universal but individualistic market level. A civil market would need something like what anthropologist Marshall Sahlins calls a "coefficient of sociability"[32] added onto the background market price. Truly civil prices would have to reflect factors beyond global moral absolutes (e.g., prohibitions on slavery) as well as the universal concatenation of individual plans, either of which are invariant for any buyer-seller pair. Market exchanges that directly promote political and other relational goods would have to vary also according to the forms of common action uniting particular buyers and sellers. Different communal contexts, different prices. Arguably, we see this basic structure on the margins of contemporary markets, when buyers are willing to pay somewhat more for a local product just because of the benefits to the local community.[33] It is such concerns that explain the premium prices in fancy farmers' markets or the wholesome photos of farmers on upscale milk jugs.

According to a doctrine of "social coefficients," the basic civil bargain would take roughly the following form: "Here is my offer, which is the background market price +/- adjustments based on our shared communal concerns." From this point of view, the numbers themselves could tell you quite a bit: local *variance* in prices could reflect reciprocity and concern for the common good in a way that absolute price levels could not. This would yoke together two morally asymmetrical components into a single numerical figure: the background market price as a quasi-natural fact that seems, as Hayek puts it, "neither just nor unjust"[34] and the social coefficient as a direct object of moral and political scrutiny. One might read these two components as affirmations of abstract human equality and concretely shared goods, respectively. They combine to yield what I call "reciprocity pricing."

Civil prices with these two components could also be helpfully understood as a mixture of bargain and gift. We usually think of exchanges as a binary: either bargains or gifts. But there is no reason why a single transaction could not be both, inasmuch as the prevailing market price represents the bargain, while the departure from that price adds the element of gift.[35] It might seem that tough-minded merchants could simply ignore the gift element, but construing the social component as a gift is not incompatible with regarding it as compulsory. Are family Christmas gifts optional? On the classic account of Marcel Mauss, a gift is an exchange that reflects an ongoing moral relationship: "In theory such gifts are voluntary, but in fact they are given and repaid under obligation."[36] In reciprocity pricing, paying the "social coefficient" is an obligation to some community, not an individual entitlement of any individual. Contrariwise, the receiving merchant could well look on the social component as a gift to herself, which in turn imposes a reciprocal obligation on her—not to her particular counterparty, but to that common good in light of which it was given.

The notion of reciprocity pricing moves the civil economy ideal one step closer to the real world, by sketching how dynamic market coordination could take account of common goals. Building shared concerns directly into prices would usefully lessen the moral and informational burden on civil merchants, if it can be done effectively. But I will not pretend to have shown where and how social coefficients could be concretely institutionalized or who would design and enforce specific mechanisms. A great deal more research, as they say, is required.

REACHING FOR UTOPIA?

With the "spirit of the gift" or the "social coefficient," civil markets aspire to a win-win combining prosperity with virtue. Lest this sound too good to be true, we should consider both the practicalities and the limits of markets as common action. Who is paying for this free lunch? As with many civic republican proposals, the main cost lies in the formation and maintenance of moral culture. One selling-point of the Smithian market is that it requires little in the way of virtue or personal sacrifice. The "crooked timber of humanity" is a fine fuel for the SSS market engine. The civic cost of SSS exchange is not up-front difficulties of getting off the ground, but the potential damage to individuals or civic cultures on the back end, and thus also the problem of long-term sustainability that Bas van Bavel observes in historical market systems. Civil economy requires more refined inputs, in terms of taut political institutions and personal virtue, with the promise of less waste in the end.

This higher tone implies that the tradition of civil economy is indeed utopian in some important way. It is best seen, in my view, as in part a descriptive theory about markets as they actually are, and in part a vision of markets as they might or ought to be. Zamagni and Bruni acknowledge that no national economies, much less the international scene, could be described as civil in Genovesi's sense. Yet they argue that the raw ingredients for a civil economy are always present, because they are rooted in human nature. And many real-world institutions are already notably "civil," even if their social aspects are ignored, marginalized, or misinterpreted by the individualistic rhetoric of markets.

Consider the motives and norms that typify farmer's markets or locally owned stores, which reflect and sustain a web of multifaceted relationships. My grandfather, the son of Sicilian immigrants, owned a corner grocery called Louis Market in downtown Detroit in the 1950s and '60s. When his customers were in a hard spot, he was generous (to a fault, or so my grandmother complained) about extending them credit and otherwise lending a hand. This may have helped his bottom line in the long run (though again, Grandma demurred), but it was clearly more than that. During the Detroit summer riots of 1967, he refused to put bars on his store windows even as neighboring shops were looted or burned. Louis Market emerged unscathed, because the locals knew what kind of merchant he was, and evidently some were willing to defend the store or deflect anger elsewhere. Corner groceries are very nearly a thing of the past in the United States, but similar norms of market sociality are not limited only to quaint or bygone corners of the economy. An acquaintance of mine works in a private equity firm in Philadelphia. Even in the hard-nosed world of pure finance, he informs me, a trader who flouts norms of reciprocity by sharp dealing with clients or colleagues is apt to be shunned or stigmatized.

Larger signs pointing toward a civil economy can be found in the "care industries," such as nursing and home health services, as well as the nonprofit and social business sectors.[37] These sectors make up a large and growing fraction of industrialized economies, sometimes more than a third. At a still larger scale, coordinated market economies on the German and Nordic models are built around reciprocity at the national level, which makes up in political heft what it may lack in personal connection.[38] What is actual is possible, so examples like these show that aspects of the civil ideal can be realized. Of course, the civil economy remains an idealistic, reforming proposal and not merely a moralized redescription of the facts on the ground. Yet it can plausibly claim to be more than a daydream, because it builds on the proven advantages and aspirations of the market economy, unlike communism or other utopias of the left.

The seeds of a civil market have not disappeared, then, but how and how far can they be expanded? Most of today's attempts to humanize the market economy turn a moralizing eye onto the individual: what we need is the "patient investor," or the "conscious capitalist." But the civil economy tradition retains a classic republican awareness of the effects of normative institutions—and common goods—upon character and culture. Personal rectitude is not enough. Even if we could fill today's markets with thoroughly "fraternal" individuals, likely we would only reproduce the emphasis on private goods that is embodied in markets' present social form. To "fraternize" such markets adequately entails changing the prevailing norms and institutions such that the intention of mutual assistance is not an individual option, to be adopted at will by virtuous individuals, but a social requirement baked into the ground-rules of exchange.[39] Ultimately, what the civil economists are after is an (almost) entirely new market culture, not a few tweaks here or there.

As a rough parallel, consider the well-known Mondragòn Cooperative in Spain.[40] It began as an effort to conduct small industrial firms on an employee-controlled, mutualist paradigm, quite in the spirit of civil economy. The larger business environment was uncomprehending or hostile, and Mondragòn was eventually obliged to create an entire alternate ecosystem of banking, insurance, and education in order for its core enterprises to remain true to their own cooperative mission.[41] Despite its success, Mondragòn's multilayered solution has proven nearly impossible to replicate elsewhere. Moralizing individuals would seem easier, to be sure.

Even setting practical challenges aside, we should not construe the civil market's ideals as obviously superior to the spontaneous or civil approaches simply in virtue of emphasizing common goods. Here the rigorous logic of Aristotelian pluralism can help to remedy the legacy of "analytic imprecision"[42] left by the optimist Genovesi. Not all exchange can be "civilized" because civil markets depend precisely upon common action. The contours and limits of common action thus set the frontiers of a civil exchange. It cannot be effective where there is no possibility for meaningful solidarity among merchants or where there are no encompassing communities to guide and norm exchange. In anonymous global commodity markets, for instance, there would be few meaningful common goods to account for. In such cases the "social coefficient" would be close to zero, so the "reciprocity price" would be the same as the prevailing market price. In far-flung global markets the civil ideal is largely otiose, except in exhorting merchants to trade in a generous and cheerful spirit.

Furthermore, even where we could enact markets as solidarity, it might not be best to do so. The more exchange is "fraternal," the more it is susceptible to all the potential drawbacks of real-world common action: inequality, abuse of power, bias, high transaction costs. SSS markets have their own difficulties, as we have seen, but they are relatively immune to pathologies of this kind. Immigrants and other persons on the margins know all too well that treatment as a stranger can be a small price to pay for treatment as an equal. Civil markets among real, flawed humans might deny them this basic justice, so there are moral as well as material costs to market fraternity. There will always be room for prudential judgment and debate about the proper location and overall value of civil exchange and its common goods.

A MULTICHAPTER CONCLUSION: PLURALISTIC MARKETS

The last three chapters of this book have laid out a three-way contest between rival views of markets and common goods: Hayek's spontaneous model, Polanyi's instituted approach, and Italian civil economy. But no winner has been declared. Which interpretation should we adopt? Partisans of various full-scale moral doctrines may not find it hard to decide: champions of individual liberty would likely crown the spontaneous ideal, while advocates of communal harmony would back the civil economists. But both triumphs would be rigged, in the sense that they would keep score based on something beyond the basic rules of common action. Fair decision demands a standard of judgment that does not tip the scales in favor of one conception or another. Taking a leaf from the social science playbook, I propose that one should choose the model that best "fits the data," since they all claim to capture the empirical reality of markets as well as a normative ideal, and indeed to build their ideals upon that reality. And what are the data? As a starting point, ordinary discourse and practice take politics as preeminently a zone of common action, and markets not. By this yardstick, the instituted model's patchwork of private versus shared interests makes for the most immediately plausible general account of markets and politics. Hayek's consistently individualist model privileges an aspect of politics that is normally subordinate, while the civil market's consistently communal view does the same for exchange. The "inconsistent" instituted model affirms both parts of the commonsense view, so it best fits the dominant social imaginary of the market.

Yet if the instituted model is more often accurate, it is not always so. Its framework admirably captures the real estate market, say, or online shopping, or the innumerable other markets where basically anonymous exchange is backed by political forces and laws that establish contractual forms, impose taxes, and police the limits of what can and cannot be exchanged. The common good of some sustaining polity might well take preference here. But the same could hardly be said of long-distance global commerce, which is beholden to multiple polities with potentially conflicting interests. Nor could we plausibly hold that intense, long-term economic collaboration—another prominent feature of thriving market systems—leaves merchants as mutually indifferent as the instituted model supposes them to be. These are paradigm cases for the spontaneous and civil models, respectively, and they constitute standing counterexamples against generalizing the initially preferable instituted approach.

What does this empirical variety imply about the moral architecture of markets—that all rigorous analysis is bound to fail, so choose your own adventure? The better lesson to draw, in my view, is that the level of common action involved in particular markets can vary. In other words, markets are pluralistic, so different cases need different analytic models. If no single account can capture the relevant structure of common goods in every modality of the market, then the pretensions to universality shared by all three models turn out to be a significant liability. By the same token, there is good reason to calibrate one's arguments about the common good to the variant at hand.

In thinking about markets and their variety, we can learn from the same economic sociologists who earlier illuminated the Uber Problem. Recall that Gereffi and his coauthors persuasively distinguish several modes of economic transacting that vary based on the goods changing hands.[43] Here again is their basic typology:

1. *Markets*: simple, standardized exchanges governed by price
2. *Modular chains*: highly capable suppliers perform complex but codifiable tasks
3. *Relational chains*: complex tasks that cannot be codified bring high-capacity firms into long-term contact

4. *Captive chains*: low-capacity suppliers are beholden to lead firms in carrying out complex tasks
5. *Hierarchy*: complex coordination under authority

As we see here, impersonal, price-guided exchange is one market mode, but not the only one. Hence it is worth asking why classic arm's-length SSS arises where it does. "Strangers and equals" transact most effectively where products are standardized, deals are simple, and the relevant knowledge and metrics are well codified and public. Under these conditions, merchants can be relatively indifferent about *whom* to bargain with, because they'll be getting the same product either way: price competition is intense and the cost of switching partners is low. Little explicit coordination is needed, so transactions can proceed efficiently at greater distance. But as Gereffi and coauthors explain, where products and deals are not standardized or merchants rely on tacit, local knowledge and expertise, businesses seldom coordinate simply via impersonal prices. Here we find "relational value chains" in which merchants opt for longer-term collaboration and greater relationship-specific investment. Costs of switching partners are high, and spatial proximity is often crucial in facilitating complex collaboration. This latter type of market coordination looks much more like common action. (As argued in part 1 of the book, hierarchical firms and captive chains like Uber involve so much nonprice coordination that we shouldn't think of them as markets at all.)

The connection of exchange to its legal-political frame also varies considerably across political contexts, as the "varieties of capitalism" literature has amply shown.[44] The rules for long-range commodity trade are often set by multilateral treaties, such as NAFTA, rather than by a single authoritative center. Because multiple nations must assent, the terms of such treaties are only indirectly controlled by political forces animating a given nation. Despite the importance of treaty-governed markets, the most consequential laws, tariffs, and regulations remain those set unilaterally by national governments. Political input is particularly prominent when it comes to markets that touch on questions of higher social salience, such as labor markets or armaments, or matters of local particularity, such as cultural and environmental goods. No politician wants to admit that the self-governing

TABLE 7.1. A Rough Guide to Real-World Rival Markets

Model	Spontaneous	Instituted	Civil
Scale	Large (International)	Medium (National)	Small (Local/ Regional)
Salience/ Particularity	Low	Medium to high	High
Main Contribution	Private goods	Mix of private and common goods	Preponderance of common goods

people has given up control of its own common life or bargained away deep-shared concerns to foreign powers.

These considerations suggest two empirical variables as handy guides for locating common action in market institutions and thus for applying the three rival versions: scale and social salience/particularity. The spontaneous model obtains where there is little common action either in exchange or in politics; hence it will apply best to exchange at the largest volume or longest distance, where political salience/particularity is low—for example, in international commodity exchange. The instituted model applies most directly where standardized products enable relatively impersonal, price-focused exchange, but social salience and political intervention are significant. Its paradigmatic case would be the midlevel scale of national markets, which still make up arguably the most important market contexts (hence the initial appeal of the instituted account). Finally, the civil model is most apt in relatively close-range situations where political salience is high and/or contractual standardization is difficult, necessitating more intense coordination among merchants.

The relative importance of common and private goods in these cases varies with the importance of common action. The appropriate standard for global, high-volume market relations—that is, that which makes up their key contribution to implicated persons and communities—will be efficient coordination of private goods, which can benefit parties at any distance. But common action plays a larger role in constituting a national market, whose proper contribution must be reckoned in both common and private goods (in varying proportions). Regional markets are constituted in larger measure by common action, so a larger share of their societal contribution lies in common goods beyond private gain—for example, innovation in industry, educational gains, flourishing communities. Due to the limited portability of common goods, these relational benefits will likely be limited to the same localities or regions where the features of common action most clearly obtain. Which of these plural market forms and normative ideals will apply concretely depends, of course, on the case at hand.

PLURALISTIC AUTO MARKETS

In the interest of having a case in hand, I turn lastly to the automotive industry as an illustration of pluralistic common-action analysis, drawing on the empirical work of Timothy Sturgeon and his collaborators.[45] At first glance, one might think that a single industry ought to answer to a unified normative standard, since its contribution to society is basically a single end product. Yet the making and selling of cars involves so many different tasks and components, and so many transactions at different scales, that any adequate assessment will have to draw on more than one model of common goods and markets.

Today, virtually no cars are made all in one place, or even one county. The 2023 Ford Escape, for instance, rated as only 47 percent made in America.[46] Auto manufacturers rely on a dispersed, international network for standardized or modular components, from paint to screws to tires. With a large number of suppliers bidding for major contracts, geography frequently yields to price and capacity considerations. The political salience of such deals is low, and their legal underpinnings lie in private contract backed by multilateral trade agreements. What these component transactions can or should contribute to society at large is well captured by the spontaneous model, focused on efficiency or wealth generation. Far-flung factor markets have little potential for reflecting or generating solidarity around common interests at any level, so they are rightly oriented to private goods.

Though many manufacturers have sought to offshore final assembly of cars, as General Motors does in Mexico, there remains major political pressure in many regions to "build where you sell." Unlike components, completed cars and their makers are highly visible politically. Governments often invest substantially to attract auto firms, and end manufacturers cannot afford to be seen as totally disconnected from national projects. In spring 2023, for instance, Ford ran prime-time TV ads touting its position as the "most American automaker,"[47] presumably to strengthen the brand's position with patriotic buyers as well as the trade unions with which Ford was negotiating at the time. Car manufacturers still compete on performance and price, of course, but both external actors and the firms themselves apparently regard political contributions as a relevant additional metric of success. To describe and assess a market like this—where common action underwrites otherwise-impersonal transactions—we need the resources of the instituted model, with its patchwork of common and private goods.

Beyond global and national vectors, auto manufacturing remains in many respects tied to regional centers such as Detroit. Like Silicon Valley in the tech world, automotive clusters develop dense social ecologies of tacit knowledge and expertise that are essential for innovation in complex areas such as engineering or design. It is no coincidence that foreign suppliers like Bosch as well as lead brands like Nissan generally maintain R&D operations in the Detroit area even when their final-assembly plants are elsewhere, to take advantage of the education pipelines, professional networks, and other close-range relational advantages of presence in the region. In these complex, long-term interactions, firms and other regional actors draw more than cheap inputs from, and contribute more than wealth outputs to, one another. A fully anonymous SSS model is blind to the relational concerns and benefits that drive these exchanges; what is needed is a civil model that admits common action at the level of commercial collaboration.

From this brief glimpse we can already see that assessing even one complex industry brings all three rival versions of the market into play. Insisting on SSS or indeed on any single model of common and private goods would only obscure some important dimension of how auto manufacture should or does work. As I have tried to emphasize throughout this book, privileging one or another common-action model for a given institution does not dictate any final judgment; it only points up the persons, patterns, and goals to be considered. Wherever the auto industry merits normative praise or condemnation, it does so by promoting or violating the objectives and logics built into its various social forms and into the private or common goods to which they are rightly oriented. It would not be cynical or reductive to exempt Ford's far-flung supplier network from the standards of an elusive solidarity that such relations could never reasonably generate. On the other hand, any sober-minded realist (be she a legislator, a local mayor, or an armchair theorist) should admit that the logic of common goods does strictly apply to Ford and other automakers in other respects: first as major players in and beneficiaries of national market-making, and more emphatically as participants in the communal project of a region such as Detroit. Here common action may well contribute positively to market "efficiencies," as it does in firms, provided that one recognize the common goods at stake alongside private gain. In sum, the social forms and ends of the market are multiple, and they should remain so as long as making and selling cars, or provisioning human society in general, involves an irreducibly diverse array of goods and coordinating relationships.

What shall we finally conclude? Are common goods pervasive at all levels of the market, or found only in politics, or nowhere to be seen? I would argue tentatively for the instituted approach as a default option, yet as a fully general model it is no more serviceable than its rivals. The world of the market is just too various to fit in any one box. But the conversation need not end with pluralism and a theoretical shrug, since the variety of market institutions is not haphazard; it already tracks human concerns and could be made to do so better. Different degrees of common action appear where Strangers Selling Stuff can more or less effectively bargain, where the goods in question are more or less standardized and free of communal entanglements. The simplest single indicator of common action is scale, so one might summarize the spontaneous, instituted, and civil models as markets writ Large, Medium, and Small.

Moral analysis of markets should be sensitive to empirically measurable variation, but not slavishly deferential. Quantitative considerations such as size or complexity are not themselves moral factors, but only clues that the "social facts" of different markets involve categorically different human relations, dominant goals, and normative claims. If markets are not all alike in their basic social form, it would be a mistake to apply a blanket moral standard to them all. Prudence and practical efficacy may commend any of the three proposed patterns of cooperation and exchange as the best answer for grasping a given market and guiding it toward greater human flourishing. The conceptual framework of common action and private exchange fits the contours of market institutions like hand in glove, even if it promises no easy answers about what various markets are and should be like.

CONCLUSION

Toward a Pluralist Political Economy

The large goal of this book has been to recast the moral architecture of the business corporation and the market (and, by implication, the political economies that they dominate) as transformative modes of common action, for good and ill. Because of their underlying solidarities, these familiar economic institutions are not, and could not be, only about "making money" in any crude sense. They draw merchants and citizens, often unwittingly, into common projects answering the deepest political questions of how to live together.

With this deeper dimension in mind, it should come as no surprise that millennials seek jobs with a purpose beyond the paycheck, or that factory workers in eastern China feel wounded by their alienation from the cultural contexts where their products are ultimately used, or that populists around the globe plead the cause of cultural integrity against the liquid forces of the market. These may seem like sentimental objections against a rationalized system of economic coordination, but they are more than that. At a human level, they are pleas for fuller participation in a shared economic life that cannot be explained, much less justified, in the language of self-interest. Such anomalies invite us to look past a private-good analysis to consider the many and various shared goals that are already at stake in familiar institutions, whether generally acknowledged or not. We are closer than one might think to a pluralist political economy—that is, to an economic order built around the multiple shared goods of human life and work.

The real challenge, which no amount of argument can achieve on its own, is to protect the goods and rectify the evils that come to light once we admit the morally transformative shared ends built into institutions such as the market and the business corporation. I have sketched a framework of Aristotelian pluralism in order to provoke further discussion, not as a definitive solution to these challenges. This book's account is incomplete in several key ways. In the first place, my grammar of common action has been focused on the analytic distinction between private and common goods, which indicates only formal structures, not substantive content. A full-fledged normative theory or policy proposal would have to flesh out formal blueprints both with principles of justice and with the social facts of particular institutions. I have deliberately left these further questions as open as possible, the better to reach the proponents of opposing political ideals with my alternative framework, and to enrich the terms of their debate.

In itself, the logic of common action does not settle disputes between, say, liberal, progressive, traditionalist, and anarchist views, except to mark out the terrain that they can most fruitfully contest. The proper question to dispute is not *whether* firms and markets should embody irreducibly social, formative ends. All contending camps should be Aristotelian pluralists on this foundational matter, since common ends are built into emergent social realities and it is vain to wish them away. Any partisan answer that adverted only to private goods or universal human rights would be hopelessly impoverished on its own terms, having ignored a major chunk of the relevant considerations. Whatever conception of justice one may hold, one ought not to abstract away from the teleological drift of particular institutions toward ends held in common. The real question to debate is, then, *Which* ends? Every conclusion about the proper role of, say, workers in firm governance or of rent control in housing enacts some answer to the great question of common action: *Who are we to become together?* A grammar of common action should help us to think more clearly about this complex question, so I have broken it into three more tractable ones: (1) *What is the goal or end of the endeavor?* (2) *Who are the members?* (3) *How can they justly pursue their common goal together?* Patiently asking these questions about particular institutions is one way to identify the common goals already present, quite directly in the corporation and more diffusely in market exchange, and to pursue them together with fuller justice.

In order to find transformative common action at the heart of the market economy as we know it, one need look no farther than the main merchant of our day, the business corporation. To appreciate business as a rich human project requires first setting aside the notion of the firm as an ingenious device of coordinated self-interest. For the Chicago school, the most rigorous exponent of this notion, (1) the overriding goal of any business is to return profits (2) to stockholders, its owners, (3) who should divvy up the pile by equity stake, while honoring their contractual obligations (with workers and others). This elegant but reductive theory leads in practice to an "imperial oligarchy" that prioritizes one dimension of business (profit) and one peripheral constituency (investors) at the expense of the whole. In reality, far from being a modality of the market or an elaborate piece of property, the corporate firm is a site of publicly empowered, morally formative cooperation under authority.

Firms are valuable alternatives to the market precisely because their communal form lets them draw on the goods (and, unfortunately, also the evils) of working together. Profit can be justly pursued only as one dimension of a multifaceted solidarity that is an end in itself. Here as elsewhere, common projects may enrich or deform, but they are never only instruments of private gain. We need a quite different set of answers in order to respect the built-in common ends of business: (1) The proper goal of any firm is the rightly ordered joint achievement of four types of common goal: Property, Power, Product and, centrally, Practice. (2) It is primarily workers who share these ends as common—that is, as regulative ideals shaping their own character and cooperation, so the claims of other constituencies should be read through the flourishing of workers' common action. (3) Workplace democracy is promising, though not usually required (and not always feasible), as a way for firms to pursue their common ends in a just fashion. Whether de facto authority rests with employees, managers, or dispersed investors, their first responsibility is to the overall flourishing of the firm in all its dimensions.

Within the world of business, the logic of morally formative common ends is not confined to the four walls of the firm, thanks to the rise of disaggregated global businesses like Apple, Nike, and Uber. They rely on a highly supervised network of market suppliers to do work that might once have been done in-house by their own employees. The common action of lead firms in global value chains thus extends well beyond their formal legal boundaries. Justice demands the priority of common ends in the context of common action, whether in the firm, in supply chains, or elsewhere. But it is no simple matter to discern what ends are held in common, and by whom, in a shifting world of revisable contracts. If it is difficult to flourish together within an organization such as a business corporation, it is exponentially harder to achieve common goods—genuinely worthy and justly shared—outside of durable legal and social forms. Dispersed, unacknowledged communities of production can hardly hope to be truly just. Lead firms cannot have it both ways, both pursuing efficiency through contractual coordination and at the same time wielding tools of authority and status that can be justified only in light of common goods. We can expect more shared wrongs than flourishing collaboration in a network like Uber's, so long as it remains an uneasy mongrel of prices and power.

On the spectrum of common action, flexible and transitory market exchange is even more remote from the authority and solidity of the hierarchical firm than is Uber. The centrality of things, not persons, in a system of Strangers Selling Stuff is precisely what makes markets so dynamic and so useful as an alternative to the slower ways of solidarity in the state or in the firm. Yet we cannot rightly forget shared goods even at this individualistic end of the spectrum. To focus exclusively on private goods is to ignore the market's "moral ecology," and so to obscure both the foundations and the ultimate ends of exchange. It is very much to his credit that a market partisan such as Friedrich Hayek recognizes that the price system truly epitomizes individual freedom only where the wider society, which sets the rules of the market game, is itself an instrumental order without ends of its own. Unfortunately for Hayek's project, the notion of a political society without common ends is doomed to collapse under its own weight, since politics is always a project of solidarity in some form or other. Still, Hayek and his kindred economists make a good case that market exchange in its familiar impersonal mode is not a form of common action in its own right. And there are excellent reasons to affirm anonymous markets in their proper place—not all human interaction needs to aim at common goods;

indeed, some should not—especially far-flung global trade and other markets that lie outside and across any communal boundaries.

Yet common action and its ends enjoy a roundabout priority over most markets even in those cases where individualistic exchange performs wonders of coordination that deserve citizens' support. Price-centered markets are not self-justifying any more than they are self-standing. As Karl Polanyi and other economic historians have shown, markets have always been publicly constructed spaces of private action, instituted in service of a common vision. Self-interested merchants are unwitting participants in a political project of creating competitive exchange in some good or service. The overall success of markets should be assessed in light of the broader common ends of the citizens who underwrite exchange systems, not only by the aggregate of private goods that the prototypical SSS merchant has in view. The moral calculus is complicated by the fact that these standards can coincide. In some cases, flourishing common life may be best served by treating certain markets as no more than public utilities, efficient instruments for coordinating private action. But in other cases the opportunity cost of individualistic exchange, in terms of common goods forgone, is not worth paying. Which is which? That is a matter for political judgment, not a technical matter to be turned over to experts. Any market within a social and political frame is a dimension of a moral economy and thus part of a formative common project oriented finally to a shared vision of flourishing together.

A normative grammar of common action cannot dictate the proper shape of markets, yet it does rule out one option: essentially common goods cannot be rightly ordered by individualistic private exchange. Polanyi is quite right that the history of overzealous markets tells against an exclusive reliance on anonymous prices, since those goods that never function as merely private concerns cannot be long left to the mercy of the market. But unbridled self-interest is not the only way to play the market game, and the Italian civil economists reimagine exchange as itself a form of solidarity, in which merchants consciously aim to promote their own shared ends as well as larger common goods, precisely in their price-centered bargains. The civil economist's ideal makes a refreshing departure from tired appeals for top-down regulation, which seem unable to envision democratic solidarities apart from the centralized state. Refreshing, but dangerous: without a whole ecosystem of mature political institutions full of virtuous merchant-citizens, the risks of oppression and inefficiency that stem from politicizing exchange would be liable to outweigh the benefits of a civil market.

Thinking about markets through the lens of common action doesn't yield universal models or solutions since markets are themselves pluralistic. Some forms of exchange are anonymous, while others mix in aspects of common action. Some are interwoven within political projects, while others stand outside. According to the ideology of private goods, relational forms of exchange look like failures to attain full efficiency. But this ideology is blind in one eye. The logic of common action can be essential to coordination and innovation, depending on the scale and the social setting of the goods at hand. It is as harmful to exclude common goods from our thinking about markets as it is to ignore the benefits of impersonal exchange.

The true challenge is to figure out where each belongs, and indeed where they are already at work. Where do we need to adjust our thinking to take fuller account of common goals already operative on the ground? And where do we need to adjust the social form of our action to make shared goods more (or less!) prominent? Clarifying and resolving these tensions is the stuff of practical deliberation as well as scholarly theorizing. For the Aristotelian pluralist, "The Common Good" serves not as the name of the definitive order to end all conflicts, which will always elude us, but as a reminder that flourishing together always involves a complex hierarchy of solidarities around a vast and shifting range of human goods.

PLURAL ORDERS

"To sum up, The Common Good involves tensions, and they ought to be resolved in a just fashion"—this is either a laughably banal conclusion, or else an invitation to carry forward the argument for Aristotelian pluralism into concrete forms of public and private order. This book has begun the spadework by rearticulating the market and the firm in terms of a grammar of common action. Markets and firms do not need to be changed or improved in order to start playing the common-goods game, in which moral allegiance is given (or extracted), character is formed, visions of justice or right conduct are brought home to human lives. No, firm and market as we know them are already playing that game in their own ways. The modern state—their umpire, sponsor, and regulator—is playing as well. The three play in tandem, almost by necessity given the importance and mutual dependence of government, corporate business, and the price-mechanism of the market. Reforming or even reimagining any one of them involves shifting the others to bring the whole constellation to a new equilibrium.

Consider two of the ideologies I have criticized in this book: self-regulating markets and the shareholder-value corporation. Both overemphasize private goods, and in that sense they are mutually supporting: you should expect to find corporations of this sort in a market context of this kind, and vice versa. A further aspect of their continuing appeal and influence (often in the teeth of the facts) is their affinity with liberal ideals of free choice, private property, and self-determination. You might also predict an exaggerated emphasis on private goods where the language of individual rights and autonomy is the political mother tongue. Of course, one-sided redactions of the firm and the market represent a certain betrayal of the legitimate liberal ideals on which they trade, as ideologies always do. But the unjust distortions of a private-goods analysis can hardly be recognized and remedied without acquiring some fluency in the grammar of common action, as a kind of public second language.

Citizens who can articulate their own common ends can better recognize and order the common goods of other domains as more than heaps of individual benefit. A key goal of any pluralist politics should be to uphold the various goods of solidarity and the communities in which they are anchored. The firm is one such community, and value-chain networks such as Uber should often be seen in the same light. Markets may not have common ends all their own, but they uniquely reflect and affect the ends of much adjacent common action. Of course, the integrity of economic communities as moral projects does not fully detach them from the common action and ends of politics. A key dimension of citizens' public project is the authoritative "spin" that is put on economic institutions, encouraging this genre of business or that pattern of markets in the service of some architectonic vision. Rather than ignoring the ends we cannot avoid sharing in firms and markets, we should make them central to public celebration, deliberation, and lament.

Moving toward a pluralist political economy is in part a matter of upholding the common goods that we already share in the firm and the market, in part rectifying the injustices that stem from the normative mechanisms of economic common action, and in part envisioning new forms of solidarity that can better achieve the goals of human communion. We inhabit a world of intertwined common projects, in our dominant economic institutions no less than in private associations or politics proper. The difficulty of clearly seeing and justly pursuing our common goods in an accelerating, interconnected world does not excuse us from living up to the full human meaning of working together. On the contrary, it is an invitation to try.

NOTES

Preface

1. See Redmon, *Beads, Bodies, and Trash*, chaps. 1–2, and also his documentary film *Mardi Gras: Made in China.*

Introduction

1. In 2018, the *gilets jaunes* donned yellow traffic vests to protest overcentralization and neglect of rural concerns in France. During her 2016 presidential campaign, Hillary Clinton referred to Donald Trump's supporters as bigoted "deplorables." See Galston, *Antipluralism*, chap. 3.

2. Gallup, Inc., "How Millennials Want to Work and Live," 13–55.

3. See Silva, *Coming Up Short*, chap. 4.

4. Smith, *Inquiry into the Nature and Causes of the Wealth of Nations*, 1.4. Hereafter cited as *Wealth of Nations.*

5. Just as any physical structure reflects some sort of overall design, so I assume that all ideal or actual social forms have some "moral structure" delineating the normative stakes between members. The metaphor comes from Booth, *Households.*

6. This expansionist project was epitomized in Gary Becker's confident declaration that "all human behavior can be viewed as involving participants who maximize their utility from a stable set of preferences and accumulate an optimal amount of information and other inputs in a variety of markets." *Economic Approach to Human Behavior*, 14.

7. For a critique of market commodification as potentially corrupting or "noxious," see Sandel, *What Money Can't Buy*; Satz, *Why Some Things Should Not*

Be for Sale. For a broad countercritique, see Brennan and Jaworski, *Markets without Limits.*

8. See Bratton, "Anatomy of Corporate Legal Theory"; Singer, "Political Nature of Firms."

9. See Taylor, "Market Freedom as Antipower"; Pettit, "Freedom in the Market." For older republican views, see Gourevitch, *From Slavery to the Cooperative Commonwealth*, 1–17.

10. Happily, this register of debate has been regaining ground that it had long ceded to technocratic analysis. See Sandel, "Market Reasoning as Moral Reasoning."

11. Taylor, *Modern Social Imaginaries*, chap. 5.

12. To date, normative theory has not sufficiently incorporated empirical findings on the practical efficacy of pluralistic communal governance. See Ostrom, "Beyond Markets and States"; Aligica and Tarko, "Co-production, Polycentricity, and Value Heterogeneity."

13. Figgis, *Churches in the Modern State*, 89.

14. Even in a brute physical sense, ensemble music is more than a set of solo performances, because the sound waves of particular instruments interact to generate sounds that were not previously present.

15. For a historical overview, see Hibst, *Utilitas publica – gemeiner Nutz – Gemeinwohl.*

16. If some judge that this language still smacks of oppression or overpoliticization, little will be lost if they mentally translate "common" to "social": social ends, social goods, socially shared goals, etc.

17. As a representative example, see Garver, *Aristotle's Politics*, 74.

18. This suspicion is usually tacit. For an explicit critique, Hellman, "Gemeinwohl und Systemvertrauen."

19. For an alternative view that reads rather more moral content into the basic ground rules of common-goods discourse, compare Riordan, *Grammar of the Common Good.*

20. There is a further important question about *why* and *where* we should seek common goods in the first place, which demands full-scale moral argument. In applying my normative grammar, I take patterns of common action (which already pervade all our lives) as more or less given.

21. Polanyi, *Great Transformation*, 56.

22. It is a relation of exchange, since each party "offers a benefit in order to induce a response" (Lindblom, *Politics and Markets*, 33), but not every kind of exchange is a market relation.

23. On "exit" as the primary means of control in the market, see Hirschman, *Exit, Voice, and Loyalty*, chap. 1.

24. Economic historians offer similar baseline definitions. "Generally . . . markets are defined as systems for exchanging and allocating resources by way of monetary transactions, with prices primarily determined by the forces of supply and demand, and with multiple, competing buyers and sellers who are mainly geared towards maximizing their own utility or profit." Van Bavel, *Invisible Hand?*, 3.

25. Daniel K. Finn defines "the market" in this broad sense as "that form of economic organization which allows individuals the freedom to do what they wish, to freely make and respond to offers, provided they avoid a list of abusive behaviors prohibited by law." *Moral Ecology of Markets*, 116.

26. This point is contested. See Ciepley, "Authority in the Firm."

27. Simon, "Common Good and Common Action," 208.

28. No doubt there are good arguments to be made about desirable solidarities in areas where prices now prevail, but they demand more than the baseline conditional rule "*if* common action, *then* common goods."

29. "Ciepley, "Anglo-American Misconception of Stockholders," 10.

30. Weil, *Fissured Workplace.*

Part 1. Doing Business

1. Simon, "Organizations and Markets," 56–57.

2. In the USA, the relative importance of corporations as against markets has only grown in recent decades through a marked increase in monopoly power in industries such as telecom, air travel, and e-commerce. See Philippon, *Great Reversal.*

3. On Smith and Marx, see Singer, *Form of the Firm*, chap. 2. For Hayek, see chapter 5 of this study.

Chapter One

1. Kimes, "At Sears, Eddie Lampert's Warring Divisions Model Adds to the Troubles."

2. As representive examples from these fields, see Singer, "Political Nature of Firms"; Bratton, "Anatomy of Corporate Legal Theory"; Williamson, "Economics of Organization."

3. See Mirowski and Van Horn, "Chicago School of Economics."

4. For an elegant and concise history of economic theories of the business firm up through the Chicago school, see Singer, *Form of the Firm*, chaps. 2–6.

5. Berle and Means, *Modern Corporation and Private Property*. Lauded in "Credit Manager."

6. Jensen and Meckling, "Theory of the Firm," 311.

7. Alchian and Demsetz, "Production, Information Costs, and Economic Organization," 777.

8. Friedman, "Social Responsibility of Business."

9. Manne, "Mergers and the Market for Corporate Control."

10. For an agency-cost theorist such as Jensen, a moral notion of duty is otiose, since he regards the terms of managers' agreement with stockholders as the only effective constraint on managers' self-seeking.

11. Jensen, "Value Maximization, Stakeholder Theory," 236.

12. Jensen and Meckling ("Theory of the Firm," 311) casually refer to "the private corporation or firm" as though they were identical. Singer likewise conflates the terms in the title and subtitle of his insightful book: *The Form of the Firm: A Normative Political Theory of the Corporation*. Singer defends this conflation explicitly, arguing that for most purposes the distinction is morally irrelevant. "Corporation's Governmental Provenance."

13. Robé, "Legal Structure of the Firm," 3, 7.

14. Radin, "Endless Problem of Corporate Personality."

15. Zingales, "In Search of New Foundations," 1643.

16. Trustees of Dartmouth College v. Woodward, 17 U.S. (4 Wheat.) 518 (1819).

17. On the perpetual minority of corporate persons, see Kantorowicz, *King's Two Bodies*, 374–80.

18. Ciepley, "Is the U.S. Government a Corporation?," 418.

19. Ciepley, "Beyond Public and Private," 141 (emphasis added). All these rights are clear in the corporate law of Delaware and other important jurisdictions, as Ciepley shows. This paragraph and the following draw heavily on his arguments.

20. See Hansmann and Squire, "Law and the Rise of the Firm," 1336.

21. In the matter of limited liability, for example, even if it were possible in practice to limit the owners' contractual liability to the value of the firm itself, the assets of owners would still be subject to tortious liability, which is not a matter of prior contract. For a contrary view of corporations as contractual boilerplate, see Easterbrook and Fischel, "Corporate Contract."

22. Roy, *Socializing Capital*, 83.

23. Ciepley, "Beyond Public and Private," 141.

24. Ciepley, "Authority in the Firm."

25. Coase, "Nature of the Firm."

26. Lindblom, *Politics and Markets*, 19.

27. Alchian and Demsetz, "Production, Information Costs, and Economic Organization," 777.

28. Robé, "The Legal Structure of the Firm," 38.

29. Coase, "Nature of the Firm," 391 (emphasis original).

30. Rajan and Zingales, "Power in a Theory of the Firm," 36.

31. Cheung, "Contractual Nature of the Firm," 17, 18.

32. Coase, "Nature of the Firm," 389.

33. See Coase, 394–95.

34. See Singer, *Form of the Firm*, chaps. 7–8.

35. Figgis, "Churches in the Modern State," 116, 125.

36. Bratton, "New Economic Theory," 1480, 1482.

37. Singer, "Political Nature of Firms," 842.

38. See Heath, *Morality, Competition, and the Firm*, chap. 7.

39. E.g., Blair and Stout, "Team Production Theory of Corporate Law"; Ireland, "Company Law and the Myth of Shareholder Ownership"; Chassagnon and Hollandts, "Who Are the Owners of the Firm."

40. Ciepley, "Beyond Public and Private," 150.

41. See Ciepley, "Anglo-American Misconception of Stockholders."

42. See Hart, "Economist's Perspective on the Theory of the Firm"; Easterbrook and Fischel, *Economic Structure of Corporate Law*, 68–69.

43. Honoré, "Ownership."

44. Speaking precisely, there are also intermediate forms such as the LLP or LLC, where there is a partial legal separation between natural persons and the business entity, which lowers the mutual risk of investment. But such forms do not allow to passive outside investors the pretense of being "members" or "owners" of the firm.

45. If the corporate firm is just a matter of market agreements involving privately owned property, its goals should not be of greater public interest than the brand of soap I buy. Yet public interest in the corporation is greater, and the huge practical influence of the business corporation calls for a more explicit account of its goals.

46. Easterbrook and Fischel, *Economic Structure of Corporate Law*, 35–36.

47. There are also questions of how much income to reinvest and how much to distribute, but these do not make it onto the bumper-sticker version of the

theory. Hayek proposes that stockholders decide this as well. See "The Corporation in a Democratic Society."

48. See Jensen, "Value Maximization, Stakeholder Theory."

49. This conclusion was drawn by no less than a sitting chief justice of the Supreme Court of Delaware, the most important jurisdiction for corporate law in the USA. Strine, "Dangers of Denial," 792–93.

50. Simon, "Common Good and Common Action," 208.

51. Ciepley's full argument is presented in "Anglo-American Misconception of Stockholders."

52. See Ciepley, "Is the U.S. Government a Corporation?"

53. Santa Clara v. S. Pacific R.R., 118 U.S. 394 (1886) at 396. For a historical overview of the debate, see Horwitz, *Transformation of American Law*, chap. 3.

54. Anderson, *Private Government*; Ferreras, *Firms as Political Entities*.

55. Stout, *Shareholder Value Myth*; Ciepley, "Beyond Public and Private"; Bratton, "The 'Nexus of Contracts' Corporation."

56. The finally dominant argument was an anti-intellectual one, that of the pragmatist John Dewey ("Historic Background of Corporate Legal Personality"). On the unsettled questions that remain at the heart of corporation law, see Bratton, "Anatomy of Corporate Legal Theory."

57. For an account of the multiple rationalities at work in a firm, see Ferreras, *Firms as Political Entities*, chap. 6.

58. For further discussion, see Landemore and Ferreras, "In Defense of Workplace Democracy."

59. Maitland, "Translator's Introduction (to Gierke)," xxx.

60. John P. Davis's historical definition runs as follows: "A corporation is a body of persons upon whom the state has conferred such voluntarily accepted but compulsorily maintained relations to one another and to all others that as an autonomous, self-sufficient and self-renewing body they may determine and enforce their common will, and in the pursuit of their private interest may exercise more efficiently social functions both specially conducive to public welfare and most appropriately exercised by associated persons." *Corporations*, 34.

61. See Williams, *Taming the Octopus*.

62. Lerner, "Economics and Politics of Consumer Sovereignty," 259. Lerner continues, "Economics has gained the title of queen of the social sciences by choosing *solved* political problems as its domain."

63. The epigraph at the beginning of this section is from Berry, "Total Economy," 185–86.

64. For two canonical defenses of this general outlook, see Simon, *General Theory of Authority*; Fessard, *Autorité et Bien Commun*, chap. 1.

Chapter Two

1. I use "community" as a generic word for social orders of any size or theme, translating Aristotle's use of *koinōnia.* On this term see on Yack, *Problems of a Political Animal,* chap. 1.

2. Hoipkemier, "Where (Not) to Begin with the Common Good."

3. The Greek proverb that is the subheading of this section is referred to by Plato at *Republic* 423e; Aristotle quotes it in his *Nicomachean Ethics* 1159b32.

4. The tale is masterfully recounted in Flyvbjerg, *Rationality and Power.*

5. Aristotle, *Nicomachean Ethics* 1160a10–11. Hereafter I will cite this work as *NE,* followed by the Bekker number.

6. I have borrowed the terminology of convergent vs. common goods from Taylor, "Cross-Purposes," 190–92.

7. MacIntyre, *Ethics in the Conflicts of Modernity*, 168–69.

8. Taylor, "Cross-Purposes," 190.

9. Allen, *Talking to Strangers*, 127.

10. Aristotle, *NE* 1155b31–34.

11. Aristotle, *NE* 1156b8.

12. Aristotle, *NE* 1169b5.

13. Aristotle, *NE* 1162b17–18.

14. For a fuller defense of this interpretive line on the lower forms of friendship, see Cooper, "Aristotle on the Forms of Friendship"; Cooper, "Political Animals and Civic Friendship."

15. Aristotle, *NE* 1159b27–32.

16. Yack, *Problems of a Political Animal,* 27.

17. The "ethics of care" movement was launched by an insight along these lines, though apparently not gleaned from Aristotle. As Carol Gilligan puts it, "All human relationships, public and private, can be characterized both in terms of equality and in terms of attachment, and . . . both equality and detachment constitute grounds for moral concern." "Moral Orientation," 20.

18. For a fictionalized illustration of this point, concerning the Italian army retreating from Russia, see Corti, *Il cavallo rosso.*

19. Aristotle, *NE* 1169b8–10.

20. See Aristotle, *NE.*

21. Aristotle, *Politics* 1253a28.

22. For a seminal example from psychology, see Baumeister and Leary, "Need to Belong."

23. Aristotle's image of man apart from politics is every bit as bleak as that of Hobbes: "When separated from law and adjudication [*dikē*], [the human being]

is the worst of all animals," since "[the virtue of] justice [*dikaiosynē*] is a thing belonging to the city." *Politics* 1252a32, 38.

24. For helpful modern discussion of the same point, see Taylor, "Nature and Scope of Distributive Justice."

25. For prominent examples in Anglo-American philosophy, see Searle, *Construction of Social Reality*; Gilbert, *On Social Facts*.

26. Maitland, "Moral Personality and Legal Personality," 193.

27. Maitland, "Moral Personality and Legal Personality," 198.

28. On the political theory of the pluralists, see Runciman, *Pluralism and the Personality of the State*. On the fortunes of guild socialism, see Rogan, *Moral Economists*, chap. 1.

29. Figgis, "Churches in the Modern State," quoted in Hirst, *Pluralist Theory of the State*, 113.

30. Maitland, "Translator's Introduction," xxx.

31. Maitland, "Moral Personality and Legal Personality," 197–98.

32. Figgis, "Churches in the Modern State," 117.

33. Figgis, "Churches in the Modern State," 117.

34. Figgis, "Churches in the Modern State," 125.

35. Maitland, "Moral Personality and Legal Personality," 193.

36. Citizens United v. Federal Election Commission, 558 U.S. 310 (2010). See also Pollman, "Reconceiving Corporate Personhood."

37. For instance, "as purposive groups, they are psychic organisms, possessing not a fictitious but a real psychic personality." Barnes, *Sociology and Political Theory*, 29–30. When handled with greater care, such claims are not as outrageous as they may seem. See Douglas, *How Institutions Think*.

38. "Bhaskar's emergence theory allows us to conceive of real, irreducible wholes which are both composed of parts that are themselves real irreducible wholes, and are in turn parts of large wholes, with each level of this hierarchy of composition having its own peculiar mechanisms and emergent powers." Collier, *Critical Realism*, 117.

39. For the debate on stronger and weaker forms of emergence, see Clayton and Davies, *Re-Emergence of Emergence*.

40. Bhaskar, *Possibility of Naturalism*, 31.

41. To think otherwise is to fall into the error that Margaret Archer calls "social hydraulics." She notes that in fact all social influences "are mediated to people by shaping the situations in which they find themselves." *Realist Social Theory*, 199, 196. This way of distinguishing between biological and social things is not new. Thomas Aquinas, commenting on Aristotle, writes that social things have only a

"unity of order" as opposed to the physical unity of a natural substance, because "a part of this whole can have an operation that is not the operation of the whole, as soldier in an army has activity that does not belong to the whole army." Aquinas, *Commentary on the Ethics* 1.5.

42. Or at least "coauthors." See Smith, *What Is a Person?*, chap. 1.

43. For a more extended engagement with critical realism, see my "Critical Realism and Common Goods."

44. Simon, "Common Good and Common Action," 210.

45. Simon, "Common Good and Common Action," 208.

46. Natural law theorist John Finnis defines the common good of a community as "the factor or set of factors . . . which as considerations in someone's practical reasoning, would make sense of or give reason for his collaboration." Finnis, *Natural Law and Natural Rights*, 154.

47. Hittinger, "Coherence of the Four Basic Principles," 799. I have substituted "community" for Hittinger's original "society" as a generic word for social realities.

48. These two dimensions are characteristically linked. An orchestra with failing internal relations is not likely to produce great ensemble music for long, and I suspect that musical failures are likely to lead to strife and discord among previously cordial relationships.

49. The key passage in Aristotle is *Metaphysics* 12.10, 1075a11–15. On the medieval developments, see Kempshall, *Common Good.*

50. Simon, "Common Good and Common Action," 208.

51. Simon, *Philosophy of Democratic Government*, 64.

52. Simon distinguishes genuine common action and mere partnership by their modes of governance, quality of relations, and need for communication. *Philosophy of Democratic Government*, 36–72.

53. This explains why a sharp fact-value distinction has no purchase in an Aristotelian teleological scheme. A thing's having a certain end or good is one important fact about it.

54. Finnis, *Natural Law and Natural Rights*, 153.

55. Bhaskar, *Reclaiming Reality*, 78.

56. Aristotle, *Politics* 1309b14–17.

57. Aristotle, *NE* 1094a1–3.

58. For the contemporary debate around Aristotle's claim, see Raz, "On the Guise of the Good."

59. See Mayhew, "Part and Whole in Aristotle's Political Philosophy."

60. For sophisticated twentieth-century examples, see Utz, *Sozialethik*; De Koninck, "On the Primacy of the Common Good."

61. Gregory Froelich has persuasively argued that these two anchors generate a significant equivocation in the medieval use of the term "common good." See Froelich, "Equivocal Status."

62. Aquinas begins with the individual person, "but from there onward the argumentation moves deductively to ask what the goal is, to which the individual is oriented on the basis of its belonging to a common nature." Utz, *Sozialethik*, 1:191.

63. The classic study is Lovejoy, *Great Chain of Being*.

64. Augustine, *City of God* 12.1. On God as the extrinsic common good of the universe in the thought of Aquinas, see Verpaalen, *Der Begriff des Gemeinwohls*.

65. "Political thought when it is genuinely medieval starts from the Whole, but ascribes an intrinsic value to every Partial Whole down to and including the Individual." Gierke, *Political Theories of the Middle Ages*, 7.

66. Simon, "Common Good and Common Action," 215.

67. For a fuller interpretation see my "Justice, Not Happiness."

68. The introductions of Aristotle's discussions are illustrative. He begins his treatment of the best regime by asking "what the most choiceworthy way of life is" (*Politics* 1323a15–16), an obviously metaphysical question. The treatment of regime types, where the standard of common good is crucial, begins in a much more empirical key: "For one investigating the regime, virtually the first investigation concerns the city, to see what the city actually is." *Politics* 1274b33. On border walls, see *Politics* 1276a29, 1330b18–1331a17.

69. Aristotle, *Politics* 1274b30. This phrase occurs in the first sentence of *Politics*, book 3.

70. Aristotle, *Politics* 1279a20–21.

71. Aristotle, *Politics* 1279a31–32.

72. For Aristotle, the orientation of human affairs to some good is the foundational fact, with which he opens both his major works of practical philosophy: "Every craft and every investigation, and likewise every action and decision, seems to aim at some good." *NE* 1094a1–2. "Every partnership [*koinōnia*] is constituted for the sake of some good." *Politics* 1252a2.

73. Alasdair MacIntyre puts the point this way: "It is thus only within those systematic forms of activity within which goods are unambiguously ordered and within which individuals occupy and move between well-defined roles that the standards of rational action directed toward the good and the best can be embodied." *Whose Justice?*, 141.

74. On the transition between eudaimonistic and juridical notions of obligation, see Abizadeh, *Hobbes and the Two Faces of Ethics*, 1–11.

75. See, for example, Pettit, "Common Good."

76. Sokolowski, "What Is Natural Law?," 521.

77. Sokolowski, "What Is Natural Law?," 508. Irreducibly social ends arise "only when there are human beings," but the enduring common ends are independent of the intentions of particular individuals.

78. Sokolowski, "What Is Natural Law?," 521–22. Notice that Sokolowski does not claim that the force of these ends depends on their being "natural" in the sense of existing prior to human choice or action.

79. See MacIntyre, "Heedlessness."

80. Figgis, "Churches in the Modern State," 116, 125.

81. See Lear, *Radical Hope.*

82. MacIntyre, *Dependent Rational Animals*, 109.

83. Aristotle, *Politics* 1318b1–3.

84. Flyvbjerg, *Rationality and Power*, 223.

85. Flyvbjerg comments, "There is considerable evidence to indicate that Aalborg's overall situation would have been better if the Aalborg Project had not been implemented at all." *Rationality and Power*, 224.

Chapter Three

1. Business Roundtable, *Statement on the Purpose of a Corporation.*

2. Business Roundtable, *Statement on Corporate Governance.*

3. Business Roundtable, *Statement on Corporate Responsibility.*

4. One should not overlook the importance of rhetoric for legitimacy and formation. See Ghoshal, "Bad Management Theories."

5. For arguments along the same lines, but which rely on a theologically inspired doctrine of the common good, see the essays collected by S. A. Cortright and Michael Naughton (*Rethinking the Purpose of Business*) and the work of Alejo Sison and Joao Fontrodona ("Common Good of the Firm"; "Participating in the Common Good of the Firm").

6. Sison and Fontrodona, "Common Good of the Firm," 227.

7. Aristotle, *NE* 1094a5. By "better" Aristotle means something like, "farther down the chain of 'for-the-sake-of' intentions."

8. Macintyre, *After Virtue*, 190–91. MacIntyre adopts terminology of excellence versus effectiveness in later work (cf. *Whose Justice?*, chap. 3).

9. Alejo Sison argues for a "strict parallelism" between "the objective dimension of work and external goods, on the one hand, and . . . the subjective dimension of work and internal [common] goods on the other." "Revisiting the Common Good of the Firm," 106. Sison is using the term "internal goods" to describe goods that are internal to persons (e.g., virtues, skills) as opposed to intrinsic to social

orders, which is how the longer Aristotelian tradition uses the term. See Kempshall, *Common Good*, 99–110.

10. A similar table is discussed in Naughton and Alford, *Managing as If Faith Mattered*, 64–69. Naughton and Alford rely on a particular/common distinction rather than extrinsic/intrinsic distinction, which in my view obscures the distinctive product-orientation of cooperative work in business.

11. For an excellent book-length treatment on the right ordering of goods as crucial to good management, see Moore, *Virtue at Work*.

12. This is not to deny that, in a wider sense, money is an intrinsically common affair. I expound this claim briefly in chapter 6 of this study. For a full-dress treatment, see Desan, *Making Money*.

13. See Macintyre, *After Virtue*, chaps. 6–8.

14. There are two schools of thought on the question whether all communities do in fact aim at extrinsic ends. On the negative side, Michael Oakeshott argues that the "enterprise association" does while the "civil association" does not. *On Human Conduct*, 124. A more Platonic line of thinking argues that although friends and fellow citizens may not aim at external material outcomes, they are oriented to extrinsic transcendental goods such as truth, love, or justice. (See De Koninck, "On the Primacy of the Common Good.")

15. Aristotle, *Politics* 1318b1–3.

16. A philosophically satisfactory definition of "business" as a human domain is surprisingly elusive. For example, Donaldson and Walsh conclude that the goal of business is "optimized collective value." If this is another word for "common good," then it in no way distinguishes business from other social domains. Their alternate suggestion of "prosperity, broadly construed" is more promising, if vague. Donaldson and Walsh, "Toward a Theory of Business," 202.

17. Freeman, *Strategic Management*, 46.

18. Freeman et al., *Stakeholder Theory*, 28.

19. See Donaldson and Preston, "Stakeholder Theory of the Corporation," 67, 85–87.

20. Freeman et al., *Stakeholder Theory*, 12.

21. Sison and Fontrodona, "Participating in the Common Good of the Firm," 618.

22. Quoted in Freeman, *Strategic Management*, 31.

23. Aristotle, *Politics* 1278a2.

24. As I will argue in chapter 7, it is the impersonality of typical market exchanges that precludes common action, so if the two sides were offering one another special prices or services, we might well see a common good at stake here.

25. Robé, "Legal Structure of the Firm," 32.

26. For a powerful argument about democracy in the overall regulation of capitalism, see Rahman, *Democracy against Domination.*

27. Landemore and Ferreras, "In Defense of Workplace Democracy," 56.

28. Henry Hansmann has argued, for instance, that workplace democracy is currently feasible where workers are relatively homogenous in terms of skills and roles and that it generally fails otherwise. *Ownership of Enterprise*, chaps. 5–6.

29. For a full-scale interpretation, see Hoipkemier, "Justice, Not Happiness."

30. How much stranger this already strange picture would be if stockholders adopted a *mission civilatrice* vis-à-vis the firm: business colonialism! Ciepley, "Anglo-American Misconception of Stockholders," 10.

31. The corporation's treasury benefits from selling equity only when it issues new shares; otherwise the proceeds go to the previous stockholder.

32. "For a regime is an arrangement in cities connected with the offices, [establishing] the manner in which they have been distributed, what the authoritative element of the regime is, and what the end of the partnership is in each case." Aristotle, *Politics* 1289a14–17.

33. See Dahl, *Preface to Economic Democracy*; Walzer, *Spheres of Justice*, chap. 12.

34. See Hansmann, *Ownership of Enterprise*, chaps. 1–3.

35. Madison, Hamilton, and Jay, *Federalist*, no. 10.

36. See, for instance, Nell-Breuning, *Mitbestimmung, Wer mit Wem?*

37. Singer, *Form of the Firm*, chap. 8.

38. Aristotle, *Politics*, 1281a20.

39. In a similar vein, John Rawls remarks that "laws and institutions no matter how efficient and well-arranged must be reformed or abolished if they are unjust." *Theory of Justice*, 3.

40. Simon, *Philosophy of Democratic Government*, 55.

41. See Hoipkemier, "Architectonic Pluralism."

42. See Hall and Soskice, *Varieties of Capitalism*, introduction.

43. Thelen, "Varieties of Capitalism."

Chapter Four

1. For example, in September 2020, the Supreme Court of Spain ruled that the riders for Glovo, an app-based delivery service headquartered in Barcelona, are employees, not contractors.

2. Rosenblat, *Uberland*, 21–40. More broadly, see Heller, "Is the Gig Economy Working?"

3. In Uber's early days, drivers had to be employed by licensed limousine or taxi companies in order to use the app. This remains true in some jurisdictions,

such as Germany and the UAE. Uber's competitor Lyft pioneered the use of noncommercial drivers, and Uber followed suit. See Isaac, *Super Pumped*, chap. 9.

4. Rosenblat, *Uberland*, 91–98. According to Rosenblat, after a policy change in 2016, drivers who turned down too many fares were given a "time-out" rather than suspension.

5. Calo and Rosenblat, "Taking Economy," 1668–70. Drivers have their choice of three GPS programs—Google Maps, Waze, and the in-app Uber service.

6. Rosenblat, *Uberland*, 133.

7. This paragraph draws on Dubal, "Wage Slave or Entrepreneur?," 131–34.

8. On Uber's disruptive politics, see Collier, Dubal, and Carter, "Disrupting Regulation, Regulating Disruption."

9. Weil, *Fissured Workplace*, chap. 1.

10. Weil, *Fissured Workplace*, 58–60.

11. Rosenblat, *Uberland*, 13.

12. See Sweeney, "Uber Drivers across the U.S."

13. Dubal, "Wage Slave or Entrepreneur?," 110.

14. Rosenblat, *Uberland*, 139.

15. As of November 2020, Proposition 22 in California limits drivers to twelve consecutive hours, followed by a six-hour break.

16. White, "Uber and Lyft Threaten."

17. Isaac, *Super Pumped*, chap. 16.

18. Rosenblat, *Uberland*, 87–91. Some drivers called this "Uber math."

19. On the Toyota model, see Rothfelder, "At Toyota, the Automation Is Human-Powered"; Womack, Roos, and Jones, *Machine That Changed the World*.

20. Gereffi, Humphrey, and Sturgeon, "Governance of Global Value Chains," 83–87.

21. For development of this theme, see my "Inseparable Rivals."

22. Dubal, "Winning the Battle, Losing the War?," 766–68.

23. Dubal, "Winning the Battle, Losing the War?," 796–99.

Part 2

1. For the statistical increases and the putative role of the market therein, see McCloskey, *Bourgeois Virtues*, chap. 1.

Chapter Five

1. See Kennedy, "Paul Samuelson."

2. Hayek, *Social Justice, Socialism, and Democracy*, 13.

3. Bowles, "What Markets Can—and Cannot—Do," 13.

4. Knight, *Risk, Uncertainty, and Profit*, 79. Knight's formula need not imply that merchants have no culturally formed desires, only that the quality of their relations is kept out of view.

5. Smith, *Wealth of Nations*, 1.2.

6. As did Edgeworth, *Mathematical Psychics*, 1881. See Screpanti and Zamagni, *Outline of the History of Economic Thought*, chaps. 5–6.

7. "What makes it an economic transaction is that I am not considering you except as a link in the chain. . . . The economic relation does not exclude from my mind every one but me, it potentially includes every one but you. You it does indeed exclude." Phillip Wicksteed, *Common Sense of Political Economy*, 174.

8. Buchanan and Tullock, *Calculus of Consent*, 17–18. Buchanan and Tullock explicitly reference Wicksteed's non-tuism in the same passage.

9. Hayek, *Law, Legislation, and Liberty*, 2:116.

10. Hayek, "Use of Knowledge in Society," 86. Karl Polanyi agrees that "money is a system of symbols, similar to language, writing, or weights and measures" ("Semantics of Money Uses," 175), though he highlights the relative complexity of premodern monies.

11. Hayek, "Use of Knowledge in Society," 79.

12. Smith, *Wealth of Nations*, 4.2.

13. Hayek, *Law, Legislation, and Liberty*, 1:46.

14. Hayek, *Law, Legislation, and Liberty*, 2:108.

15. See Hayek, *Law, Legislation, and Liberty*, 1:38: "Such orders are relatively *simple* or at least necessarily confined to such moderate degrees of complexity as the maker can still survey; they are usually *concrete* in the sense just mentioned that their existence can be intuitively perceived by inspection; and, finally, having been made deliberately, they invariably do (or at one time did) *serve a purpose* of the maker.

16. Hayek, *Law, Legislation, and Liberty*, 1:50.

17. Hayek, *Law, Legislation, and Liberty*, 1:36.

18. For an excellent exposition and critique of the concept, see Luban, "What Is Spontaneous Order?"

19. The quote originally appeared in Ferguson, *Essay on the History of Civil Society*, 187.

20. Hayek, *Law, Legislation, and Liberty*, 1:46.

21. "The particular content of the order will depend on the concrete circumstances known only to the individuals who obey the rules and apply them to facts known only to them." Hayek, *Law, Legislation, and Liberty*, 1:46.

22. Hayek, *Law, Legislation, and Liberty*, 1:30. It is worth noting that Hayek's notion of social purpose here is narrow and extrinsic, in that it depends on an

outside agency intending a given order for some specific purpose of its own. For the Aristotelian, by contrast, both natural and social realities can have an intrinsic telos, which is apt to go beyond the conscious intentions of any particular individuals.

23. Hayek, *Law, Legislation, and Liberty*, 2:78.

24. Hayek, *Law, Legislation, and Liberty*, 2:110.

25. Hayek, *Law, Legislation, and Liberty*, 2:64.

26. Hayek, *Law, Legislation, and Liberty*, 2:31.

27. Hayek, *Law, Legislation, and Liberty*, 2:70.

28. Prominent neo-republicans such as Philip Pettit have exploited a similar parallel to argue that markets promote freedom as nondomination. For a critical overview of the neo-republican use of the market-weather analogy see Sagar, "Liberty, Nondomination, Markets," 413–25.

29. Hayek, *Law, Legislation, and Liberty*, 1:69, 37.

30. Hayek, *Law, Legislation, and Liberty*, 2:69.

31. Hayek, "Competition as a Discovery Procedure," 9–10. "The only reason we use competition at all has as its necessary consequence the fact that the validity of the theory of competition can never be empirically verified for those cases in which it is of interest."

32. Zamagni, "Catholic Social Thought," 71.

33. Hayek, *Law, Legislation, and Liberty*, 1:38 (emphasis original).

34. Hayek, *Constitution of Liberty*, 221.

35. Simon, *Tradition of Natural Law*, 91.

36. Von Mises, *Human Action*, 236, 232.

37. On crowding-out, see Sandel and respondents, "How Markets Crowd Out Morals."

38. Burke, *Reflections on the Revolution in France*, 8.

39. Hayek, *Road to Serfdom*, 87.

40. Hayek, *Law, Legislation, and Liberty*, 1:40 (emphasis removed).

41. Hayek, *Law, Legislation, and Liberty*, 1:113 (emphasis original).

42. Hayek, *Law, Legislation, and Liberty*, 1:48.

43. See Hayek, *Law, Legislation, and Liberty*, 3:55–56.

44. Hayek, *Road to Serfdom*, 90.

45. Hayek, *Law, Legislation, and Liberty*, 1:98.

46. Hayek, *Law, Legislation, and Liberty*, 2:114–15.

47. Hayek, *Road to Serfdom*, 150.

48. Keynes, *Tract on Monetary Reform*, 80.

49. Hayek, *Road to Serfdom*, 156.

50. Hayek, *Social Justice, Socialism, and Democracy*, 13.

51. Hayek, *Social Justice, Socialism, and Democracy*, 13.

52. Hayek, *Road to Serfdom*, 115.

53. "The main point is not that the masses have in most instances no idea of the values which a man's activities have to his fellows. . . . It is that *nobody* knows except in so far as the market tells him." Hayek, *Law, Legislation, and Liberty*, 2:77. This claim is plausible in long-range or large-scale decisions, but Hayek oversells the usefulness of the insight.

54. Hayek, *Law, Legislation, and Liberty*, 2:16–17.

55. Contrast Michael Oakeshott, whose social ontology of "enterprise" and "civil" associations otherwise runs in close parallel to Hayek's "spontaneous" and "made" orders: "The conditions of civil association are moral conditions in not being instrumental to the satisfaction of substantive wants." *On Human Conduct*, 122. Oakeshott's law-governed "civil condition" is valued as a certain mode of relationship, period, not because we are ignorant of the ends to which rights may be put.

56. See Beiner, *What's the Matter with Liberalism?*, 22.

57. Hayek, *Law, Legislation, and Liberty*, 1:48.

58. Hayek, *Law, Legislation, and Liberty*, 2:111.

59. Hayek, *Law, Legislation, and Liberty*, 2:109.

60. Hayek, *Law, Legislation, and Liberty*, 2:112.

61. Aristotle, *Politics* 1252al–2.

62. Aristotle, *Politics* 1292a32.

63. Aristotle, *Politics* 1272a40.

64. See Manent, *Metamorphoses of the City*, chap. 3.

65. The liberal perfectionist Steven Macedo writes, "To a greater extent than liberals usually allow, freedom is a way of life. . . . The point of a publicly justified liberal politics is the realization of a common, substantive moral vision." *Liberal Virtues*, 266, 271.

66. See Vogel, *Marketcraft*, chap. 1.

67. Berger, "Epistemological Modesty," 973.

68. This is Daniel Mahoney's paraphrase of Aron's judgment. See editorial note by Mahoney in Aron, *In Defense of Political Reason*, 68. For a similar assessment, see also Finn, *Moral Ecology of Markets*, chap. 2.

Chapter Six

1. The trading shorthand comes from another great open-cry exchange: London, where it was codified in an official manual. Quoted in Pardo-Guerra, "Creating Flows of Interpersonal Bits," 90. Details about the Chicago pits are from

Roscoe, *How to Build a Stock Exchange*, episode 5. See also the work of Caitlin Zaloom: *Out of the Pits*; "Derivative World."

2. As an anonymous reviewer observed, discrete markets might spring up more or less spontaneously—e.g., around a new technology—leaving governments to shape and regulate them after the fact. This is consistent with the causal priority of common action since the individual merchants would still draw on preexisting shared understandings and practices of exchange.

3. Finn, *Moral Ecology of Markets*, chaps. 2 and 7.

4. Sen, "Rational Fools."

5. For a recent overview, see Rogan, *Moral Economists*.

6. Evans-Pritchard, Introduction to *The Gift*, ix. I have deliberately misquoted Evans-Pritchard, the great midcentury anthropologist. He referred to the modern switch to a "rational" economic system, a term that is just as misleading as "moral economy" because they suggest that nonmodern systems are *irrational*, and modern markets are *immoral* or *a-moral*. Neither is true. By declining to ask what version of rationality or morality is at work, these two unhelpful terms roughly map the sterile distinction between equity and efficiency that structures much contemporary public discourse, in which one side is tarred as wicked and the other as ignorant.

7. For an excellent overview and critique of the key concepts, see Booth, "On the Idea of Moral Economy."

8. Polanyi, *Great Transformation* (hereafter *GT*). See also Polanyi, "Market Mentality," 65.

9. On the contemporary case, see Scott, *Moral Economy of the Peasant*.

10. See Polanyi, *GT*, chap. 4.

11. Mead, "Arapesh of New Guinea," 31–32.

12. Polanyi, *GT*, 48.

13. The classic study of the *kula* trade is Malinowski, *Argonauts of the Western Pacific*.

14. Mauss, *Gift*, 29.

15. Frank Knight, godfather of the Chicago school, made use of the Crusoe story (*Risk, Uncertainty, and Profit*, chap. 3.), as did many eminent economists down to the mid-twentieth century.

16. Aside from divine providence, capital-N Nature is the main, or perhaps the only, source of the "spontaneous." On one plausible reading of Hayek's spontaneous order, the chief contrast is between following the grain of one's own constitution (or "using one's own knowledge for one's own purposes" as he prefers to put it) and being moved from without (by "planning").

17. Marcel Mauss puts it this way: "It was the societies of the Western world that turned man into an economic animal, in very recent times." Cited in Braudel, *Wheels of Commerce*, 229.

18. Historians quarrel with Polanyi's focus on the Speenhamland system and other matters of detail. On the reception of Polanyi among his peers and historians today, see Rogan, *Moral Economists*, 78–83; van Bavel, *Invisible Hand?*, 8–18. For our purposes, and for Polanyi's overall project, his broad and less contested outline is much more important.

19. Many historians would agree this broad statement, while quarreling with just how "recently" the market gained real prominence. See Braudel, *Wheels of Commerce*, 223–31.

20. Polanyi, *GT*, 61.

21. Polanyi, *GT*, 63, 65. Towns were indeed bastions of market trade, but *Bürger* wanted to retain their privileges and control over the market, so they "raised every possible obstacle to the formation of that national or internal market for which the capitalist wholesaler was pressing" (65). A classic full-length treatment is Braudel, *Civilization and Capitalism, 15th–18th Century*.

22. Polanyi, *GT*, 66.

23. Polanyi, *GT*, 68.

24. Polanyi, *GT*, 76.

25. Polanyi, *GT*, 127.

26. Polanyi, *GT*, 140.

27. Polanyi, *GT*, 141.

28. Polanyi, *GT*, 132.

29. We find it, for example, in political responses to the intrusions of global markets. See Rodrik, *Globalization Paradox*.

30. Polanyi encapsulates the resigned attitude of the nineteenth-century market partisan. "Essentially economic society was founded on the grim realities of nature." *GT*, 125. Or even this: "The laws of commerce were the laws of nature and hence the laws of God." *GT*, 122. The term "Great Disembedding" can be found in Charles Taylor (*Modern Social Imaginaries*, chaps. 3–4), though it obviously owes much to Polanyi.

31. Polanyi, *GT*, 68.

32. Polanyi, *GT*, 69.

33. Polanyi, *GT*, 72.

34. As Joao Rodriguez comments, "The neoliberals recognized early on that the creation of new markets is a political process, requiring the intervention of an organized power." "Where to Draw the Line," 1008.

35. Polanyi, *GT*, 57.

36. Polanyi, *GT*, 71.

37. Polanyi, *Livelihood of Man*, 10.

38. Klein, "Fictitious Freedom," 858.

39. Polanyi, "Market Mentality," 69.

40. Polanyi, "Market Mentality," 65, 69 (emphasis added).

41. Polanyi, *GT*, 147.

42. Polanyi, *GT*, 186.

43. Bentham, *Manual of Political Economy*, 3.23.3.

44. Polanyi, *GT*, 159.

45. Polanyi, *GT*, 187.

46. Polanyi, *GT*, 76.

47. See Eich, "Between Justice and Accumulation."

48. The role of central banks has always been controversial. See Wood, *History of Central Banking*.

49. Polanyi, *GT*, 140.

50. Vogel, *Marketcraft*. The wider literature is sampled in Barma and Vogel, *Political Economy Reader*.

51. Vogel, *Marketcraft*, 6.

52. Smith, *Wealth of Nations*, 1.2.1.

53. Polanyi, *GT*, 149.

54. Finley, *Ancient Economy*, 162–64. Polanyi cautions against casually equating trade and markets in Athens, because the former was not carried on by citizens. See Polanyi, *Livelihood of Man*, 189–98.

55. Grundy, *Thucydides and the History of His Age*, cited in Polanyi, *Livelihood of Man*, 203. Aristotle notes that public revenues and the *trophē* are among the top priorities of any statesman (cf. *Rhetoric* 1360a12).

56. Polanyi, *Livelihood of Man*, 205.

57. Polanyi writes, "The peril to solidarity involved in making selfish gain at the expense of the food of one's brother had first to be removed by eliminating the invidious element inherent in such exchanges. This was achieved through the declaration of equivalences in the name of the representative of the godhead itself." *Livelihood of Man*, 61. This may be part of the explanation of Aristotle's cryptic comment about the temple of the Graces above the *agora* (*NE* 1133a3–4), on which see Gallagher, "Role of Grace in Aristotle's Theory of Exchange."

58. *Livelihood of Man*, 234–35. The same broad points about the dominance of political ends can be made about the internal markets in Athens. Polanyi notes that "in an emergency, the market could be—and was—transformed at a moment's

notice into a redistributive device," citing evidence that "cases were fixed, coinage doubled, halved or otherwise altered, goods collected or rationed—and invariably with instant effect—peremptorily and without exemptions." *Livelihood of Man*, 169–70.

59. As William James Booth felicitously puts it, commenting on *Odyssey* 13.158–68. "On the Idea of Moral Economy," 660.

60. Polanyi comments: "The significant fact is that mere aggregates of the personal behaviors in question do not by themselves produce such structures. . . . Acts of exchange on the personal level produce prices only if they occur under a system of price-making markets, an institutional setup which is nowhere created by mere random acts of exchange. . . . The supporting pattern may *seem* to result from a cumulation of a corresponding kind of personal behavior, but the vital elements of organization and validation are necessarily contributed by an altogether different type of behavior." "Economy as an Instituted Process," 150. This alternate type is none other than common action.

61. Obviously, many merchants would be aware of the political situation and goals of Athens, but promoting or hindering such goals is only incidental to the merchant's goal of driving a bargain.

62. MacIntyre, *Dependent Rational Animals*, 109.

63. Aristotle remarks that "to spend much time on such matters [of business and trade] is crude." *Politics* 1258b35.

64. Opportunity cost is not measured against what *has* been done, but what *could* be done. So, it is certainly the case that markets enable new forms of exchange that were not present in more embedded economies, and in this sense they add to rather than transforming what was already there. Still, the choice to engage in new market relations is a choice not to engage in new common action, so common goods factor into the opportunity cost even where no prior community was present. Thanks to Gladden Pappin for this objection.

65. One might say that the difference in price is how much the relational goods are "worth," but the attempt to treat relational goods as marketable typically deforms them. See Sandel, "What Money Shouldn't Buy."

66. Hirschman, "Rival Interpretations of Market Society."

67. MacGilvray, *Invention of Market Freedom*, chap. 3.

68. Constant, "Liberty of the Ancients."

69. Manent, *Intellectual History of Liberalism*, 61.

70. Some Aristotelians would disagree, notably Alasdair MacIntyre. For an exposition and critique of MacIntyre's views, see Hibbs, "MacIntyre, Aquinas, and Politics."

71. Beiner, *What's the Matter with Liberalism?*, 25, 22. The so-called liberal perfectionists amplify, and endorse, Beiner's point. See Macedo, *Liberal Virtues*; Galston, *Liberal Purposes*.

72. Polanyi defines economic liberalism as "the organizing principle of a society in which industry is based on the institution of a self-regulating market." *GT*, 149.

73. Steuart, *Inquiry into the Principles of Political Oeconomy*, 1:278–79, cited by Albert Hirschman in his classic history of the early defenses of capitalism in political rather than material terms, *Passions and the Interests*, 85.

74. I borrow the image from Kukathas, *Liberal Archipelago*.

75. See Friedman, *Lexus and the Olive Tree*, chap. 7.

76. Polanyi, *GT*, 79.

77. Ignatieff, *Needs of Strangers*, 136. Polanyi writes in a similar vein: "The market has been the outcome of a conscious and often violent intervention on the part of government which imposed the market organization on society for noneconomic ends." *GT*, 250.

78. See Bourdieu, *Habitus and Field*.

79. For an argument that Polanyi and Hayek share a great deal in terms of dichotomizing vision, see Mirowski, "Polanyi vs. Hayek?"

80. Drucker, *Adventures of a Bystander*, 137.

81. Aristotle, *Politics* 1280a21. Aristotle equates democracy with the rule of the free poor, which he regards as a defective regime that tends to unjust, populistic appropriations of wealth.

82. Polanyi, *GT*, 57.

83. Drucker writes, "It was my willingness . . . to settle instead for an adequate, bearable, but free society that Karl at the time criticized and rejected as a tepid compromise. In such a society—and it may be the best we can possibly hope for—we would maintain freedom by paying a price: the disruption, the divisiveness, and alienation of the market." *Adventures of a Bystander*, 140.

84. Polanyi, *GT*, 46.

85. The best-known treatment in the sociology literature is Granovetter, "Economic Action and Social Structure."

Chapter Seven

1. To be fair, H. J. Heinz has extensively invested in the city of Pittsburgh, where it is headquartered. In Fallows and Fallows, *Our Towns*, see "Holland, Michigan."

2. Smith, *Wealth of Nations*, 1.2.

3. Smith, *Wealth of Nations*, 4.2.

4. This reflects Hayek's explanation of the invisible hand. Smith himself does not explain its mechanism in any detail.

5. For an example of merchants deviating from price signals for civic reasons, in declining to trade oil with Russian Bolsheviks in the 1920s, see Yergin, *Prize*, chap. 13.

6. See, for example, Galston, *Antipluralism*, chaps. 1, 3, 4.

7. See Kennedy, "Paul Samuelson."

8. Smith, *Wealth of Nations*, 3.4.

9. Smith, *Wealth of Nations*, 1.2.

10. For fuller interpretations on these lines, see Herzog, *Inventing the Market*, chap. 2; Cropsey, *Polity and Economy*, chap. 3.

11. Smith, *Wealth of Nations*, 4.2.

12. See Satz, *Why Some Things Should Not Be for Sale*, chap. 2.

13. On the prospects of democratic oversight of (financial) markets, see Rahman, *Democracy against Domination*.

14. Van Bavel, *Invisible Hand?*

15. See Heilbroner, "Paradox of Progress."

16. For a broad comparison of the Scottish and Italian Enlightenments, see Robertson, *Case for Enlightenment*, chap. 7 and passim.

17. Bruni and Zamagni, *Civil Economy: Another Idea of the Market*; Sugden, *Community of Advantage*, chaps. 9–11; Milbank and Pabst, *Politics of Virtue*, chap. 4.

18. Hume, "Essay VI: Of the Independency of Parliament."

19. Genovesi, *Lezioni*, 22 (1.1.16).

20. See Bruni and Sugden, "Fraternity."

21. Genovesi, *Lezioni*, 439 (conclusione).

22. Bruni and Sugden, "Fraternity," 55–57.

23. See Murphy, "Equality in Exchange," 107.

24. "All human behavior can be viewed as involving participants who maximize their utility from a stable set of preferences and accumulate an optimal amount of information and other inputs in a variety of markets." Becker, *Economic Approach to Human Behavior*, 14.

25. Ironically, the civil economist could concur with Becker to the effect that mathematical models can capture key social domains like family and education with the same degree of insight as they can shed light on markets—but for Becker this is high, for the civil economist rather low.

26. Genovesi, *Lezioni*, 352 (2.10.16).

27. I have argued this case in my "Machiavelli and the Double Politics of Ambition."

28. See Bruni and Sugden, "Reclaiming Virtue Ethics for Economics."

29. Genovesi, *Lezioni*, 341 (2.10.1).

30. Genovesi, *Lezioni*, 343 (2.10.3).

31. Genovesi, *Lezioni*, 341n121, 342 (2.10.1).

32. Sahlins, *Stone Age Economics*, 183.

33. What is less common, to my knowledge, is sellers who are willing to take *less* from local buyers because of *costs* to the local community. These costs are sometimes made good through gestures of reparation, like corporate charity, but in theory a civil market could respond through the price mechanism.

34. Hayek, *Law, Legislation, and Liberty*, 2:70.

35. For insights on this combination, see Murphy, "Equality in Exchange," 100–113.

36. Mauss, *Gift*, 1.

37. See Bruni and Zamagni, *Civil Economy: Efficiency, Equity, Public Happiness*, chap. 6.

38. Hall and Soskice, *Varieties of Capitalism*, chap 1.

39. Consider the broadside of changes—from cooperative land-use to professional guilds—commended in Milbank and Pabst, *Politics of Virtue*, chap. 4.

40. See Whyte and Whyte, *Making Mondragon*, chaps. 5, 8.

41. See Bruni and Zamagni, *Civil Economy: Efficiency, Equity, Public Happiness*, chap. 7; Zamagni and Zamagni, *Cooperative Enterprise*.

42. Robertson, *Case for Enlightenment*, 381.

43. Gereffi, Humphrey, and Sturgeon, "Governance of Global Value Chains."

44. Thelen, "Varieties of Capitalism."

45. Sturgeon, Van Biesebroeck, and Gereffi, "Value Chains, Networks, and Clusters."

46. Kogod School of Business, "2023 Made in America Auto Index."

47. "Ford Strengthens Position as 'America's Automaker.'"

BIBLIOGRAPHY

Abizadeh, Arash. *Hobbes and the Two Faces of Ethics*. Cambridge: Cambridge University Press, 2018.

Alchian, Armen, and Harold Demsetz. "Production, Information Costs, and Economic Organization." *American Economic Review* 62, no. 5 (1972): 777–95.

Aligica, Paul Dragos, and Vlad Tarko. "Co-production, Polycentricity, and Value Heterogeneity: The Ostroms' Public Choice Institutionalism Revisited." *American Political Science Review* 107, no. 4 (2013): 726–41.

Allen, Danielle. *Talking to Strangers: Anxieties of Citizenship since Brown v. Board of Education*. Chicago: University of Chicago Press, 2004.

Anderson, Elizabeth. *Private Government: How Employers Rule Our Lives (and Why We Don't Talk about It)*. Princeton: Princeton University Press, 2017.

Aquinas, Thomas. *Commentary on the Ethics*. Translated by C. I. Litzinger. Chicago: Henry Regnery, 1964.

Archer, Margaret. *Realist Social Theory: The Morphogenetic Approach*. Cambridge: Cambridge University Press, 1995.

Aristotle. *Nicomachean Ethics*. Translated by Terence Irwin. Indianapolis: Hackett, 1985.

———. *Politics*. Translated by Carnes Lord. Chicago: University of Chicago Press, 1984.

Aron, Raymond. *In Defense of Political Reason*. Edited by Daniel Mahoney. Lanham, MD: Rowman & Littlefield, 1994.

Augustine. *The City of God against the Pagans*. Cambridge: Cambridge University Press, 1998.

Barma, Naazneen, and Steven K. Vogel. *The Political Economy Reader: Markets as Institutions*. New York: Routledge, 2008.

Barnes, Harry. *Sociology and Political Theory*. New York: Knopf, 1924.

Baumeister, Roy, and Mark Leary. "The Need to Belong: Desire for Interpersonal Attachments as a Fundamental Human Motivation." *Psychological Bulletin* 117, no. 3 (1995): 497–523.

Becker, Gary. *The Economic Approach to Human Behavior*. Chicago: University of Chicago Press, 1978.

Beiner, Ronald. *What's the Matter with Liberalism?* Berkeley: University of California Press, 1992.

Bentham, Jeremy. *A Manual of Political Economy*. Vol. 3 of *Works of Jeremy Bentham*. Edinburgh: Henry Tait, 1843.

Berger, Peter. "Epistemological Modesty." *Christian Century*, October 29, 1997.

Berle, Adolf, and Gardiner Means. *The Modern Corporation and Private Property*. New York: Harcourt, Brace, and World, 1932.

Berry, Wendell. "The Total Economy." In *What Matters? Economics for a Renewed Commonwealth*, 177–86. Berkeley: Counterpoint, 2010.

Bhaskar, Roy. *The Possibility of Naturalism*. Atlantic Highlands, NJ: Humanities Press, 1979.

———. *Reclaiming Reality: A Critical Introduction to Contemporary Philosophy*. London: Routledge, 2010.

Blair, Margaret, and Lynn Stout. "A Team Production Theory of Corporate Law." *Virginia Law Review* 85, no. 2 (1999): 247–328.

Booth, William James. *Households: On the Moral Architecture of the Economy*. Ithaca, NY: Cornell University Press, 1993.

———. "On the Idea of Moral Economy." *American Political Science Review* 88, no. 3 (1994): 653–67.

Bourdieu, Pierre. *Habitus and Field: General Sociology*. Vol. 2, *Lectures at the Collège de France, 1982–1983*. Translated by Peter Collier. London: Polity, 2023.

Bowles, Samuel. "What Markets Can—and Cannot—Do." *Challenge* 34, no. 4 (1991): 11–16.

Bratton, William. "An Anatomy of Corporate Legal Theory." *Research in Law and Economics* 24 (2009): 24–41.

———. "The New Economic Theory of the Firm: Critical Perspectives from History." *Stanford Law Review* 41, no. 6 (1989): 1471–1527.

———. "The 'Nexus of Contracts' Corporation: A Critical Appraisal." *Cornell Law Review* 74 (1989): 407–65.

Braudel, Fernand. *Civilization and Capitalism, 15th–18th Century*. Translated by Siân Reynolds. 3 vols. New York: Harper & Row, 1981–1984.

———. *The Wheels of Commerce*. Translated by Sian Reynolds. Vol. 2 of *Civilization and Capitalism, 15th–18th Century*. New York: Harper & Row, 1982.

Brennan, Jason, and Peter Jaworski. *Markets without Limits*. New York: Routledge, 2015.

Bruni, Luigino, and Robert Sugden. "Fraternity: Why the Market Need Not Be a Morally Free Zone." *Economics & Philosophy* 24 (n.d.): 35–64.

———. "Reclaiming Virtue Ethics for Economics." *Journal of Economic Perspectives* 27, no. 4 (2013): 141–64.

Bruni, Luigino, and Stefano Zamagni. *Civil Economy: Efficiency, Equity, Public Happiness*. Oxford: Peter Lang, 2007.

———. *Civil Economy: Another Idea of the Market*. Newcastle: Agenda Publishing, 2016.

Buchanan, James, and Gordon Tullock. *The Calculus of Consent*. Vol. 3 of *The Collected Works of James M. Buchanan*. Indianapolis: Liberty Fund, 1999.

Burke, Edmund. *Reflections on the Revolution in France*. Edited by Frank Turner. New Haven: Yale University Press, 2003.

Business Roundtable. *Statement on Corporate Governance*. Washington, DC: Business Roundtable, 1997.

———. *Statement on Corporate Responsibility*. Washington, DC: Business Roundtable, 1981.

———. *Statement on the Purpose of a Corporation*. Washington, DC: Business Roundtable, 2019. https://opportunity.businessroundtable.org/our commitment/.

Calo, Ryan, and Alex Rosenblat. "The Taking Economy: Uber, Information, and Power." *Columbia Law Review* 117, no. 6 (2017): 1623–90.

Chassagnon, Virgile, and Xavier Hollandts. "Who Are the Owners of the Firm: Shareholders, Employees or No One?" *Journal of Institutional Economics* 10, no. 1 (2014): 47–69.

Cheung, Steven. "The Contractual Nature of the Firm." *Journal of Law and Economics* 26, no. 1 (1983): 1–21.

Ciepley, David. "The Anglo-American Misconception of Stockholders as 'Owners' and 'Members': Its Origins and Consequences." *Journal of Institutional Economics* 16, no. 5 (2019): 1–20.

———. "Authority in the Firm (and the Attempt to Theorize It Away)." *Critical Review* 16, no. 1 (2004): 81–115.

———. "Beyond Public and Private: The Political Theory of the Corporation." *American Political Science Review* 107, no. 1 (2013): 139–58.

———. "Is the U.S. Government a Corporation? The Corporate Origins of Modern Constitutionalism." *American Political Science Review* 111, no. 2 (2017): 418–35.

Clayton, Philip, and Stephen Davies, eds. *The Re-emergence of Emergence*. Oxford: Oxford University Press, 2006.

Coase, Ronald. "The Nature of the Firm." *Economica* 4, no. 16 (1937): 386–405.

Collier, Andrew. *Critical Realism*. London: Verso, 1994.

Collier, Ruth, V. B. Dubal, and Christopher Carter. "Disrupting Regulation, Regulating Disruption: The Politics of Uber in the United States." *Perspectives on Politics* 16, no. 4 (2018): 919–37.

Constant, Benjamin. "The Liberty of the Ancients Compared with That of the Moderns." In *Political Writings*, edited by Biancamaria Fontana, 308–28. Cambridge: Cambridge University Press, 1988.

Cooper, John. "Political Animals and Civic Friendship." In *Reason and Emotion*, 356–77. Princeton: Princeton University Press, 1999.

Cooper, John W. "Aristotle on the Forms of Friendship." *Review of Metaphysics* 30, no. 4 (1977): 619–48.

Corti, Eugenio. *Il cavallo rosso*. Milan: Ares, 1983.

Cortright, S. A., and Michael Naughton, eds. *Rethinking the Purpose of Business: Interdisciplinary Essays in the Catholic Social Tradition*. Notre Dame, IN: University of Notre Dame Press, 2002.

"Credit Manager." *Time*, April 24, 1933.

Cropsey, Joseph. *Polity and Economy: An Interpretation of the Principles of Adam Smith*. The Hague: M. Nijhoff, 1957.

Dahl, Robert. *A Preface to Economic Democracy*. Berkeley: University of California Press, 1985.

Davis, John P. *Corporations: A Study of the Origin and Development of Great Business Combinations and of Their Relation to the Authority of the State*. New York: Capricorn Books, 1905.

De Koninck, Charles. "On the Primacy of the Common Good: Against the Personalists." In *The Collected Works of Charles de Koninck*, edited by Ralph McInerny, 63–108. Notre Dame, IN: University of Notre Dame Press, 1997.

Desan, Christine. *Making Money: Coin, Currency, and the Coming of Capitalism*. Oxford: Oxford University Press, 2014.

Dewey, John. "The Historic Background of Corporate Legal Personality." *Yale Law Journal* 35, no. 6 (1926): 655–73.

Donaldson, Thomas, and Lee Preston. "The Stakeholder Theory of the Corporation: Concepts, Evidence, and Implications." *Academy of Management Review* 20, no. 1 (1995): 65–91.

Donaldson, Thomas, and James P. Walsh. "Toward a Theory of Business." *Research in Organizational Behavior* 35 (2015): 181–207.

Douglas, Mary. *How Institutions Think*. Syracuse, NY: Syracuse University Press, 1986.

Drucker, Peter. *Adventures of a Bystander*. New York: Harper & Row, 1978.

Dubal, V. B. "Wage Slave or Entrepreneur? Contesting the Dualism of Legal Worker Identities." *California Law Review* 105, no. 1 (2017): 101–59.

———. "Winning the Battle, Losing the War? Assessing the Impact of Misclassification Litigation on Workers in the Gig Economy." *Wisconsin Law Review*, no. 4 (2017): 739–802.

Easterbrook, Frank, and Daniel Fischel. "The Corporate Contract." *Columbia Law Review* 89, no. 7 (1989): 1416–48.

———. *The Economic Structure of Corporate Law*. Cambridge, MA: Harvard University Press, 1991.

Edgeworth, Francis Y. *Mathematical Psychics*. London: Kegan Paul, 1881.

Eich, Stefan. "Between Justice and Accumulation: Aristotle on Currency and Reciprocity." *Political Theory* 47, no. 3 (2019): 363–90.

Evans-Pritchard, E. E. Introduction to *The Gift*, by Marcel Mauss, translated by Ian Cunnison, v–x. Glencoe, IL: Free Press, 1954.

Fallows, Deborah, and James Fallows. *Our Towns*. New York: Pantheon, 2018.

Ferguson, Adam. *An Essay on the History of Civil Society*. London, 1767.

Ferreras, Isabelle. *Firms as Political Entities*. Cambridge, MA: Harvard University Press, 2016.

Fessard, Gaston. *Autorité et Bien Commun*. Edited by Frederic Louzeau. Paris: Ad Solem, 2015.

Figgis, John Neville. *Churches in the Modern State*. London: Longmans, Green, 1913.

———. "Churches in the Modern State." In *The Pluralist Theory of the State*, edited by Paul Q. Hirst, 111–30. London: Routledge, 1993.

Finley, Moses. *The Ancient Economy*. Berkeley: University of California Press, 1973.

Finn, Daniel K. *The Moral Ecology of Markets*. Cambridge: Cambridge University Press, 2006.

Finnis, John. *Natural Law and Natural Rights*. Oxford: Clarendon, 1980.

Flyvbjerg, Bent. *Rationality and Power*. Chicago: University of Chicago Press, 1998.

"Ford Strengthens Position as 'America's Automaker' with Most Hourly Workers, US-Assembled Vehicles and Exports." Ford Newsroom, April 10, 2023. https://media.ford.com/content/fordmedia/fna/us/en/news/2023/04/10/ford-strengthens-position-as-americas-automaker-with-most-hourly.html.

Freeman, R. Edward. *Strategic Management: A Stakeholder Approach*. Cambridge: Cambridge University Press, 2010.

Freeman, R. Edward, Jeffrey Harrison, Andrew Wicks, Bidhan Parmar, and Simone De Colle. *Stakeholder Theory: The State of the Art*. Cambridge: Cambridge University Press, 2010.

Friedman, Milton. "The Social Responsibility of Business Is to Increase Its Profits." *New York Times Magazine*, September 13, 1970.

Friedman, Thomas. *The Lexus and the Olive Tree*. New York: Farrar, Straus and Giroux, 1999.

Froelich, Gregory. "The Equivocal Status of Bonum Commune." *New Scholasticism* 63, no. 1 (1989): 38–57.

Gallagher, Robert. "The Role of Grace in Aristotle's Theory of Exchange." *Methexis* 26, no. 1 (2013): 143–92.

Gallup, Inc. "How Millennials Want to Work and Live." Washington, DC: Gallup, Inc., 2016. https://www.gallup.com/workplace/238073/millennials-work-live.aspx.

Galston, William. *Antipluralism: The Populist Threat to Liberal Democracy*. New Haven: Yale University Press, 2018.

———. *Liberal Purposes*. Cambridge: Cambridge University Press, 1991.

Garver, Eugene. *Aristotle's Politics: Living Well and Living Together*. Chicago: University of Chicago Press, 2011.

Genovesi, Antonio. *Lezioni di Economia Civile*. Edited by Francesca Dal Degan. Milan: Vita & Pensiero, 2013.

Gereffi, Gary, John Humphrey, and Timothy Sturgeon. "The Governance of Global Value Chains." *Review of International Political Economy* 12, no. 1 (2005): 78–104.

Ghoshal, Sumantra. "Bad Management Theories Are Destroying Good Management Practices." *Academy of Management Learning and Education* 4, no. 1 (2005): 75–91.

Gierke, Otto von. *Political Theories of the Middle Ages*. Translated by F. W. Maitland. Cambridge: Cambridge University Press, 1900.

Gilbert, Margaret. *On Social Facts*. London: Routledge, 1989.

Gilligan, Carol. "Moral Orientation and Moral Development." In *Women and Moral Theory*, edited by Eva Kittay and Diana Meyers, 19–35. Totowa, NJ: Rowman and Littlefield, 1987.

Gourevitch, Alex. *From Slavery to the Cooperative Commonwealth: Labor and Republican Liberty in the Nineteenth Century*. Cambridge: Cambridge University Press, 2014.

Granovetter, Mark. "Economic Action and Social Structure: The Problem of Embeddedness." *American Journal of Sociology* 91, no. 3 (1985): 481–510.

Grundy, G. B. *Thucydides and the History of His Age*. London: J. Murray, 1911.

Hall, Peter, and David Soskice, eds. *Varieties of Capitalism: The Institutional Foundations of Comparative Advantage.* Oxford: Oxford University Press, 2001.

Hansmann, Henry. *The Ownership of Enterprise.* Cambridge, MA: Belknap Press, 1996.

Hansmann, Henry R., and Richard Squire. "Law and the Rise of the Firm." *Harvard Law Review* 119, no. 5 (2006): 1333–1403.

Hart, Oliver. "An Economist's Perspective on the Theory of the Firm." In *Organization Theory: From Chester Barnard to the Present and Beyond,* edited by Oliver Williamson, 154–71. Oxford: Oxford University Press, 1990.

Hayek, Friedrich. "Competition as a Discovery Procedure." *Quarterly Journal of Austrian Economics* 5, no. 3 (1968): 9–23.

———. *The Constitution of Liberty.* Chicago: University of Chicago Press, 2011.

———. "The Corporation in a Democratic Society: In Whose Interest Ought It to and Will It Be Run?" In *Studies in Philosophy, Politics, and Economics,* 300–312. Chicago: University of Chicago Press, 1967.

———. *Law, Legislation, and Liberty.* Vol. 1, *Rules and Order.* Chicago: University of Chicago Press, 1973.

———. *Law, Legislation, and Liberty.* Vol. 2, *The Mirage of Social Justice.* Chicago: University of Chicago Press, 1976.

———. *The Road to Serfdom.* Chicago: University of Chicago Press, 2007.

———. *Social Justice, Socialism, and Democracy.* Turramurra: Centre for Independent Studies, 1977.

———. "The Use of Knowledge in Society." In *Individualism and Economic Order.* Chicago: University of Chicago Press, 1948.

Heath, Joseph. *Morality, Competition, and the Firm: The Market Failures Approach to Business Ethics.* Oxford: Oxford University Press, 2014.

Heilbroner, Robert L. "The Paradox of Progress: Decline and Decay in *The Wealth of Nations.*" *Journal of the History of Ideas* 34, no. 2 (1973): 243–62.

Heller, Nathan. "Is the Gig Economy Working?" *New Yorker,* May 15, 2017.

Hellman, Kai-Uwe. "Gemeinwohl und Systemvertrauen: Vorträge Zur Modernisierung Alteuropâischer Begriffe." In *Gemeinwohl und Gemeinsinn: Rhetoriken und Perspektiven Sozial-Moralischer Orientierung,* edited by Herfried Münkler and Karsten Fischer, 77–110. Berlin: Akademie Verlag, 2002.

Herzog, Lisa. *Inventing the Market.* Cambridge: Cambridge University Press, 2013.

Hibbs, Thomas S. "MacIntyre, Aquinas, and Politics." *Review of Politics* 66, no. 3 (2004): 357–83.

Hibst, Peter. *Utilitas publica – gemeiner Nutz – Gemeinwohl.* Frankfurt: Peter Lang, 1991.

Hirschman, Albert. *Exit, Voice, and Loyalty*. Cambridge, MA: Harvard University Press, 1970.

———. *The Passions and the Interests*. Princeton: Princeton University Press, 1977.

———. "Rival Interpretations of Market Society: Civilizing, Destructive, or Feeble?" *Journal of Economic Literature* 20, no. 4 (1982): 1463–84.

Hirst, Paul. *The Pluralist Theory of the State: Selected Writings of G.D.H. Cole, J.N. Figgis, and H.J. Laski*. London: Routledge, 1993.

Hittinger, Russell. "The Coherence of the Four Basic Principles of Catholic Social Doctrine: An Interpretation." *Nova et Vetera* 7, no. 4 (2009): 791–838.

Hoipkemier, Mark. "Critical Realism and Common Goods." *Journal of Critical Realism* 15, no. 1 (2016): 53–71.

———. "Inseparable Rivals: On the Social Ontology of Practices and Institutions." In *MacIntyre and the Practice of Governing Institutions*, edited by Dulce Redin and Garrett Potts. Dordrecht: Springer, 2025.

———. "Is an Architectonic Pluralism Possible?" In *Polycentric Governance and the Good Society: A Normative and Philosophical Investigation*, edited by David Thunder and Pablo Paniagua, 41–62. Lanham, MD: Lexington, 2024.

———. "Justice, Not Happiness: Aristotle on the Common Good." *Polity* 50, no. 4 (2018): 547–74.

———. "Machiavelli and the Double Politics of Ambition." *Political Studies* 66, no. 1 (2018): 245–60.

———. "Where (Not) to Begin with the Common Good." *Public Discourse*, June 2020. https://www.thepublicdiscourse.com/2020/06/64241/.

Honoré, A. M. "Ownership." In *Oxford Essays in Jurisprudence*, 107–47. Oxford: Oxford University Press, 1961.

Horwitz, Morton. *The Transformation of American Law, 1870–1960*. Oxford: Oxford University Press, 1992.

Hume, David. "Essay VI: Of the Independency of Parliament." In *Essays, Moral and Political*, 117–21. Edinburgh: Cadell, 1748.

Ignatieff, Michael. *The Needs of Strangers*. New York: Picador, 2001.

Ireland, Paddy. "Company Law and the Myth of Shareholder Ownership." *Modern Law Review* 62, no. 1 (n.d.): 32–57.

Isaac, Mike. *Super Pumped: The Battle for Uber*. New York: W.W. Norton, 2019.

Jensen, Michael. "Value Maximization, Stakeholder Theory, and the Corporate Objective Function." *Business Ethics Quarterly* 12, no. 2 (2002): 235–56.

Jensen, Michael, and William Meckling. "Theory of the Firm: Managerial Behavior, Agency Costs, and Ownership Structure." *Journal of Financial Economics* 3 (1976): 305–60.

Kantorowicz, Ernst. *The King's Two Bodies: A Study in Medieval Political Theology.* Princeton: Princeton University Press, 1957.

Kempshall, Marshal. *The Common Good in Late Medieval Political Thought.* Oxford: Oxford University Press, 1999.

Kennedy, Gavin. "Paul Samuelson and the Invention of the Modern Economics of the Invisible Hand." *History of Economic Ideas* 18, no. 3 (2010): 105–19.

Keynes, John Maynard. *A Tract on Monetary Reform.* London: Macmillan, 1923.

Kimes, Mina. "At Sears, Eddie Lampert's Warring Divisions Model Adds to the Troubles." *Bloomberg Businessweek,* July 11, 2013.

Klein, Steven. "Fictitious Freedom: A Polanyian Critique of the Neo-Republican Revival." *American Journal of Political Science* 61, no. 4 (2017): 852–63.

Knight, Frank. *Risk, Uncertainty, and Profit.* Boston: Houghton Mifflin, 1921.

Kogod School of Business. "2023 Made in America Auto Index." https://kogod.american.edu/autoindex/2023.

Kukathas, Chandran. *The Liberal Archipelago: A Theory of Diversity and Freedom.* Oxford: Oxford University Press, 2007.

Landemore, Hélène, and Isabelle Ferreras. "In Defense of Workplace Democracy: Toward a Justification of the Firm-State Analogy." *Political Theory* 44, no. 1 (2016): 53–81.

Lear, Jonathan. *Radical Hope: Ethics in the Face of Cultural Devastation.* Cambridge, MA: Harvard University Press, 2008.

Lerner, Abba. "The Economics and Politics of Consumer Sovereignty." *American Economic Review* 62, no. 1/2 (1972): 258–66.

Lindblom, Charles. *Politics and Markets.* New York: Basic Books, 1977.

Lovejoy, Arthur O. *The Great Chain of Being.* Cambridge, MA: Harvard University Press, 1936.

Luban, Daniel. "What Is Spontaneous Order?" *American Political Science Review* 114, no. 1 (2020): 68–80.

Macedo, Stephen. *Liberal Virtues.* Oxford: Clarendon, 1990.

MacGilvray, Eric. *The Invention of Market Freedom.* Cambridge: Cambridge University Press, 2011.

MacIntyre, Alasdair. *After Virtue.* Notre Dame, IN: University of Notre Dame Press, 1981.

———. *Dependent Rational Animals.* Chicago: Open Court, 1999.

———. *Ethics in the Conflicts of Modernity.* Cambridge: Cambridge University Press, 2016.

———. "Heedlessness." Public lecture, University of Notre Dame, 2014. Available at https://www.youtube.com/watch?v=ccwTDBMn9Fs.

———. *Whose Justice? Which Rationality?* Notre Dame, IN: University of Notre Dame Press, 1988.

Madison, James, Alexander Hamilton, and John Jay. *The Federalist.* Edited by George Carey and James McClellan. Indianapolis: Liberty Fund, 2001.

Maitland, Frederic. "Moral Personality and Legal Personality." *Journal of the Society of Comparative Legislation* 6, no. 2 (1905): 192–200.

———. "Translator's Introduction." In *Political Theories of the Middle Ages*, by Otto von Gierke. Cambridge: Cambridge University Press, 1900.

Malinowski, Bronisław. *Argonauts of the Western Pacific.* New York: E.P. Dutton, 1961.

Manent, Pierre. *An Intellectual History of Liberalism.* Translated by Rebecca Balinski. Princeton: Princeton University Press, 1995.

———. *Metamorphoses of the City.* Translated by Marc LePain. Cambridge, MA: Harvard University Press, 2010.

Manne, Henry. "Mergers and the Market for Corporate Control." *Journal of Political Economy* 73, no. 2 (1965): 110–20.

Mauss, Marcel. *The Gift: The Form and Reason for Exchange in Archaic Societies.* Translated by W. D. Halls. London: Routledge, 1990.

Mayhew, Robert. "Part and Whole in Aristotle's Political Philosophy." *Journal of Ethics* 1, no. 4 (1997): 325–40.

McCloskey, Deirdre. *The Bourgeois Virtues.* Chicago: University of Chicago Press, 2006.

Mead, Margaret. "The Arapesh of New Guinea." In *Competition and Cooperation among Primitive Peoples*, edited by Margaret Mead, 20–50. New York: McGraw-Hill, 1937.

Milbank, John, and Adrian Pabst. *The Politics of Virtue: Post-Liberalism and the Human Future.* Lanham, MD: Rowman & Littlefield, 2016.

Mirowski, Philip. "Polanyi vs. Hayek?" *Globalizations* 15, no. 7 (2018): 894–910.

Mirowski, Philip, and Robert Van Horn. "The Chicago School of Economics and the Rise of Neoliberalism." In *The Road from Mont Pelerin: The Making of the Neoliberal Thought Collective*, edited by Dieter Plehwe and Philip Mirowski, 139–80. Cambridge, MA: Cambridge University Press, 2009.

Moore, Geoff. *Virtue at Work.* Oxford: Oxford University Press, 2019.

Murphy, James Bernard. "Equality in Exchange." *American Journal of Jurisprudence* 47 (2002): 85–121.

Naughton, Michael, and Helen Alford. *Managing as If Faith Mattered.* Notre Dame, IN: University of Notre Dame Press, 2001.

Nell-Breuning, Oswald von. *Mitbestimmung, Wer Mit Wem?* Freiburg: Herder, 1969.

Oakeshott, Michael. *On Human Conduct*. Oxford: Clarendon, 1975.

Ostrom, Elinor. "Beyond Markets and States: Polycentric Governance of Complex Economic Systems." *American Economic Review* 100, no. June (2010): 641–72.

Pardo-Guerra, Juan Pablo. "Creating Flows of Interpersonal Bits: The Automation of the London Stock Exchange, c. 1955–90." *Economy & Society* 39, no. 1 (2010): 84–109.

Pettit, Philip. "The Common Good." In *Justice and Democracy: Essays for Brian Barry*, edited by Keith Dowding, Robert E. Goodin, and Carole Pateman, 150–69. New York: Cambridge University Press, 2004.

———. "Freedom in the Market." *Politics, Philosophy, and Economics* 5, no. 2 (2006): 131–49.

Philippon, Thomas. *The Great Reversal: How America Gave Up on Free Markets*. Cambridge, MA: Belknap Press, 2019.

Polanyi, Karl. "The Economy as an Instituted Process." In *Primitive, Archaic, and Modern Economies*, 139–74. Boston: Beacon, 1968.

———. *The Great Transformation*. Boston: Beacon, 1964.

———. *The Livelihood of Man*. New York: Academic Press, 1977.

———. "Our Obsolete Market Mentality." In *Primitive, Archaic, and Modern Economies*, 59–77. Boston: Beacon, 1971.

———. "The Semantics of Money Uses." In *Primitive, Archaic, and Modern Economies*, 175–206. Boston: Beacon, 1971.

Pollman, Elizabeth. "Reconceiving Corporate Personhood." *Utah Law Review*, no. 4 (2011): 1629–75.

Radin, Max. "The Endless Problem of Corporate Personality." *Columbia Law Review* 32, no. 4 (1932): 643–67.

Rahman, Sabeel. *Democracy against Domination*. Oxford: Oxford University Press, 2017.

Rajan, Raghuram, and Luigi Zingales. "Power in a Theory of the Firm." NBER Working Paper w6274, National Bureau of Economic Research, Cambridge, MA, 1997. https://ssrn.com/abstract=226031.

Rawls, John. *A Theory of Justice*. 2nd ed. Cambridge, MA: Harvard University Press, 1996.

Raz, Joseph. "On the Guise of the Good." In *Desire, Practical Reason, and the Good*, edited by Sergio Tenenbaum, 111–35. Oxford: Oxford University Press, 2010.

Redmon, David. *Beads, Bodies, and Trash: Public Sex, Global Labor, and the Disposability of Mardi Gras*. London: Routledge, 2014.

———. *Mardi Gras: Made in China*. Carnivalesque Films, 2005. https://carnivalesquefilms.com/films/mardi-gras-made-china. Or see https://www.kanopy.com/en/product/mardi-gras-made-china-0?vp=dbrl.

Riordan, Patrick. *A Grammar of the Common Good: Speaking of Globalization*. London: Continuum, 2008.

Robé, Jean-Philippe. "The Legal Structure of the Firm." *Accounting, Economics, and the Law* 1, no. 1 (2011): 1–86.

Robertson, John. *The Case for Enlightenment: Scotland and Naples, 1680–1760*. Cambridge: Cambridge University Press, 2005.

Rodriguez, Joao. "Where to Draw the Line between State and Market? Institutionalist Elements in Hayek's Political Economy." *Journal of Economic Issues* 46 (2012): 1007–34.

Rodrik, Dani. *The Globalization Paradox: Democracy and the Future of the World Economy*. New York: W.W. Norton, 2011.

Rogan, Tim. *The Moral Economists*. Princeton: Princeton University Press, 2017.

Roscoe, Philip. *How to Build a Stock Exchange*. Podcast. https://philiproscoe.net/podcast-archive.

Rosenblat, Alex. *Uberland: How Algorithms Are Rewriting the Rules of Work*. Berkeley: University of California Press, 2018.

Rothfelder, Jeff. "At Toyota, the Automation Is Human-Powered." *Fast Company*, September 5, 2017.

Roy, William G. *Socializing Capital: The Rise of the Large Industrial Corporation in America*. Princeton: Princeton University Press, 1997.

Runciman, David. *Pluralism and the Personality of the State*. Cambridge: Cambridge University Press, 1997.

Sagar, Paul. "Liberty, Nondomination, Markets." *The Review of Politics* 81, no. 3 (2019): 409–34.

Sahlins, Marshall. *Stone Age Economics*. Chicago: Aldine-Atherton, 1972.

Sandel, Michael J. "How Markets Crowd Out Morals." *Boston Review* 37, no. 3 (2012): 12–30.

———. "Market Reasoning as Moral Reasoning: Why Economists Should Re-engage with Political Philosophy." *Journal of Economic Perspectives* 27, no. 4 (2013): 121–40.

———. *What Money Can't Buy*. New York: Free Press, 2012.

———. "What Money Shouldn't Buy." *Hedgehog Review* 5, no. 2 (Summer 2003): 77–98.

Satz, Debra. *Why Some Things Should Not Be for Sale*. Oxford: Oxford University Press, 2010.

Scott, James C. *The Moral Economy of the Peasant*. New Haven: Yale University Press, 1976.

Screpanti, Ernesto, and Stefano Zamagni. *An Outline of the History of Economic Thought*. 2nd ed. Oxford: Oxford University Press, 2005.

Searle, John. *The Construction of Social Reality*. New York: Free Press, 1994.

Sen, Amartya. "Rational Fools: A Critique of the Behavioral Foundations of Economic Theory." *Philosophy and Public Affairs* 6, no. 4 (1977): 317–44.

Silva, Jennifer. *Coming Up Short: Working Class Adulthood in an Age of Uncertainty*. Oxford: Oxford University Press, 2013.

Simon, Herbert. "Organizations and Markets." In *The Firm as an Entity: Implications for Economics, Accounting, and the Law*, edited by Yuri Biondi, Arnoldo Canziani, and Thierry Kirat. London: Routledge, 2007.

Simon, Yves. "Common Good and Common Action." *Review of Politics* 22, no. 2 (1960): 202–44.

———. *A General Theory of Authority*. Notre Dame, IN: University of Notre Dame Press, 1962.

———. *Philosophy of Democratic Government*. Notre Dame, IN: University of Notre Dame Press, 1993.

———. *The Tradition of Natural Law*. Edited by Vukan Kuic. New York: Fordham University Press, 1965.

Singer, Abraham. "The Corporation's Governmental Provenance and Its Significance." *Economics & Philosophy* 35, no. 2 (2019): 283–306.

———. *The Form of the Firm: A Normative Political Theory of the Corporation*. Oxford: Oxford University Press, 2019.

———. "The Political Nature of Firms and the Cost of Norms." *Journal of Politics* 80, no. 3 (2018): 831–44.

Sison, Alejo. "Revisiting the Common Good of the Firm." In *The Challenges of Capitalism for Virtue Ethics and the Common Good*, edited by Alejo Sison and Kleio Akrivou. Cheltenham, UK: Edward Elgar, 2016.

Sison, Alejo, and Joan Fontrodona. "The Common Good of the Firm in the Thomistic-Aristotelian Tradition." *Business Ethics Quarterly* 22, no. 2 (2012): 211–46.

———. "Participating in the Common Good of the Firm." *Journal of Business Ethics* 113 (2013): 611–25.

Smith, Adam. *An Inquiry into the Nature and Causes of the Wealth of Nations*. Indianapolis: Liberty Fund, 1981.

Smith, Christian. *What Is a Person?* Chicago: University of Chicago Press, 2010.

Sokolowski, Robert. "What Is Natural Law? Human Purposes and Natural Ends." *The Thomist* 68, no. 4 (2004): 507–29.

Steuart, James. *An Inquiry into the Principles of Political Oeconomy*. London, 1767.

Stout, Lynn. *The Shareholder Value Myth*. New York: Berrett-Koehler, 2012.

Strine, Leo E., Jr. "The Dangers of Denial: The Need for a Clear-Eyed Understanding of the Power and Accountability Structure Established by the Delaware General Corporation Law." *Wake Forest Law Review* 50, no. 3 (2015): 761–93.

Sturgeon, Timothy, Johannes Van Biesebroeck, and Gary Gereffi. "Value Chains, Networks, and Clusters: Reframing the Global Automotive Industry." *Journal of Economic Geography* 8, no. 3 (2008): 297–321.

Sugden, Robert. *The Community of Advantage*. Oxford: Oxford University Press, 2018.

Sweeney, Sam. "Uber Drivers across the U.S. Are Manipulating Fares to Create Artificial Price Surges." WJLA, June 13, 2019. https://wjla.com/news/local/uber-drivers-nationwide-manipulating-fares-artificial-surges.

Taylor, Charles. "Cross-Purposes: The Liberal-Communitarian Debate." In *Philosophical Arguments*, 181–203. Cambridge, MA: Harvard University Press, 1995.

———. *Modern Social Imaginaries*. Durham, NC: Duke University Press, 2004.

———. "The Nature and Scope of Distributive Justice." In *Philosophy and the Human Sciences*, 289–317. Cambridge: Cambridge University Press, 1985.

Taylor, Robert S. "Market Freedom as Antipower." *American Political Science Review* 107, no. 3 (2013): 593–602.

Thelen, Kathleen. "Varieties of Capitalism: Trajectories of Liberalization and the New Politics of Social Solidarity." *Annual Review of Political Science* 15 (2012): 137–59.

Utz, Arthur. *Sozialethik*. Vol. 1. Heidelberg: F. H. Kerle, 1958.

van Bavel, Bas. *The Invisible Hand? How Market Economies Have Emerged and Declined since 500 AD*. Oxford: Oxford University Press, 2016.

Verpaalen, Antoine. *Der Begriff des Gemeinwohls bei Thomas von Aquin*. Heidelberg: F.H. Kerle, 1954.

Vogel, Steven K. *Marketcraft*. Oxford: Oxford University Press, 2018.

von Mises, Ludwig. *Human Action*. Indianapolis: Liberty Fund, 2007.

Walzer, Michael. *Spheres of Justice*. New York: Basic Books, 1983.

Weil, David. *The Fissured Workplace: Why Work Became So Bad for So Many, and What Can Be Done about It*. Cambridge, MA: Harvard University Press, 2014.

White, Jeremy B. "Uber and Lyft Threaten to Take Their Cars and Go Home." Politico, August 19, 2020. https://www.politico.com/states/california/story/2020/08/19/uber-and-lyft-threaten-to-take-their-cars-and-go-home-1310414.

Whyte, William F., and Kathleen K. Whyte. *Making Mondragon: The Growth and Dynamics of the Worker Cooperative Complex*. Ithaca, NY: ILR Press, 1991.

Wicksteed, Phillip. *The Common Sense of Political Economy*. London: Macmillan, 1910.

Williams, Kyle. *Taming the Octopus: The Long Battle for the Soul of the Corporation*. New York: W.W. Norton, 2024.

Williamson, Oliver. "The Economics of Organization: The Transaction Cost Approach." *American Journal of Sociology* 87, no. 3 (1981): 548–77.

Womack, James T., Daniel Roos, and Daniel T. Jones. *The Machine That Changed the World*. New York: Free Press, 1990.

Wood, John H. *A History of Central Banking in Great Britain and the United States*. Cambridge: Cambridge University Press, 2005.

Yack, Bernard. *The Problems of a Political Animal*. Berkeley: University of California Press, 1993.

Yergin, Daniel. *The Prize: The Epic Quest for Oil, Money & Power*. New York: Free Press, 2009.

Zaloom, Caitlin. "The Derivative World." *Hedgehog Review* 12, no. 2 (Summer 2010): 20–27.

———. *Out of the Pits: Traders and Technology from Chicago to London*. Chicago: University of Chicago Press, 2006.

Zamagni, Stefano. "Catholic Social Thought, Civil Economy, and the Spirit of Capitalism." In *The True Wealth of Nations*, edited by Daniel K. Finn, 63–94. Oxford: Oxford University Press, 2010.

Zamagni, Stefano, and Vera Zamagni. *Cooperative Enterprise: Facing the Challenge of Globalization*. Cheltenham: Edward Elgar, 2011.

Zingales, Luigi. "In Search of New Foundations." *Journal of Finance* 55, no. 4 (2000): 1623–53.

INDEX

MARK HOIPKEMIER is an assistant professor in the program on Politics, Philosophy, and Economics at the University of Navarra.

www.ingramcontent.com/pod-product-compliance
Ingram Content Group UK Ltd.
Pitfield, Milton Keynes, MK11 3LW, UK
UKHW020219290926
15470UKWH00001B/269

9 780268 208974